D1739945

"*Rewriting the North* breaks new ground. This critically-informed and prescient study of the contemporary literary North moves deftly between cultural politics and literary aesthetics in order to propose an alternative future for the field."

– **James Procter**, Newcastle University, UK.

"*Rewriting the North* registers the erratic pulse of contemporary British politics, especially in the post-Brexit moment. Ashbridge considers a range of understudied but significant texts, highlighting literature's ability to help clarify regional politics and the reverberations of devolution."

– **Simon Lee**, Texas State University, USA.

"Devolution is about the political meaning of Not Being England. But as Ashbridge brilliantly shows, adjusting the UK constitutional order places new pressures on England's own nationhood and voice, sparking new questions of place, belonging and citizenship. (It turns out that a lot of England is also Not Being 'England'.) If Brexit underscores the ailments of British Literature as a critical paradigm, this path-breaking study shrewdly examines what – other than alternative literary nationalisms – might come next."

– **Scott Hames**, University of Stirling, UK.

Rewriting the North

This book shows how twenty-first-century writing about Northern England imagines alternative democratic futures for the region and the English nation, signalling the growing awareness of England as a distinct and variegated political formation. In 2016, the Brexit vote intensified ongoing constitutional tensions throughout the UK, which have been developing since the devolution of Scotland, Wales, and Northern Ireland in 1997. At the same time, British devolution developed a distinctively cultural registration as a surrogate for parliamentary representation and an attempt to disrupt the status of London as Britain's cultural epicentre. *Rewriting the North* shifts this debate in a new direction, examining Northern literary preoccupation with devolution's constitutional implications. Through close readings of six contemporary authors – Sunjeev Sahota, Sarah Hall, Anthony Cartwright, Adam Thorpe, Fiona Mozley, and Sarah Moss – this book argues that literary engagement with the North emphasises regional devolution's limited constitutional charge, calling instead for an urgent abandonment of the British centralised state form.

Chloe Ashbridge is Lecturer in Modern and Contemporary Literature at Newcastle University, where her research concerns the interplay between British literature and politics. She is the author of several publications on working-class writing and neoliberalism, regional uneven development in Brexit literature, and the relationship between the literary North and Black Britishness. Chloe is currently researching the function of regional literary awards in the context of Britain's devolving cultural and creative economy. *Rewriting the North* is her first book.

Twenty-First Century Perspectives on British Literature and Society

Twenty-First Century Perspectives on British Literature and Society is home to cutting-edge research into transitions in British culture and society as seen through literary texts, including novels, plays, poetry and life writing. Exploring key works from the canon as well as lesser-known or historically marginalised voices, the books in this series tackle topics such as race, migration, gender, class and Brexit, looking at how major texts respond to and anticipate these contemporary issues. The series offers an insight into the multicultural landscape of Britain today and the ways in which it has transformed over the centuries.

Terry Pratchett Could Save the World
Rebecca Ann Bach

Rewriting the North
Contemporary British Fiction and the Cultural Politics of Devolution
Chloe Ashbridge

For more information about this series, please visit: https://www.routledge.com/Twenty-First-Century-Perspectives-on-British-Literature-and-Society/book-series/21BLS

Rewriting the North

Contemporary British Fiction and the
Cultural Politics of Devolution

Chloe Ashbridge

Routledge
Taylor & Francis Group

NEW YORK AND LONDON

First published 2023
by Routledge
605 Third Avenue, New York, NY 10158

and by Routledge
4 Park Square, Milton Park, Abingdon, Oxon OX14 4RN

Routledge is an imprint of the Taylor & Francis Group, an informa business

© 2023 Chloe Ashbridge

The right of Chloe Ashbridge to be identified as author of this work has been asserted in accordance with sections 77 and 78 of the Copyright, Designs and Patents Act 1988.

All rights reserved. No part of this book may be reprinted or reproduced or utilised in any form or by any electronic, mechanical, or other means, now known or hereafter invented, including photocopying and recording, or in any information storage or retrieval system, without permission in writing from the publishers.

Trademark notice: Product or corporate names may be trademarks or registered trademarks, and are used only for identification and explanation without intent to infringe.

ISBN: 978-1-032-43660-9 (hbk)
ISBN: 978-1-032-48502-7 (pbk)
ISBN: 978-1-003-38872-2 (ebk)

DOI: 10.4324/9781003388722

Typeset in Sabon
by Taylor & Francis Books

Contents

Acknowledgements

This book started life as a doctoral thesis in the School of English at the University of Nottingham, and thanks are due to Midlands4Cities for funding my research. I am grateful to Joe Jackson, Dominic Head, Adam Rounce, and Corinne Fowler for their guidance and conversations that helped me think about literature in new ways. Particular thanks to Joe for urging me to pursue a politically alert scholarship and for providing incisive comments on the later drafts of this work. Michael Gardiner and Joel Evans gave invaluable readings of the final version of the thesis that helped it to become a book.

I would never have applied for a PhD without support from the Literature department at York St John University, who always encouraged me to believe that I had something to say. Conversations with Alex Beaumont during my MA helped set me on this path, and Anne Marie Evans has been a model of everything an academic should be.

The School of English Literature, Language and Linguistics at Newcastle University has felt like home for the past two years. Special thanks to my students on Contemporary Cultures, whose enthusiasm and ideas have invariably strengthened my readings and offered light from the isolation of writing.

I did not expect that moving to Nottingham for my PhD would bring both intellectual collaboration and friendship. I am grateful to Gemma Edwards for challenging me to think with more care and for reminding me that there is more to life than academia. I was lucky to find Laurie Dempsey in the move to Beeston, whose kindness and cheerleading brightened my doctoral days. Much of the research for this project was completed amidst a national lockdown, and Beth Robinson offered company, endless emotional support, and friendship during periods that would otherwise have been spent alone.

The challenges of precarious academic labour in the UK have meant that this book was largely written in evenings, at weekends, and on holidays. Despite my occasional neglect, my family have shown me unending patience, love, and support, especially my mum, Janet, and my dad, Richard.

My greatest debt is to Ricky Carr – my partner in this, and in all things. Without him, this book simply would not exist.

Declaration

Earlier drafts of selected material from Chapter 2 appear in Ashbridge, Chloe. 'Post-British Politics and Sarah Hall's North', *Sarah Hall: Critical Essays*. ed. by Alexander Beaumont and Elke D'hoker (Canterbury: Gylphi, 2023)

Extracts from Chapter 3 were published in Ashbridge, Chloe. 'It aye like London, you know': The Brexit Novel and the Cultural Politics of Devolution, *Open Library of Humanities*. 6.1 (2020), n.p. <http://doi.org/10.16995/olh.463>

I am grateful to Gylphi and the Open Library of Humanities for their permission to reproduce this material.

Introduction

Placing the Cultural Politics of Devolution

Why has the North of England dominated British politics during the first two decades of the twenty-first century? How has England's North–South divide preserved the Union in the wake of devolved parliaments in Scotland, Wales, and Northern Ireland? And why might the North be crucial in activating a post-British England? *Rewriting the North* suggests that these questions are both literary and political, and that the answers reside in an unacknowledged interplay between British constitutional culture and the literary North. A central argument advanced in this book is that literary constructions of the North of England have served a state-supporting function in suppressing the emergence of an independent England. Twenty-first-century political shifts demonstrate the ways in which the North of England has functioned in Britain's national consciousness less as a geographical territory and more as a spatial metaphor for England's 'left behind'. In this context, Northern England's longstanding literary, cultural, and political history as the nation's internal 'other' has represented England as a nation in flux, unable to reconcile its internal poles of 'North' and 'South'. It is hard to overstate the constitutional implications of resolving England's Northern question. In the current period of ongoing constitutional weakening – from Westminster's parliamentary concessions in 1997 to the deepening stress fractures between the four nations since the 2016 Brexit vote – a coherent English civic nationalism would pose a significant threat to the Union if not end it altogether.

By placing constitutional questions at the centre of its analysis, this book shows how twenty-first-century writing about Northern England imagines alternative democratic futures for the region and the English nation, signalling the growing awareness of England as a distinct and variegated political formation. The following chapters offer close readings of six contemporary authors – Sunjeev Sahota, Sarah Hall, Anthony Cartwright, Adam Thorpe, Fiona Mozley, and Sarah Moss – tracing the development of Northern literary preoccupation with Britain's constitutional fractures in the post-devolutionary period. Democratic deficit, regional uneven development, political agency, and representation are thematic concerns to which these writers consistently return. What these works have in common is that they place

DOI: 10.4324/9781003388722-1

several, differentiated geographies across Northern England as key drivers of democratic renewal amidst Britain's constitutional instability and fragmentation. Throughout the two decades following the devolutionary moment, literary engagement with 'the North' increasingly stages democratic alternatives to the centralised British state form, only to prematurely foreclose their political actualisation. This retreat from regional emancipatory politics registers a scepticism towards devolution's democratic potential, emphasising its limitations as a form of contained, partial freedom. Read alongside a literary thematic concern with devolution as a constitutional principle, this aesthetic articulation of 'incomplete' or 'failed' regional political projects is what I call the 'cultural politics of devolution'.

Brexit and the Two English Questions

While devolution on a national scale began more than twenty years ago, the North of England has been at the forefront of a growing appetite for devolved powers in the English regions. From the Jarrow March in 1936, the Miners' Strikes in the 1970s and 1980s, to the North-East's devolution referendum in 2004 and the establishment of the Northern Independence Party in 2021, places across the North have long been constructed as 'a region of discontent'. David Peace's fictionalisation of the Yorkshire Moors murders in the *Red Riding Quartet* – later popularised by its adaptation for ITV – captures the image of an ungovernable North, with the now-infamous assertion 'THIS IS THE NORTH. WE DO WHAT WE WANT!' (Peace, 1999, p. 265). Andy Burnham evoked this history during his first major speech as Mayor of Greater Manchester when he declared regional devolution 'the best answer to Brexit' (Burnham, 2018). Emphasising a long-standing democratic deficit across Northern England, Burnham deplored the way English regional development projects had, unlike Scotland and Wales, stalled due to Whitehall's preoccupation with Brexit negotiations. Burnham's speech evidences Brexit-fuelled devolutionary energy in the North, proposing that 'the time has come to free up places like Greater Manchester to chart our own path and our own way of responding to the uncertainty it brings' (Burnham, 2018). Though overlayed with Manchester exceptionalism, Burnham's speech offers a useful starting point in invoking the two versions of what is often termed the 'English Question': on the one hand, a national question about rebalancing England's place in the Union post-devolution and, on the other, a regional question about England's internal socio-economic and geographical fault-lines (see Hazell, 2000, p. 221).

In 2016, Brexit saw the regional English Question work its way into the heart of Britain's political and cultural imaginary. A dominant narrative of Brexit holds that the referendum provided a form of democratic participation for England's socio-economic peripheries and the opportunity to seize power, if only temporarily, from Westminster's political elite. These accounts approach Brexit as having less to do with Brussels' administrative stranglehold than a London-based polity who were out of touch with life beyond the para-meters of the M25.[1] From the campaigns to the political fallout from the referendum result, Brexit reactivated discussion of the North–South divide and positioned a geographically undefined, discursive version of the North as a synonym for the Leave vote.[2] Echoing Thatcher's demonisation of trade unions in the 1970s and 1980s, Brexit's media and political commentary reflected the primacy of the North as a so-called regional backwater that had failed to shake off the effects of deindustrialisation. All at once the region operated in the national consciousness as a 'revolting rustbelt' (Hazeldine, 2017), 'distressed locality' (MacLeod and Jones, 2018), home of the 'the left behind' (Tomaney and Pike, 2018) and, in the case of Sunder-land, England's 'Brexit city' (Rushton, 2017). This narrative of Brexit as an anti-establishment 'revolt' is, of course, a symptom of longstanding eco-nomic inequality in formerly industrial towns, rural villages, and neglected coastal towns due to successive waves of uneven development that dis-proportionately affected Northern England. At the same time, though, it also makes visible the overdetermined status of 'the North' as the 'senior representative'r of a much larger left-behind England distributed across its entire geography (Hazeldine, 2020, p. 12).[3] The political association of the North with England's 'left behind' was matched in the literary sphere by a wave of post-Brexit literary and cultural production that primarily con-centrated on working-class communities, broadly located in the North of England. In the year immediately following the vote, Anthony Cartwright's commissioned response to the referendum, *The Cut* (2017), Adam Thorpe's *Missing Fay* (2017), Jon McGregor's *Reservoir 13* (2017), Amanda Craig's *Lie of the Land* (2017), Douglas Board's *Time of Lies* (2017), and Kenneth Stevens' *2020* (2017) all retreated to England's socio-economic margins to get the measure of a nation that had voted to cut ties with the world's lar-gest trading bloc. Put simply, the development of a post-Brexit-vote literary culture saw the North's status as the inward-looking counterpart of London reaffirmed in the national consciousness.

If Brexit raised the question of a politically dissident North, it also brought Britain's competing internal nationalisms into sharp relief. Despite wrangles over the Irish border and ongoing pressures for Scottish independ-ence, it was English nationalism that gained widespread attention after 2016. The fact that the Leave vote was so readily interpreted as a populist English 'revolt' against the political elites of both Westminster and Brussels turned the spotlight onto the absence of an English national parliament and inspired a surge of studies on what Englishness meant today.[4] Anthony Barnett pinpoints Brexit as a constitutional rupture, with 'England-without-London' at the forefront of the UK's 'overdue' fragmentation (Barnett, 2017), while Ben Wellings suggested that Brexit wedded Euroscepticism to the 'Anglosphere' as a named English ideology (Wellings, 2019). Aisla Hen-derson and Richard Wyn Jones captured the wider critical mood in pro-posing that Englishness is now the 'motor force' behind the remaking of

British politics. Henderson and Jones' discussion points up the unique character of English nationalism that 'combines both concern about England's place in the Union as well as fierce commitments to a particular version of England's past, present, and future' (Henderson and Jones, 2021, p. 4). The nostalgic (often reactionary) connotations tainting Englishness are not new, but they provide evidence of a nation struggling to detach its identity from its imperial past.[5] Much critical discussion of Englishness after Brexit developed in this vein, employing what Michael Kenny describes as a 'blanket characterization of an emergent form of ethno-national consciousness' (Kenny, 2021, p. 6). A deep aversion to considering the political potential and diverse character of an English civic nationalism underpins Alex's Niven's push for British regional federalism in *New Model Island*. For Niven, England is 'a backward-looking, self-hating place' (Niven, 2019, p. 33) too tarnished by its imperial past, leaving a 'progressive culture' for the English regions unthinkable without abandoning the idea of England altogether.[6] Niven's anti-nationalist stance evidences the continuing hold of England's overdetermined status (see Baucom, 1999) which has, since the decline of Empire, prevented serious consideration of Englishness as a progressive political project.

Brexit's regional and national English Questions date back to intellectual developments in political science between the 1960s and 1990s. Alongside New Left collaborator, Perry Anderson, Tom Nairn elaborated a distinctive evolution of the Britain as an 'absorptive', rather than a federal, unitary state form that depended on England's constitutional invisibility as the naturalised core of Anglo-Britishness (Anderson, 1964, 1992; Nairn, 1977). In the Nairn-Anderson thesis, England was 'defined by absence' (Nairn, 1977, p. 305), with Nairn endorsing England's political revolution as a critical component of upheaving Britain's *ancient regime* (see Nairn, 2000). Twenty years before the devolutionary moment, Nairn's *The Break-Up of Britain* (1977) predicted that the post-imperial British state was in crisis, unable to unify its competing internal nationalisms in the wake of the dissolution of the Empire. Evidence of Britain's exhaustion materialised in the latter half of the 1990s when New Labour proposed devolution for Scotland, Wales, and Greater London in an attempt to pacify energies for independence. Yet, as Nairn and others have argued, devolution could never deliver the democratic renewal it promised because it is fundamentally wedded to preserving the unitary state form.[7] Nairn's predictions on this matter appear to have held true. Scottish devolution has not dispelled momentum for a clean break from Westminster that might be achieved through independence, and Nairn's reflections on the potential for a progressive English civic nationalism have increasingly gained critical traction. The constitutional adjustments of 1997 not only re-energised discussion surrounding 'the break-up of Britain', but, as Claire Westall and Michael Gardiner have identified, raised the question as to whether membership of the Union could be re-negotiated from the inside out – England included (Westall and Gardiner, 2013, p. 119).

Consequently, in devolutionary Britain, England became less 'the gaping hole' in the devolution question and has increasingly taken centre-stage in the debates about Britain's perceived imminent break-up.[8]

Devolution as Literary Culture

Between 1990 and 2020, literary culture was a key site where devolutionary English questions played out. In 1992, Robert Crawford proposed that the university discipline of English Literature has a particularly centralised register which has depended on England as a synonym for Britain. As he puts it, 'the development of the subject "English Literature" has constantly involved and reinforced an oppressive homage to centralism. As such, English Literature is a force which must be countered continually by devolutionary momentum' (Crawford, 1992, p. 7). Michael Gardiner's proposition of English literary 'reprovincialisation' is one example of such a devolutionary momentum. In *The Return of England in English Literature* (2012) and his follow-up essay, *The Constitution of English Literature* (2013), Gardiner offers a cultural historiography of the discipline of English Literature as a bulwark of the unified British state. In this account, English Literature is not the literature of England, but rather a 'universalising principle dependent on displaced and ideal images of England for the ends of empire and social class' (Gardiner, 2012, p. 1). Gardiner argues that the discipline of English Literature has, in the close relationship between canonicity and Empire, prevented a politically activated England, providing a 'constitutional glue' for the Union.[9] As he explains:

> The modern British constitution and the discipline of English Literature have been mutually supporting: both arose from the need to bolster the informal State between the late seventeenth century and the dangers at the end of the eighteenth, and both came into question with the post-colonial unravelling of welfare consensus at the end of the twentieth.
>
> (Gardiner, 2013, p. 1)

What is crucial here is the particular way in which English Literature provided the modern British state with a constitutional *culture* that can, in the absence of a formally codified constitution, change invisibly to suit political projects. Preservation of the political status quo, centralisation of political power, protection of the state form, containment of radical politics, and the suppression of a post-imperial civic England have all been the task of the discipline during its developmental phase.

As Gardiner's account makes clear, the discipline of English Literature is actively antagonistic to the literary and political actualisation of a national England. The discipline has relied on an 'a-political', 'placeless', and 'stretchy' (Gardiner, 2013, p. 1) version of imperial England played out in the cultural sphere and, in turn, upheld a constitutional structure in which

England has no distinctive parliamentary basis.[10] In this context, Gardiner proposes a Deleuzian notion of reprovincialisation which would 'return experience to local contexts, working between dialects and showing the connectedness of the many facets of the state' (Gardiner, 2012, p. 6). Gardiner's thesis makes a literary registration of post-imperial England more thinkable than ever before, but the spatial mythology of the North presents an obstacle to a unitary national re-provincialisation. A potential blocker to a 'thoroughly reprovincialised' literature of England is the way the literary North has developed and operated in the national consciousness as a mythological principle, rather than a geographical territory. This book aims to build on Gardiner's initiation of a 're-provincialised national reading', taking the view that placing the twenty-first-century literary North is a necessary precondition to a national literature of England. By providing a place-based engagement with the region's twenty-first-century literary status, the analysis that follows seeks to detach the North from the mythology of the North–South divide and, in turn, allow a reprovincialised literature of England to emerge.

There has been little sustained attempt to disentangle Englishness from Britishness in regional literary studies. Beyond Claire Westall and Michael Gardiner's *Literature of an Independent England* (2013) 'devolutionary' criticism to date responds to London's parallel (and not entirely unrelated) centralism as Britain's commercial and cultural core. The spatial biases of British literary studies are, of course, partly a consequence of the commercial dominance of London. As Claire Squires points out, the disproportionate concentration of major publishing houses in London, including the 'big five' – Bertelsmann, Pearson, HarperCollins, Hodder Headline, and Hachette – limits access to mainstream publishing houses while reproducing a canon of already successful writers (Squires, 2007, p. 21). However, this trend also speaks to a centralised logic underpinning dominant understandings of literary value and prestige throughout Britain. In 'A Tale of Two Novels', Corinne Fowler makes the case that fiction viewed as 'regional' tends to enjoy nowhere near the same degree of commercial or critical attention as novels located in London or the South East, whose location is not considered a defining characteristic (Fowler, 2008). Indeed, this bias pertains not only to the cultural industries but the academic discipline. Scholarly approaches to contemporary British literature are equally London-centric, where England's capital city constitutes an entire subfield within British literary and cultural studies today.[11]

Existing attempts to regionally 'devolve' the discipline have focused on Black British writing. For example, James Procter's *Dwelling Places* (2003) provides a pioneering contribution to developing a spatially differentiated analytic, proposing a literary methodology attuned to 'the politics of location' (Procter, 2003, p. 164). Procter argues that the lack of regional difference in Black Britain is largely due to the 'deterritorialising tendencies of diaspora discourse', which have been facilitated by a 'slippage' between London and Britain (Procter, 2003, p. 164). As a result, the former 'provides the only sustaining setting for an excavation and interrogation of Black culture, the only available archive and inventory' (Procter, 2003, p. 164). In this sense, London has occupied a 'deterritorialised' yet simultaneously national status in diasporic discourse, operating as the default site for a racially diverse Britishness. While Procter focuses on Black British writing, his account is instructive in emphasising that it is not just the internal nations of the UK that require a devolved lens that would, for example, recognise England's own highly differentiated socio-economic and cultural demography. As he puts it, '[e]ven within England the notion of "two nations" – the affluent, silicon South and the once-Industrial North where the impact of structural unemployment has been its greatest remains a key imagined geography' (Procter, 2003, p. 3). Echoing Procter, Lynne Pearce, Corinne Fowler, and Robert Crawshaw's *Postcolonial Manchester* (2013) seeks to promote 'a newly devolved canon of English literature which embraces not only ethnic and cultural difference but also *regional* difference' (Fowler and Pearce, 2013, p. 3). *Postcolonial Manchester* retains a critical eye on 'diasporic' writings from lesser-known Black and Asian authors in Manchester, suggesting that the city's 'devolved literary cultures challenge and revise our collective sense of Manchester, of diaspora space and, indeed, of Britain itself' (Pearce, Fowler, and Crawshaw, 2013, pp. 4–5). Such an emphasis on a revised notion of Britishness acknowledges the way that the national register of 'British literary studies' has been dictated by a network of London-based writers. This is significant because it demonstrates the particular way that British literary culture has often proved amenable to a unitary British state logic and provided a cultural institutionalisation of Westminster's centralised political power.

Literary-critical attention to devolving Britain has tended to focus on Black writers. As a cultural form and academic discipline, Black British literature has, as Joseph Jackson argues, served a 'new, unified, Britishness' in the post-devolutionary period (Jackson, 2020, p. 27). However, there is an important distinction to be made between existing regional literary approaches to devolution and *Rewriting the North*. Both *Dwelling Places* and *Postcolonial Manchester* understand devolution as spatial, rather than constitutional. That is, they approach devolution as a decentralised literary politics which aims to destabilise London's literary hegemony and, consequently, pay greater attention to regional literary production. Procter and Fowler's pursuit of regional specificity is worthwhile, but it nonetheless assumes Britain's continuity in a fashion that mirrors the state's deployment of devolution to manage sub-national unrest. Jackson notes precisely this tendency in *Writing Black Scotland*, describing a conceptual conflict in which the goal of a regional differentiated Britishness cannot be squared with the political-constitutional correlates of devolution which 'thinks through, if not anticipates [Britain's] fragmentation' (Jackson, 2020, p. 45). Though Jackson attends to a specifically national devolutionary politics in Scotland, his critique brings to light a crucial mechanism in the relationship between regional literary culture and politics in Britain. That is, a spatial approach to devolution replicates a political system in which regional devolution – including Mayoralties, City Deals, and Local Enterprise Partnerships – does not pose the same kind of threat to Britishness as the concession of legislative powers to national parliaments like Holyrood. English regional devolution was never envisaged to have the same constitutional charge as national devolution in Scotland, Wales, and Northern Ireland. Instead, it had a stabilising logic that intended simply to deliver centralised policy more effectively (and in turn, pacify regional unrest), a goal which aligns with an approach to devolution as a 'fuller' account of regional specificity (Aughey, 2013).

In this context, *Rewriting the North* advances a political-constitutional understanding of regional devolution as a cultural politics. A distinctive contribution of this book is a new approach to devolving British literary culture that brings together a decentralised literary-critical practice with attention to literary engagement with devolution's constitutional contours as a symptom of Britain's territorial disintegration. More specifically, it situates Northern England at the centre of a reassessment of British literature's unitary logic by examining the various ways in which writers attempt to imagine democratic alternatives to the centralised state form. In doing so, the book proposes a literary-critical practice that accounts for the political significance of devolution as a process of British state preservation. My approach, while it retains an ambition to destabilise London as the nation's cultural epicentre, upholds a critical awareness of Britain's naturalisation in the literary sphere.

I have already alluded to a wider national context of British literary devolution in which Scotland has played the starring role. It is often argued that Scottish literary devolution preceded the nation's political devolution,[12] but Northern literary engagement with Britain's continuing constitutional crises has a much more guarded democratic vision. Rather than blazing the trail for political devolution, the texts considered throughout this book underline the limits of the kind of agency offered by devolution as a process of state preservation. Thus, *Rewriting the North* does not propose that fiction emerging from various locations in the North advocates regional devolution. Rather, it suggests an emerging Northern literary embeddedness with regionalised democratic alternatives to centralised British parliamentary politics. As the following chapters argue, the premature foreclosure of these political projects articulates precisely devolution's limited constitutional charge. Overall, then, this book maps a Northern literary ambivalence towards devolution to effect meaningful democratic reform, pointing towards a potential post-British literary consciousness to accompany the end of the Union.

Historicising the Literary North

To grasp the full implications of a devolving Northern literary consciousness in the twenty-first century, however, we need to look back. The contemporary political mobilisation of 'the North' indexes the ongoing political purchase of the region's cultural and literary past. More specifically, the fact that the North became synonymous with Brexit's Leave vote as a working-class revolt evidences how contemporary ideas of a politically dissident 'North' have been facilitated by the region's longstanding status as a set of class-inflected cultural codes, characteristics, spatial iconographies, and literary aesthetics. Nineteenth- and twentieth-century representations of Northern England repeatedly frame the region as what Philip Dodd termed a 'second-rate Lowryscape' (Dodd, 1990), a place 'consistently described in terms of dearth, authenticity, and pastness' (Davidson, 2005, p. 199). This class-inflected narrative of the North has often been associated with industrialisation and its aftermath. The Industrial Revolution was a central factor in establishing a 'sense of place' for the North, with sectoral specialisation distinguishing regions from each other and resulting in 'regional coherence centred around towns such as Manchester, Leeds, Sheffield, Newcastle, and Bradford, which became foci of economic growth' (Rawnsley, 2000, p. 7). At the same time, the social problem novels of the nineteenth century saw the city take on a metonymic role for a broader, working-class, urban-industrial North. As Dave Russell points out, Victorian social problem novels 'have done more to define the North as "other"– as harsh, bleak, industrial, and the "land of the working class" – than any other single cultural form' (Russell, 2004, p. 87). Benjamin Disraeli's *Sybil* (1845), subtitled 'the two nations', Elizabeth Gaskell's *North and South* (1854), and Charles Dickens' *Hard Times* (1854) are often credited with the nineteenth-century construction of an archetypal North as an inherently 'bleak place typified by squalor, poverty and industrial labour' in opposition to depictions of a more 'gentrified and attractive South' (Mansfield, 2010, p. 285; see also Pocock, 1979). England's status as a nation divided by both class and geography carried over to depictions of the North during the Edwardian and interwar periods. H.V. Morton's travelogue *In Search of England*, opposed 'beautiful old England' with 'industrial England' (Morton, 2000, pp. 185–186), while in *The Road to Wigan Pier* George Orwell posited that it was only 'beyond Birmingham' that 'the real ugliness of industrialism' (Orwell, 2001 [1973], p. 94) can be encountered.

The industrial North took on a new cultural and political significance from the post-war period to the 1990s. Successive waves of uneven development and governmental policies which disproportionately affected the economies of Northern England and the Midlands led to a geographically expansive 'North' which was yoked to its socio-economic status. This vision was intimately tied to deindustrialisation, poverty, and unemployment. For example, the 1950s and 1960s marked the emergence of Mersey Beat, kitchen sink drama, the films associated with the British New Wave, early Northern Soul, the plays of the so-called 'Angry Young Men', and the Movement poetry. These works contributed to a regional subgenre of class-inflected literary and cultural production referred to as 'Northern grit' which was typified by a formal reliance on social realism and regional dialect, often set

in declining urban environments and associated with a particularly homo-
genous stereotype of white working-class masculinity. John Osborne's play
Look Back in Anger (1956) and Sheila Delaney's *A Taste of Honey* (1958)
are some of the earliest notable examples of kitchen sink drama. Parallels in
British cinema include Keith Waterhouse's *Billy Liar* (1963), Lindsay
Anderson's adaptation of David Storey's *This Sporting Life* (1963), and Ken
Loach's *Kes* (1969). Here, a 'keep calm and carry on' attitude, authenticity,
nostalgia, and a strong sense of community identity associated with manual
labour were all taken to represent the everyday lives of England's 'ordinary
people'. These works frequently employed de-industrial *leitmotifs* situated
in the decaying 'sink estates' of Northern England and the Midlands, and
solidified a vision of a geographically imprecise North as a postindustrial
monolith marked by working-class dispossession and alienation.

The Thatcher period is also an important staging post in the socio-economic construction of the North. Accelerated deindustrialisation during the
1980s saw the total employment base in Northern England contract by half
a million (Hazeldine, 2020, p. 118), solidifying the cultural association of the
region with working-class politics and deindustrialised urban spatial settings. John Hill notes how, during this period,

> [t]he iconography of rows of small, terraced houses and cobbled streets
> characteristic of 1960s realism [gave] way to run-down housing estates
> with boarded-up windows (precisely the sort of estates just built in films
> such as *Saturday Night and Sunday Morning* (1960)). Factories (as in
> *Business as Usual*) have become wastelands and images of work, such as
> there are, are linked to the service sector (especially shops) rather than
> manufacturing.
>
> (Hill, 1999, p. 167)

The divisive Conservative administration and the 1984–1985 Miners' Strike
thus represented a period of vibrant renewal for Northern working-class
culture.[13] Notable engagements with these socio-political shifts include
Barry Hines', most notably, *The Price of Coal* (1979) and *Looks and Smiles*
(1981), Pat Barker's *Union Street* (1982) and *Blow Your House Down*
(1984), and Livi Michael's *Under a Thin Moon* (1992), all of which reinforced Northern England's association with working-class identity, a patriarchal hegemonic masculinity, and deindustrial spatial settings.

The 'Thatcher Revolution' came to be seen as a fulcrum in the development of the British novel more widely. Dominic Head defines the 1980s as 'a
period of renaissance in English fiction' (Head, 2008, p. 45) signalling the
widespread emergence of postmodern aesthetics in response to the onset of
neoliberalism.[14] However, this trend of self-conscious, fragmentary narrative
did not appear to extend to Northern literary engagement with the period.[15]
In fact, much Northern literary engagement with Thatcherism emerged
much later in the early 2000s. Retrospective responses to the Miners' Strike

reaffirmed the association of the North with deindustrialised spatial settings, working-class identity, and the aesthetics of social realism. A number of contemporary historical fictions appropriate a specific iconography of Northern England during the 1980s and 1990s in often nostalgic ways, imagining the region in terms of its industrial past. An awareness and subsequent use of this topography are central to Gordon Burn's *The North of England Home Service* (2003), David Peace's *Red Riding Quartet* (1999; 2000; 2001; 2002) and *GB84* (2004), Philip Hensher's *The Northern Clemency* (2008), and, most recently, Glen James Brown's *Ironopolis* (2018). These examples demonstrate the ongoing symbolic purchase of the industrial landscape as synonymous with Northern working-class disaffection. Peace's depictions of Northern England are, as Christopher Vardy argues, dominated by 'dystopian post-industrial land-scapes' and 'imbricated with nostalgia' (Vardy, 2013). The drunken toast of a corrupt police officer in Peace's *Nineteen Eighty Three*, 'To us all and to the north – where we do what we want!' (Peace, 2002, p. 228), captures what Raymond Williams describes as the 'structure of feeling' (Williams, 1977, p. 134) of a region defined by disaffection and exploita-tion. One of the most overtly political evocations of the Thatcher period and the effects of deindustrialisation is Anthony Cartwright's *How I Killed Margaret Thatcher* (2012), depicting nine-year-old Sean Bull's plan to murder the Prime Minister against a backdrop of political discontent and socio-economic decline.

In contrast to the retrospective tendency of the 'post-Thatcher novel', the North's poetry scene quickly responded to the destructive effects of Thatcherism and deindustrialisation. In Yorkshire, Ted Hughes' *Remains of Elmet* (1979), Tony Harrison's *V* (1985), and Sean O'Brien's collections *The Indoor Park* (1983) and *The Frighteners* (1987) are paradigmatic of a wider regionalist poetic response to the continued socio-economic decline in industrial towns during the Thatcher period. James Underwood identifies the devolutionary thrust of poetry in the North during the 1970s and 1980s, arguing that if 'these are the decades in which the British poetry map began to devolve, then this is in part because these are the decades in which the North of England was cast adrift from the country's political and economic powerbase in the South-East' (Underwood, 2019, p.176). While Underwood approaches devolution in the spatial, decentralising sense here, he none-theless foregrounds the relationship between a literary regional or place-bound affiliation and lived socio-economic and political inequality. There is, then, a longer history of cultural devolution in Northern England that pits the region in opposition to Westminster politics.

Cinema and television series during 1980s and 1990s also paralleled this literary political activism. Ken Loach's adaptation of Hines' *Looks and Smiles* (1981) provided one of the earliest filmic responses to the mounting levels of unemployment in industrial towns during the 1970s and 1980s, centring on three young people who are left disenchanted by the lack of opportunities in Sheffield. This disaffection also permeates Chris Bernard's Liverpool-based film *Letter to Brezhnev* (1985), and the dramaturgical output of Andrea Dunbar, among others. The development of a specific subgenre of social realism engaging with the Miners' Strike also characterised this period. Alan Bleasdale's Liverpool-set TV series, *Boys from the Blackstuff* (1982), identified many of the issues that emerged in the 1970s, and which also underpinned the strikes during the 1980s. The series lamented the end of a working-class culture heavily associated with manual labour and masculinity, with unemployed tarmac layer Yosser Hughes' catchphrase 'Gizza job!' quickly entering the public consciousness. Mike Herman's *Brassed Off* (1996) depicted unemployment in the aftermath of pit closures, while *Our Friends in the North* (1996) captured the political energies of the North-East, pitting the Metropolitan Police against the striking miners and establishing a dichotomy between North and South.[16]

The socio-economic transformations of the 1980s thus instigated a much longer cultural framing of the North as irretrievably stuck in the past. These works operate within a set of regional aesthetics in which deindustrialised urban space is the default landscape for an almost exclusively working-class North, evoking what David Forrest and Sue Vice describe as a 'Northern Chronotope' (Forrest and Vice, 2015, p. 55). Taking *The Price of Coal* (1977), *The Northern Clemency,* and *GB84* as case studies, Forrest and Vice describe a tendency in which Northern literary production operates, somewhat self-consciously, within a 'spatial narrative, which aligns the North within a working-class symbolic system in opposition to the middle-class South' (Forrest and Vice, 2015, p. 61). These works, among others, helped solidify a set of regional aesthetics that continue to permeate literary representations of Northern England in the twenty-first century. Ken Loach, Mike Leigh, and Alan Clarke paved the way for contemporary evocations of the period as the effects of Thatcher's administration continued into the new millennium. Stephen Daldry's *Billy Elliot* (2000), Shane Meadows' film *This is England* (2006), and its related television series, and Paul Abbott's *Shameless* (2004–13) are also notable examples of reworkings 'of stereotypical or comic versions of the region's history and culture' (Russell, 2004, p. 269) that mark Northern England as 'other' following the socio-political shifts of the 1980s and 1990s. *Billy Elliot*'s working-class escape narrative is also heavily tied to a recurring post-strike class narrative of 'overcoming broken communities in Northern England' (Gardiner, 2004, p. 122). Gardiner notes how the central protagonist '"escapes" a community destroyed by the Miners' Strike, and the embarrassingly provincial attitudes of his family, to dance for the Royal Ballet in a performance only his father can afford to attend' (Gardiner, 2004, p. 122), pinpointing the oppositionality between a provincial identity in the North and London as a site of British cultural capital. Notably, this motif has carried over to twenty-first century coming-of-age narratives depicting a new, upwardly mobile 'creative class' (Florida, 2014). Jessica Andrews' *Saltwater* (2019), Eliza Clark's *Boy Parts* (2020), and

Anna Glendenning's *An Experiment in Leisure* (2021) rewrite the story of working-class escape for a distinctively neoliberal millennial generation, each following young women who flee formerly industrial Northern towns in search of the cultural capital offered by London.[17] The North's regional mythology has therefore been perpetuated not only externally but also *internally* in culture. As David Law points out, among the problems of conceiving of a 'progressive' Northern literary identity are the class-based 'totalising rhetorics of the North' that are effectively 'mimicked and given by the region' (Law, 2003, p. 299).

A related barrier to transcending this historically rooted 'rhetoric of North' is the scant critical attention to Northern England's diverse, twenty-first-century literary identity. Cockin's *The Literary North* provides the most in-depth engagement with the region thus far, observing that the region 'has been subjected to stereotype, misrepresentation and myth', particularly between the nineteenth and twentieth century (Cockin, 2012, p. 1). Cockin notes how existing studies of the region favour cinematic or televisual representation over its literary output; she argues that, while the region has been examined in various cultural forms, 'the literary North of England has not hitherto been considered in any systematic way' (Cockin, 2012, p. 1). Surveying a range of literary genres – including science fiction and children's literature – emerging from various towns within Northern England between the mid-nineteenth century and the late twentieth century, the book identifies several recurring motifs and characteristics that have helped construct – and occasionally challenge – the region's cultural mythology. However, while the collection offers a valuable reassessment of myths of the North, 'making power relations taken for granted in the literary canon more visible', discussion of these 'power relations' does not concern the twenty-first-century literary North, or its role in the relationship between England and Britain (Cockin, 2012, p. 19). Beyond Cockin's edited collection and Law's PhD thesis (2003), literary-critical engagement with Northern England takes the form of book-chapter length studies that engage with the region as a spatial aesthetic or as a thematic preoccupation in author-centred studies. Though scholars have barely begun to study the region's cultural evolution in any sustained detail, twenty-first-century literary engagement with the North remains a critical omission.[18]

The self-exoticising tendencies marking Northern literary and cultural production also characterise non-fictional engagements with the region, which are often aimed at a non-academic audience. Largely taking the form of travel writing or memoir, much non-fictional discussion of the North focuses on the region's cultural fluorescence during a period of economic decline. Former Hacienda DJ Dave Haslam's *Manchester, England* describes how the rave revolution 'brought a thriving subculture to the surface' in which Manchester 'was no longer carrying the baggage of a hundred and fifty years of preconceptions, about the weather, the environment, the misery' (Haslam, 1999, p. 250). At the turn of the new millennium, Haslam's love letter to Manchester's rave scene paved the way for a wider coterie of male writers and their cultural history of the region. Dave Russell and Stephen Wagg's *Sporting Heroes of the North* (2004), Peter Davidson's *The Idea of North* (2005), Stuart Maconie's *Pies and Prejudice* (2007), Martin Wainwright's *True North* (2010), and NME writer, Paul Morley's *The North (and Almost Everything In It)* (2013) are notable examples of this trend, many of which romanticise the writer's relationship to the region. By Morely's own admission, his narrative of the North is 'a hallucination as much as it is a history' (Morely, 2013, p. 555). So while these Northern cultural histories acknowledge the region's marginalisation, they are also complicit in its mythologisation.

Christoph Ehland's *Thinking Northern* (2007) and Dave Russell's *Looking North* (2004) offer explorations of the North that go beyond this self-exoticising lens. Ehland examines the various imaginative locations associated with 'Northernness', arguing that the North of England is a region marked by a mythology and cannot escape its past. For Ehland, the North is a 'fragmented vision, somewhere along the lines of Wordsworth's daffodils, Manchester capitalism, and Beatlemania' (Ehland, 2007, p. 20). Likewise, Russell surveys twentieth-century representations of the North in a range of cultural forms, including literature, theatre, and film, seeking to 'make sense of northern England's place within national culture' (Russell, 2004, p. 9). Russell's account pinpoints the industrial novels of the 1840s, the Wigan Pier era, the kitchen sink dramas of the post-war period, and Manchester's music scene as temporary 'break-through' moments, concluding that the North 'has enjoyed some degree of agency and been celebrated, even cherished, but always on terms dictated by the centre' (Russell, 2004, p. 9). The inequality between core and periphery that Russell diagnoses in these conflicted versions of England has structural and constitutional origins, and, as we shall see, implications that have been borne out in literary culture.

Any cultural or political discussion of the North is complicated by the impossibility of delimiting geographic parameters of a region which does not constitutionally exist. After all, the UK is a unitary, not federal, multi-national state form. Helen Jewell's historical account of *The North-South Divide* identifies a line joining the River Humber, River Trent, and River Mersey to define a Southern boundary (Jewell, 1994, p. 16), while in *The Literary North*, Katherine Cockin pinpoints the construction of the M1 as an essential indicator. As Cockin notes, the Watford Gap service station has 'characterised Northern travel and featured in many media engagements with the North' (Cockin, 2012, p. 5). For Robert Shields, the North is pre-dominantly a 'space-place myth' but he eventually delimits the region with a line drawn from the River Severn to the River Wash (Shields, 1991, p. 259). Critical discussion of Northern England also often includes the Midlands. As Russell observes in his discussion of the North's cultural status, the region is often generously defined as so to embrace, amongst other areas,

D.H. Lawrence's north Nottinghamshire, Alan Sillitoe's Nottingham and Arnold Bennett's Potteries. The tendency to include the Midlands in critical discussion of the North points to how 'Northernness' operates as a short-hand for (de)industrial towns with a predominantly working-class demographic, with a kind of geographical stretchiness that, as Tom Kew points out, occludes local variances across the Midlands as a distinct region (Kew, 2017). These multiple, differing critical attempts to delimit parameters for the North testify to the region's overdetermined, mythological status.

But while existing cultural and historical studies of Northern England have attempted to define parameters for the region, my approach to 'the North' rejects a singular definition. Rather, *Rewriting the North* recognises the plural and heterogenous localities across the region. Of course, this is not to neglect the interplay between space, place, and social power in Britain; the material and cultural landscapes of the North are inseparable from the reflection and reproduction of hierarchal social relations, especially contemporary class struggle. *Rewriting the North* thus approaches the region in the spirit of what Benedict Anderson calls an 'imagined community' (Anderson, 1983, p. 6). Although Anderson's 'imagined communities' refers to nations, I am applying the term regionally here to explore literary engagement with the North of England's 'imagined' status as a complex web of changing socio-economic and geopolitical relations that transcend territorial boundaries. As we will see, Northern England is far from uniform and its internal sub-regions remain highly differentiated across complex socio-economic, cultural, and political lines. Brexit's voting demographics demonstrated that there remains vast inequalities that go beyond 'North' and 'South' with coastal areas across England emerging as key geographies of intersecting, material inequalities.[19] The regions comprising Northern England are not simply areas of economic decline. Lying between York, Leeds, and Harrogate, Yorkshire's 'Golden Triangle' encompasses economically prosperous suburban fringe towns that enjoy a largely middle-class population, while the region's major cities – such as Leeds, Manchester, Newcastle, and Liverpool – are benefitting from urban renewal and rebranding themselves as financial and cultural hubs.[20] In fact, by 'placing' various spatialities across Northern England, this book aims to offer a differentiated narrative of the region that pulls against a simplistic North–South opposition. *Rewriting the North* initiates a disciplinary shift towards England's literary reprovincialisation that might, in turn, enable a post-British literature of England to emerge.

Chapter Summaries

The chapters that follow identify four contemporary literary conceptualisations of the North which are situated within several political moments in Britain between 2001 and 2018. Part I traces the literary registration of stress fractures emerging in the relationship between the North and the British state following the Devolved Parliaments Act, departing from the 'multicultural' refashioning of Britishness under Tony Blair's New Labour government. Chapter 1 focuses on the relationship between multicultural political practice and literary culture after the 2001 'Northern race riots': specifically, the centralisation of the 'multicultural' novel in London as the singular terrain for multi-racial experience in Britain. Surveying the wider field of 'devolutionary' approaches to Black and Asian British writing, the chapter responds to the way that existing attempts to 'place' race in the nation tend to overlook devolution's constitutional implications. The chapter suggests that Sunjeev Sahota's Sheffield-based novels *Ours are the Streets* (2011) and *The Year of the Runaways* (2015) counter a state-led, racialised narrative of the urban North as a white working-class monolith, instead placing the roots of racism with British political practice at the turn of the millennium. Moving from city to country, Chapter 2 focuses on the rural North as a site of post-British potential. Taking Sarah Hall's *Haweswater* (2002), *The Carhullan Army* (2007), and *The Wolf Border* (2015) as case studies, the chapter maps the development of a distinctively post-pastoral consciousness that attempts to disentangle Englishness from the imperial formation of the pastoral idyll. From small-scale agriculture to the practices of rewilding and environmental sustainability, the chapter suggests that Hall's persistent rejection of the pastoral literary mode functions as a 'devolutionary' pull against centralised state power in Britain and attempts to imagine a politically autonomous England emerging from the North-West.

Part II focuses on literary engagement with the North after the 2016 United Kingdom (UK) European Union (EU) membership referendum. Taking this moment as a watershed for the relationship between the North and the wider nation, Chapters 3 and 4 examine works that locate regional uneven development and democratic deficit as key to Brexit as a devolutionary revolt in support of regionalised English governance. Chapter 3 explores the ways in which the North operated in the post-Brexit-vote literary imagination as a geographically vague, socio-economic metaphor for deindustrialisation. Exploring the relationship between place, region, and class, the chapter traces the link between literary constructions of the North after the Brexit-vote and the 'Little Englandism' that was perceived to lie behind England's decision to exit the EU. Examining Anthony Cartwright's *The Cut* and Adam Thorpe's *Missing Fay*, this chapter suggests that Thorpe and Cartwright's use of nostalgia and deindustrial aesthetics operates within a regional mythology in which the North functions as a localised, specifically English, antithesis to a London-centred Britishness. Another form of nostalgia is the central focus of the final chapter. Chapter 4 turns to the 'global' orientation of Britishness as a 'progressive', rearticulated state-nationalism after the Brexit vote. I identify an inward 'neo-primitive turn' emerging from post-Brexit-vote Northern literary production as a rejection of 'Global Britain' as a state-led attempt to present a unitary Britishness after the Brexit referendum. The temporal and environmental imaginaries of Sarah Moss' *Ghost Wall* (2018) and Fiona

Mozley's *Elmet* (2017) provide a neo-primitivist praxis of place in opposition to a deterritorialised governmental discourse of 'Global Britishness'. My analysis of *Elmet* and *Ghost Wall* in this chapter is indicative of a central argumentative strand running throughout this book, suggesting the need to reconceptualise the relationship between the region and the nation that goes beyond, on the one hand, a metropolitan 'Global Britain'; and, on the other, a reactionary English regionalism.

The conclusion sketches out the disciplinary implications for the future of British literary studies and explores spatial inequalities within the cultural and creative industries. This chapter examines how increasing attempts to address regional imbalances in Britain's creative economy over the past decade replicate the centralised logic of governmental initiatives. Overall, the conclusion underlines the significance of the cultural politics of devolution as both a literary aesthetic marking contemporary fiction and critical practice, both of which articulate the narrow horizon afforded by devolution as an alternative to the centralised state form. For British literary studies, the consequences go beyond the urgency of rewriting the North towards an entire methodological rethink. The 'British literature' paradigm is no longer tenable for reading the diverse literary production emerging out of Northern English geographies – these heterogenous, placed literary cultures resist mobilisation in support of a unitary national narrative.

Notes

1 An illustrative example is David Goodhart's explanation of Brexit's culture war in Goodhart (2017) *The Road to Somewhere: The Populist Revolt and the Future of Politics*. London: C. Hurst & Co.

2 See, for example, Kirsty Major (2016) 'Why the North of England Will Regret Voting for Brexit', *The Independent*, 24 June. Available at: www.independent.co.uk/voices/why-the-north-of-england-will-regret-voting-for-brexit-a7101321.html [accessed 14 July 2020] and Ben Glaze and Jack Blanchard (2016) 'Labour Heartlands Give Huge Backing to Brexit as the North Votes to Leave', *The Mirror*, 24 June. Available at: www.mirror.co.uk/news/uk-news/labour-heartlands-give-huge-backing-8271074 [accessed 14 July 2020].

3 As we will see in Chapters 3 and 4, the yoking together of the North and England's 'left behind' has been reflected since 2016 in a surge of literary production which deploys the deindustrial North as a default spatial setting for exploring Brexit.

4 Notable engagements with Englishness after the EU referendum include Anthony Barnett (2017) *The Lure of Greatness: England's Brexit and America's Trump*. London: Unbound; Stephen Haesler (2017) *England Alone: Brexit and the Crisis of English Identity*. London: Forum Press; Mike Wayne (2018) *England's Discontents: Political Cultures and National Identities*. London: Pluto; Ben Wellings (2019) *English Nationalism, Brexit and the Anglosphere: Wider Still and Wide*. Manchester: Manchester University Press; and Aisla Henderson and Richard Wyn Jones (2021) *Englishness: The Political Force Transforming Britain*. Oxford: Oxford University Press.

5 For Stuart Hall, Englishness can never be mobilised in a progressive sense, remaining emphatically opposed to 'radical appropriation'. See Jon Derbyshire

(2012) 'Stuart Hall: "We Need to Talk about Englishness"', *New Statesman*, 23 August. Available at: https://www.newstatesman.com/politics/uk-politics/2012/08/stuart-hall-we-need-talk-about-englishness [accessed: 4 September 2020].

6 See also Alex Niven (2020) 'Why It's Time to Stop Talking about English Identity', *The Guardian*, 15 July. Available at: https://www.theguardian.com/commentisfree/2020/jul/15/english-identity-patriotism-england-independent [accessed 15 September 2020].

7 Nairn's view of devolution as a form of 'virtual liberation' reflects the way in which its parliamentary affordances are reversible by Westminster at any time. See Nairn (1998 and 2000) and Vernon Bogdanor (1999) *Devolution in the United Kingdom*. Oxford: Oxford University Press.

8 Nairn influenced a body of work that began to focus on the political dimensions of English identity from the mid-2000s, forming one part of a much wider social science literature devoted to the study of nationalism. Notable contributions included monographs by Krishan Kumar (2003) *The Making of English National Identity*, Cambridge: Cambridge University Press; Arthur Aughey (2007) *The Politics of Englishness*. Manchester: Manchester University Press; Simon Featherstone (2009) *Englishness: Twentieth-Century Popular Culture and the Forming of English Identity*. Edinburgh: Edinburgh University Press; Michael Kenny (2014) *The Politics of English Nationhood*. Oxford: Oxford University Press; and Ben Wellings (2019) *English Nationalism, Brexit and the Anglosphere: Wider Still and Wider*. Manchester: Manchester University Press.

9 Gardiner's approach is indebted to Ian Baucom's influential assessment of Englishness as a series of reproducible, idealised images that were displaced in Britain's Empire. See Baucom (1999) *Out of Place: Englishness, Empire, and the Locations of Identity*. Princeton: Princeton University Press.

10 Gardiner identifies the period between the 1790s and 1810 as the time in which English Literature became 'an alternative codification' of Britishness, developing further during the nineteenth century, the First World War, and again after the decline of Empire' (2013, p. 19). Key literary figures in his thesis include Samuel Taylor Coleridge, who connected 'the permanence of a state with the land and the landed property' and William Shakespeare, who embodied 'the values of an empiricist and exceptionalist British state' (Gardiner, 2013, pp. 41, 37).

11 See, for example, Nick Hubble and Philip Tew (2016) *London in Contemporary British Fiction: The City Beyond the City*. London: Bloomsbury.

12 See most recently, Scott Hames (2020) *The Literary Politics of Scottish Devolution: Voice, Class, Nation*. Edinburgh: Edinburgh University Press.

13 See James. F. English (2005), 'Introduction: British Fiction in a Global Context' in English (ed) *A Concise Companion to Contemporary British Fiction*. Oxford: Blackwell, pp. 1–15; For dedicated discussions of Thatcherism in relation to developments in British fiction, see Joseph Brooker (2010) *Literature of the 1980s: After the Watershed*. Edinburgh: Edinburgh University Press and Kimberly Duff (2014) *Contemporary British Fiction and Urban Space: After Thatcher*. New York: Palgrave Macmillan.

14 The Thatcher period is often credited with initiating a wave of postmodern representation and narrative innovation in novels of the 1980s and 1990s. For a critical appraisal of this development, see Tew, Horton, and Wilson (eds.) (2014) *The 1980s: A Decade of Contemporary British Fiction*. London: Bloomsbury.

15 Jeff Noon's Manchester-based cyberpunk series, *Vurt* (1993, 1995, 1996, 1997) is a notable exception to this rule.

16 See David Forrest (2011) '*Our Friends in the North* and the Instability of the Historical Drama as Archive'. *The Journal of British Cinema and Television*, 8 (2), pp. 218–233.

17 See Chloe Ashbridge (2022) '"All I Need Is Myself": Spatialising Neoliberal Class Consciousness in the Northern Millennial Novel' in S. Lee (ed.) *Locating Classed Subjectivities: Intersections of Space and Working-Class Life in Nineteenth-, Twentieth-, and Twenty-First-Century British Writing.* London: Routledge, pp. 206–225.

18 See David Forrest and Sue Vice (2015) 'A Poetics of the North: Visual and Literary Geographies' in I. Franklin, H. Chignell and K. Skoog (eds.) *Regional Aesthetics: Mapping UK Media Cultures.* London: Palgrave Macmillan, pp. 55–67 and David Thompson's discussion (2011) of David Peace's North in Katy Shaw (ed.) *Analysing David Peace.* Newcastle Upon Tyne: Scholars Publishing, pp. 107–114.

19 For a critical discussion of the North–South divide as a socio-economic formation, see Danny Dorling (2010), 'Persistent North-South Divides', in N.M. Coe and A. Jones. (eds.) *The Economic Geography of the UK.* London: SAGE, pp. 12–28.

20 See, for example, Brett Christophers (2008) 'The BBC, the Creative Class, and Neoliberal Urbanism in the North of England', *Environment and Planning A: Economy and Space*, 40 (10), pp. 2313–2329.

Part I
Stress Fractures

1 Multicultural Britishness and the Urban North

In the summer of 2001, violence erupted on the streets of three former mill towns in Lancashire and West Yorkshire. Heralded as the most severe instances of urban violence since the 1980s, the disturbances in Oldham, Burnley, and Bradford were framed in a series of tabloid media and political responses as the result of increased tension between young Asian men and white extremists (Alexander, 2004, p. 526). In Oldham, the violence unfolded across three consecutive nights in May, shortly followed by disturbances in Burnley. The largest clashes were concentrated in Bradford over the weekend of 8 and 9 July, during which young White men attacked the police and Asian-owned businesses in the Arncliffe and Holmwood areas, leading to the injuries of over 300 police officers and 287 cumulative arrests. In the wake of these so-called 'Northern race riots' or 'Northern town riots', images circulated within national media and political commentary which set the town's Asian community and police officers in opposition to one another, tacitly depicting the former as antagonistic internal 'others' pitted against juridical markers of national belonging, law, and order.[1] In parallel to this racialised discourse of Northern England's Asian community, tabloids including the *Daily Mail* blamed the events on the Labour council 'funnelling' public spending 'worth millions' (Wilkies, 2006) into regenerating the predominantly Asian areas of Stoneyholme and Daneshouse. The riots are part of a historical vein of racial politics in Britain which constructed 'the North', especially Yorkshire's former mill towns, as an undifferentiated space of racial antagonism. Less than twenty years earlier, Bradford had been the site of the highly politicised burning of *The Satanic Verses* in 1989, and the 7/7 London bombings of 2005 were carried out by four young Muslim men brought up in West Yorkshire. The events of 2001 exposed the seemingly ethnically segregated, 'parallel lives' of two constructed groups, Muslims and the 'English Defence League (EDL) supporting white racists' (Miah, Sanderson, and Thomas, 2020, p. 4), both of which were attributed to failed multicultural policies in Northern towns.

The urban street is a recurring symbolic site of racialised politics in Sahota's literary imaginary. All of his novels concern Northern England in general and Sheffield in particular, exploring how experiences of race and

DOI: 10.4324/9781003388722-3

migration in the city are shaped by Northern England's position in the national consciousness. Sahota has spoken elsewhere about his interest in how, in Sheffield, the socio-economic and material implications of Thatcher's dismantling of the steel industry altered the experience of first- and second-generation inward migration:

> [A] sense of betrayal from that time still hangs in the air today in many communities in the North of England. What that does to a community, how the blame for that is fixed on a government, and the sense of displacement caused by new communities coming in, is fascinating. The children of those new groups create a new dynamic and a unique nexus of conditions that is quite specific to the North. The landscape of the North seems to lend itself to that sense of isolation, of subversion, of going against the grain …
>
> (Shaw, 2017, p. 267)

Sahota's words recall a post-Thatcherite iconography of a monolithic, deindustrialising North, but the local specificity of his work negates regional mythologisation. Instead, it is through the urban topography of the Sheffield's streets that Sahota's first two novels, *Ours are the Streets* (2011) and *The Year of the Runaways* (2015), go 'against the grain' of a prevailing narrative of 'Northern' racial hostility. Apart from occasional passages set in London, the Midlands, India, and Pakistan, both novels are intensely localised. Residential estates, local bus routes, and road signs punctuate his account of migration, with the socio-economic implications of deindustrialisation providing an intersectional class narrative that challenges an easy association of Northern England with an undifferentiated white working class.

Sahota's attempt to provide a specifically localised account of race in Northern England might be compared to the novels of Caryl Phillips, a writer whose most recent writing concentrates on the everyday lives of ethnically diverse communities in Yorkshire.[2] John McLeod suggests that Phillips has been crucial in rearticulating Northern England against a stereotype of racial prejudice:

> The northern "English somewheres" towards which [Phillips'] work travels are never idealized or glibly celebrated, but articulated in order to secure a postcolonial discourse of the North, in contradistinction to the usual clichés – one which suggests the tactics needed for a transformed future for the region.
>
> (McLeod, 2011, p. 27)

For example, Phillips' *A Distant Shore* (2003) appears to be concerned with the complexities of establishing a placed vision of England which is both regionalised and ethnically diverse. The novel opens with the statement that

'England has changed: these days it's hard to tell who's from round here and who isn't' (Phillips, 2003, p. 1), focusing on the everyday lives of a small, unnamed village in Northern England. Sahota's novels affect a similar placing and re-provincialisation. His accounts of migrant experience in Northern England expose not only the spatial biases of political multiculturalism, but also the exclusions inherent in state-sanctioned notions of citizenship. This chapter thus focuses on Sahota as a writer whose fiction might be read productively alongside the work of Phillips in that it is concerned with multicultural British citizenship and belonging in Northern towns. Like Phillips, Sahota's fictions are inseparable from Britain's uneven regional development, with what McLeod terms the 'glitzy spectacle of millennial multicultural British chic' (McLeod, 2020a, p.464) frequently problematised. This chapter thus proposes that Sahota's novels reject a vision of Northern England as a microcosm of a narrower ethno-purist Englishness and complicate the region's association with a monolithic, white working class. While *Ours are the Streets* and *The Year of the Runaways* do not attempt to present Sheffield as a place without racism, their narratives of diasporic alienation shift the foundations of racism in Britain towards the structures of British political practice and, in turn, actively denaturalise Britishness. Taken together, they constitute an ideological departure from the London-based 'multicultural novel' in which Britishness has operated as the default national setting.

Ours are the Streets tells the story of Imtiaz Raina, a second-generation immigrant living in Sheffield. Told from Imtiaz's perspective in the style of a diary cum confessional memoir, the text explores his radicalisation and plans to blow up Meadowhall following a trip to Pakistan, where he becomes involved in terror activities. Unable to forge an identity as an active participant in England, Imtiaz's lack of belonging manifests itself in an attack on Sheffield's largest shopping centre. The governmental imperatives of 'inclusion' and 'community' are registered through Imtiaz's self-surveillance, leaving his experience in Sheffield marked by alienation and culminating in his decision to detonate a bomb in Meadowhall (Cantle, 2001, p. 27; Denham, 2001, p. 1). As the title indicates, for Imtiaz, the street becomes a symbolic space to be reclaimed in order to fight back against his abjection under the British state.[3] Published four years later, *The Year of the Runaways* offers a distinctively neoliberal migrant narrative which explores the pursuit of legal British citizenship. Set in Sheffield in 2003, the novel traces the precarious lives of three Indian men (Randeep, Avtar, and Tochi) in the years leading up to the 2007–2008 global financial crisis, all of whom believe that migration to England will enable them to live what Lauren Berlant describes as 'the good life' promised by capitalist culture (Berlant, 2011, p. 1). Told through the multiple narrative perspectives of these men and one British-Indian woman (Narinder), *The Year of the Runaways* approaches 'multicultural Britain' through the asymmetrical relationship between the individual and the state in an era of neoliberalism. Connecting Sahota's protagonists is an experience of legal British citizenship as a state-sanctioned assimilatory politics with negative consequences for civic life, resulting in self-surveillance and alienation. What is notable about the depiction of Sheffield in *Ours are the Streets* and *The Year of the Runaways* is how they complicate a government-led narrative of Northern England's urban spaces as sites of racial hostility. Instead, these novels position the state's management of race and the political structures of Britishness at the core of their protagonists' lack of belonging.

These multicultural policies were a product of Tony Blair's New Labour government, which, in the aftermath of devolution in Scotland, Wales, and Northern Ireland, placed 'race' at the centre of a state-led, unitary, nationalist politics. The nation's rebirth reached its pinnacle in Blair's 'Cool Britannia' as a reinvigorated celebration of Britain as 'one nation', a 'young country' (Blair, 1995) that was forward-looking, progressive, and emphatically multicultural. In the context of Britain's ongoing constitutional fragmentation, Blair's redefinition of Britishness was necessary for New Labour to 'shore up a continued hierarchical relation between the devolved national areas and the British parliament in England's capital city' (Pitcher, 2009, p. 44). This culturally pluralist state nationalism is what Ben Pitcher calls an 'elaborated Britishness' (Pitcher, 2009, p. 44) which harnessed racial politics to maintain the nation-state after a period of constitutional weakening during the 1990s. Under the devolutionary British state, multicultural policies served to legitimate the state and facilitate a new British nationhood during a significant phase of constitutional instability. Put another way, the devolutionary period saw the state's mobilisation of 'race' in the service of Britain's refashioning as a culturally plural, but unified nation.

Amidst New Labour's pluralist nationalism, the 'Northern riots' provided the government with a pretext for setting out 'its new communitarian approach to race politics' (Pitcher, 2009, p. 87). The implied narrative here was that the North had a 'problem with race' and that the relationship between its assumed White locals and Asian population required managing by the state. In his preface to *There Ain't No Black in the Union Jack*, Paul Gilroy's interprets the riots as 'testimony to the depth of degradation found in decaying post-industrial towns', noting how industrial decline has been 'intertwined with technological change, with immigration and settlement, with ideological racism and spatial segregation along economic and cultural lines' (Gilroy, 2013, p. xvi). Gilroy's account brings to the fore how the riots are a significant moment for the position of Northern England in the British national imaginary. Tellingly, the riots were not 'British'; instead, they were English in general and Northern in particular. The riots thus appeared to represent the failure of multiculturalism, depicting the three mill towns as sites of dispossession, hostility, and racial prejudice on both sides. The 2001 riots solidified the racialisation of Northern England as an entire region which was taken to be 'a breeding ground for criminality and ideologically driven violence' (Miah et al., 2020). Shamim Miah, Pete Sanderson, and Paul Thomas propose that the North had come to symbolise racial hostility since the mid-1980s when it 'took centre stage in political and media discourse over British multiculturalism and has then accelerated markedly in the post-2001 era of concern over "parallel lives" and Islamic extremism' (Miah et al., 2020, p. 10). This longer historical discourse of Northern England as a 'failed space' of racial diversity yoked the region to a homogenous (and largely xenophobic) white working-class identity that was bound up with an ethnonationalist approach to Englishness. At the same time, the tendency to construct the working class as a race in and of itself is based on a failure to fully grasp the complex interrelationship between race and class. In any case, governmental responses to the riots contributed towards a socio-political framing of mostly deindustrialised areas of Northern England as deprived and backwards looking, both 'other' and opposed to a supposedly progressive multicultural Britishness.

The Literary Politics of British Multiculturalism

The development of the British 'multicultural novel' as a subgenre of Black and Asian British writing has been instrumental to the racialisation of the North. As both a cultural form and academic discipline, Black and Asian writing in Britain occupies a unique position in literary debates about decentralisation. Since the 1980s, it has, as Stuart Hall puts it, become increasingly 'centred' (Hall, 1987) to the extent that London takes on a national status as the singular terrain for accounts of racial diversity in Britain.[4] Existing literary-critical attempts to 'devolve' Black Britain echo Hall in seeking to conceive of a spatially differentiated approach to race in the nation. James Procter's *Dwelling Places* sought to develop a devolved spatial optic for reading Black British cultural production that recognises 'the politics of location' (Procter, 2003, p. 1). Of particular importance in Procter's account is how the lack of regional difference in Black Britain is largely due to the 'deterritorialising tendencies of diaspora discourse', which have been facilitated by a 'slippage' (Procter, 2003, p. 164) between London and Britain. As a result, the former 'provides the only sustaining setting for an excavation and interrogation of Black culture, the only available archive and inventory' (Procter, 2003, p. 164). London has dominated a contemporary canon of 'multicultural' writing in Britain, epitomised by the critical and commercial success of Hanif Kureishi's *The Buddha of Suburbia* (1990), Zadie Smith's *White Teeth* (2000) and *N.W.* (2012), and Monica Ali's *Brick Lane* (2003). In all of these works, London's cityscape becomes a metonym for a larger multicultural Britishness. As such, the capital has occupied a 'deterritorialised' but simultaneously national status in diasporic Black British discourse, operating as the default site for a racially diverse Britishness. Lynne Pearce, Corinne Fowler, and Robert Crawshaw note a similar tendency in *Postcolonial Manchester* (2013). In excavating a history of post-war Black and Asian cultural production across Manchester, they suggest that while regions in the North of England are 'not without their own long-established histories of cultural production', these outputs 'have rarely won metropolitan support or favour' (Pearce et al., 2013, p. 3). Echoing Procter, Pearce et al. pinpoint the dominance of London as Britain's 'multicultural heartland' and how diasporic literary production, dissemination, and critique persistently neglect locales which are seen to be 'provincial' (Pearce et al., 2013, p. 3).

Just as political multiculturalism has functioned as a politics of state-nationalism in devolutionary Britain, the development and critical and commercial reception of 'multicultural' writing in Britain have served the priorities of a London-centred Britishness. The treatment of Smith's debut novel, *White Teeth* (2000) is instructive here. Upon its publication, Smith was 'heralded as the new voice of British literature', and *White Teeth*, though satirical, was 'initially perceived as a celebratory examination of multicultural relations' (Shaw, 2017, p. 67). Smith's association with British literature was inextricably tied to London's status as the epicentre of an outward-facing multicultural Britishness. While, for Kristian Shaw, *White Teeth* envisions 'London's potential in establishing a "happy multicultural land" of transnational associations' (Shaw, 2017, p. 67), Corinne Fowler approaches the novel as emblematic of the relationship between British political projects and its literary economy. In a pioneering essay, 'A Tale of Two Novels' (2008), Fowler charts the vastly differing fortunes of *White Teeth* and Joe Pemberton's *Forever and Ever, Amen* (2000), which was published during the same year. Fowler attributes the unique success of *White Teeth* to the fact that it has 'proved amenable to a process of domestication that at least partially serves a celebratory cosmopolitan agenda', while Smith herself is 'readily marketable … as an apparent success story of British multiculturalism' (Fowler, 2008, p. 83). Unlike *White Teeth*, the parochial 'Northern' association of Pemberton's Moss Side setting negatively impacted its perceived marketability and, in turn, its commercial and critical success. As Fowler points out, the fact that 'Northern' writing is seen to be inherently less marketable than the London-based 'multicultural novel' provides evidence of 'the discomforting links between the political and literary economy' (Fowler, 2008, p.75). Fowler's analysis of two thematically comparable – but geographically disparate – novels illustrates the way that scholarly and commercial approaches to 'multicultural' writing in Britain have tended to reinforce the spatial biases of British *political* multiculturalism – that is, they replicate a centralised state logic that allocates capital and narrates Britishness itself in a way that is centred on London.

But while the dominance of London in Black and Asian British literary production is often noted, the symbiotic ecology of Britain's political and literary cultures has further implications for Northern literary representation. For example, the absence of a regionally differentiated Black British culture augments the racialised power relations of the North–South divide in which the North of England is 'synonymous with a (caricatured) white, provincial ethnicity', while London 'does not seem to raise the same kind of contradictions' (Procter, 2003, p. 161). As Procter explains:

> [D]ebates on empire and its aftermath have tended to flicker between metropolitan centre and postcolonial periphery while paying scant attention to the internal margins of provincial Englishness. Nevertheless, there is compelling evidence to suggest that the regional novel has played, and continues to play, a significant imaginative role during the period of the empire's passing.
>
> (Procter, 2011, p. 203)

More widely still, the ongoing centrality of London in accounts of Black British life marginalises intersectional accounts of race and class beyond the capital, ensuring the continuity of a London- and South-East-centric literary economy as a bulwark of the Union. So, just as Joseph Jackson suggests that Black British literature has seen racial diversity 'increasingly mobilised to evidence a new, unified, Britishness' (Jackson, 2020, p. 27), this centralised logic has simultaneously relied on an image of Northernness that operates outside of – and in opposition to – multicultural Britishness.

From Assimilation to Abjection: *Ours are the Streets*

Ours are the Streets is told retrospectively through Imtiaz's first-person narration, charting his journey to Islamic radicalisation following a trip to Pakistan. The narrative comes to form the apologia that Imtiaz intends to leave behind for his wife, Becka, and daughter, Noor, justifying his actions and communicating what he feels is a profound moral dilemma. Imtiaz expresses relief in the novel's opening sentence ('At last the page is stained') suggesting a confessional writing process before his death, because 'knowing you're going to die makes you want to talk' (Sahota, 2011, p. 1). *Ours are the Streets* might be read as what Sarah Ilott describes as a 'British Muslim Bildungsrome', which makes available 'a broader range of subject positions that are crucial in challenging representations of Islam as monoliths and in perpetual opposition to notions of Britishness' (Ilott, 2015, p. 29). Indeed, the narrative charts Imtiaz's journey from initially wanting to be like everyone else and 'a part of their drift towards nothing' (Sahota, 2011, p. 3) to becoming a 'new stronger Imtiaz' (Sahota, 2011, p. 64). However, while *Ours are the Streets* attempts to go beyond polarising narratives of Muslims in Britain, tracing the structures of inequality and marginalisation that contribute to Imtiaz's radicalisation, a key ideological difference between Ilott's 'British Muslim Bildungsromane' and Sahota's novel resides in the latter's rejection of an 'expanded' Britishness that might include Islam. The novel refuses to reconcile Imtiaz's subject position with a version of Britishness premised on state discourse of 'community', 'assimilation', and 'integration', making visible the exclusions inherent in multiculturalism as a politics of nation.

Imtiaz's first-person confessional prose functions as a counter-narrative to the discourse of British political multiculturalism, communicating how state approaches to race result in constant self-governing and alienation. Despite being born in England, Imtiaz feels culturally separate from both 'Britishers' (pejoratively referred to as 'Goreh') and the Asian 'freshies' around him, locating an 'in-betweenness' or 'hybridity' characteristic of migrant narratives (Sahota, 2011, pp. 165, 78). Imtiaz's social alienation can be read through Imogen Tyler's 'social abjection', a process characteristic of neoliberal governance in which individuals excluded from state-sanctioned definitions of belonging are 'abject, cast out and illegalized' (Tyler, 2013, p. 20). Imtiaz appears to be what Tyler terms a 'national abject' who exists as 'ideological conductors mobilised to do the dirty work of neoliberal governmentality' (Tyler, 2013, p. 9) and who are subsequently the target of governmental strategies of control and risk containment. As we shall see, his alienation and subsequent self-surveillance represent the ways British political multiculturalism relied on internalised others, or 'national abjects' in order to legitimate itself through the governance of an internal threat to 'national values' (Tyler, 2013, p. 9). Tyler's concept of the 'national abject' offers an appropriate critical lens through which to read the exclusory practices of state racism embedded within political multiculturalism, particularly the way that Muslims were targeted as part of the state's formalised ideology of 'managing diversity' in the Cantle and Denham Reports. Many scholars have noted how, after the events of 2001, the 'War on Terror', and 7/7, male Muslims, in particular, were criminalised as 'revolting' subjects in the manner Tyler identifies here. Yasmin Hussain and Paul Bagguley point out, for example, that the combination of the riots, the political successes of the British National Party, and the events after 9/11 'pushed British-Pakistani Muslims into the forefront of national political conflicts around citizenship, national identity and allegiance to the state' (Hussain and Bagguley, 2005, p. 407). Pitcher likewise locates the exclusory practices of British state multiculturalism, arguing that the state views Muslim communities as 'exceed[ing] the official parameters of multicultural Britain' (Pitcher, 2009, p. 146). This process led to the figure of the male British Muslim often standing as the undifferentiated face of both immigration and terrorism, enabling the state to bundle refugees, immigrants, and terrorists 'into one revolting parasitical figure' (Tyler, 2013, p. 91) to be governed in the interests of the nation.

In this context, *Ours are the Streets* becomes Imtiaz's attempt to write back to his social abjection under the British state. The aesthetics of the first-person memoir enable a kind of confessional counternarrative which goes beyond a dominant political discourse that demonises British Muslims. When Imtiaz directs the narrative at Noor, for example, he emphasises the difference between media portrayals of terrorists and the 'loneliness that takes hold of his gut' (Sahota, 2011, p. 2). He admits that she 'won't find it easy, … but don't listen to what the newspapers and TV will have said about me. None of it is true. They don't know me' (Sahota, 2011, p. 2). Here, the novel attempts to communicate how a prevailing media and political narrative of alienation and otherness has led to Imtiaz's isolation and subsequent turn to radical Islam. For Imtiaz, the textual space of *Ours are the Streets* thus becomes what Homi K. Bhabha might call a 'Third Space' (Bhabha, 1994, p. 55), which provides the 'discursive conditions of enunciation' in which social marginality can be transformed. Sahota humanises the narrative of the would-be suicide bomber through an emphasis on Imtiaz's focalising voice; this shift in emphasis, from violence to voice, both attempts to 'put a human face on the threat of jihadi violence' (Morrison, 2017, p. 574) and registers the limitations of multiculturalism as a political ideology to effect egalitarian social relations. The process of writing indicates a desire for the kind of self-actualisation that goes beyond stereotype. Imtiaz tells us how 'that's what these pages are all about …. Wanting to be found out, which is only another way of wanting to be known' (Sahota, 2011, p. 17), framing his suicide attack is less a religiously motivated act of violence than the desire to forge meaningful social and democratic participation in England.

In terms of structures that uphold the British state, *Ours are the Streets* is alert to how Englishness has operated as a closed ethno-nationalist ideology rather than a civic nationalism. When Imtiaz recalls his childhood, a self-reflexive awareness locates the imperial power structures inherent in the use of English language, the discipline of English Literature, and the act of novel writing. Reflecting on his experiences of the British education system, Imtiaz reflects how:

> I really did enjoy English and Art and stuff like that. And wondered about growing up and writing plays or something, like ones Miss Shepherd took us to see in our GCSE year. Knew it'd never happen, like. For all the usual boring brown reasons. But I'm loving writing this. It's really helping. It's like I'm normally walking round and I'm just confused about how I'm feeling or what I'm thinking. But when I'm writing it's like I'm rummaging until I find something that's not far off what it really is what I want to say.
>
> (Sahota, 2011, p. 26)

Imtiaz perceives the discipline of English Literature and the art of writing creatively as racialised structures that are out of his reach 'for all the boring brown reasons'; his rationale recalls the yoking of the education system with loyalty to nation, which was embodied in the appearance of 'British Values' on the national curriculum in 2011 as part of the government's anti-terrorism strategy. Despite his childhood ambition and the catharsis that he attributes to writing, Imtiaz assumes that such a profession is closed to him. Imtiaz's inability to imagine himself as a writer and the novel's overall concern with language demonstrates the long-standing implications of policies like the Immigration and Nationality Act of 1955, which formally set out the requirement for immigrants to be proficient in the English language. Indeed, Imtiaz's implicit association of England with Whiteness evokes a reactionary ethnonationalism that reached its peak in Enoch Powell's infamous 'Rivers of Blood' speech of 1968 and continued with the emergence of Thatcherism a decade later, both of which presented Englishness as 'a closed ethnicity rather than an open nationality'.[5]

The novel returns to this exclusionary Englishness in sporting culture. During his time in Pakistan, shortly after his father's death, Imtiaz explains to his uncle the difficulties of growing up in England as a second-generation immigrant:

> We don't really know what we're about, I guess. Who we are, what we're here for. But that weren't nothing like what I wanted to say. Even to me it just sounded like the usual crap I'd been hearing for years. I wanted to talk about why I felt fine rooting for Liverpool, in a quiet way, but not England. I wanted to talk about why I found myself defending Muslims against whites and whites against Muslims.
>
> (Sahota, 2011, p. 137)

Imtiaz substitutes national affiliation with England for a ('quiet') emphasis on the regional through football, indicating that place-based identities attached to sporting culture are more accessible to him than a narrower Englishness. The reference to sporting allegiance speaks to a particular ethnonationalist Englishness that, following the Powell and Thatcher years, was encapsulated in the Tebbit test during the 1990s. Proposed by Conservative MP Norman Tebbit, the test challenged the supposed 'national loyalty' of immigrants via their support of England's cricket team, rather than the country from which they (or their parents) emigrated. Imtiaz's inability to reconcile the two identity classifications alludes to an ideological mechanism of British multiculturalism which relies on Islam standing as a racial category in opposition to a class-inflected English whiteness; at the same time, however, Imtiaz's admission that he finds himself defending 'Muslims against whites and whites against Muslims' (Sahota, 2011, p. 137) pulls against such a racialised, governmental discourse.

Imtiaz's psychological deterioration and dispossession also articulate the impact of British state surveillance on civic life. The narrative switches frequently from past to present, with a metafictional acknowledgement early on that Imtiaz 'might be getting things mixed up a bit,' but 'this is how [he] remember[s] things' (Sahota, 2011, p. 13). This narrative fragmentation is framed as Imtiaz's growing paranoia that he is being watched by an unnamed group, culminating in a narrative interruption; he tells Becka and Noor, for example, that 'if they really are on to me then I need to get the rest of everything down quick' (Sahota, 2011, p. 202). This self-conscious narrative disjointedness works productively to foreground the imaginary status of Tarun, a security guard at Meadowhall whom Imtiaz suspects may know of his planned attack. As an authority figure, Tarun functions allegorically as a symbol of the state, an outward projection of Imtiaz's self-surveillance and paranoia within a regulatory environment of assimilationism. Invisible to Becka and other characters in the text, Imtiaz initially glimpses Tarun on the tram from Meadowhall back to Sheffield city centre, describing Tarun staring at him the way 'someone might start at a tree or a painting', but later forgetting the encounter (Sahota, 2011, p. 111). The association of Tarun with political multiculturalism is acutely visible during an exchange in which he gives Imtiaz food tokens based on 'community', causes Imtiaz to recoil – it 'always made him wince, that word' (Sahota 2011, p. 144).

The reference to 'community' is a hallmark feature of New Labour multiculturalism and the state's politics of race after the 2001 riots, providing a 'de facto mechanism through which the institutions of the state have sought to understand and deal with racialized groups' (Pitcher, 2009, p. 76). The Cantle (2001) and Denham (2001) Reports are two such examples of government legislation which effectively instructed ethnic minorities to police themselves to ensure the performance of national values aligned with British citizenship (Cantle, 2001, p. 19). The Cantle Report formed the state's earliest response to 'managing diversity' via an apparently self-empowering goal of 'community cohesion'. The word 'community' appears 377 times in the 80-page document, providing a state discourse of communal association that has no democratic or social benefit beyond governmental regulation. At the same time, this discourse was premised on a shared loyalty to state-prescribed 'national values' that turned Britishness into an integrationist and always unitary state politics. Indeed, as Pitcher notes, the use of community in the reinvention of Labour was crucial to its project as a pluralist nationalism in that it also 'had the advantage of differentiating the Party's position (at least rhetorically) from the laissez-faire policies of Thatcherite neo-liberalism' (Pitcher, 2009, p. 79). A particularly illustrative extract from the Cantle Report instructs ethnic minorities to 'develop a greater acceptance of, and engagement with, the principal national institutions' of Britain while working towards a 'meaningful concept of "citizenship"' which 'establishes a clear primary loyalty to this Nation' (Cantle, 2001, p. 20). The report prescribes a version of national 'allegiance' and 'loyalty' in which 'diversity' is assimilated into a set of state-sanctioned British values, implying the existence of delegitimised versions of citizenship that did not intrinsically perform 'allegiance' to the British nation-state. At the same time, the Cantle and Denham Reports marked the creation of a self-governing citizen responsible for their performance of 'a specific set of social goals through which the state seeks to reframe the contract between citizen and state', displacing external control with *internal* systems of domination in which the 'national abject' began to police itself in the name of both community and Nation with a capital 'N' (Burnett, 2004, p. 13).

For both Imtiaz and his parents, it is in the imperative to assimilate that the novel registers the implications of a state-led narrative that demonises Muslims. Imtiaz's father, Rizwan, is subject to racist abuse by the bride of a drunken hen party. When the group enter, Imtiaz describes this family's reactive self-regulation:

> I could feel you were nervous, though, Abba and Ammi. The way you went quiet over your food. Like you were trying to make yourselves as small and invisible as possible. And when I said I were going to the toilet, Ammi looked frightened and asked me not to go, as if any movement away from the table were asking for trouble. Like this were our little corner and we should just stick to it.
>
> (Sahota, 2011, p. 44)

This scene reflects the subordination of Muslims in the national imagination after 2001, reflecting how the 'focus shifted from the state's upholding of human rights to the responsibility of Muslims to integrate themselves into the shared values of Britishness' (Kundnani, 2007, p. 34). The bride asks Rizwan for a picture as 'a nice touch for the album', before throwing her arms around him and asking him to kiss her; the situation persists, as the woman 'jiggle[s] her tits in his face' before another member of the group asks Imtiaz's mum about her husband's sexual preferences (Sahota, 2011, p. 49). Mortified, Rizwan retreats into himself, repeatedly apologising until Imtiaz defuses the scene. Despite the bride's drunken retort that 'there isn't a racialist bone in my body!' (Sahota, 2011, p. 50), the incident testifies to a cultural environment in which Muslims are denied agency and thus prevented from challenging their marginalisation in public.

What is also worth noting about this scene, however, is the fact that it is Rizwan's inability to challenge his position that angers Imtiaz the most. Directing the narrative at his father, he reflects that 'it were like you were letting yourself be humiliated all over again. And it just fucked me off' (Sahota, 2011, p. 51). Rizwan's deference can be read within a broader national narrative of integrationism which underpinned both political multiculturalism and governmental responses to 9/11. As Kundnani suggests, the 'origins of integrationism lie in the government's response to the riots in northern towns in the summer of 2001 and to 9/11' (Kundnani, 2007, p. 31). According to Kundnani, '[w]hile the anti-terrorist legislation of the "war on terror" institutionalised anti-Muslim racism in the structures of the state, integrationism has normalised an anti-Muslim political culture' (Kundnani,

2007, p. 29).[6] References to 9/11 locate the novel within a political moment in which Muslims are demonised in the public imagination.[7] Before the conflict takes place, Rizwan ironically asserts that '[m]aybe if there were more brave enough to speak out like me we would not be having our children driving planes into buildings' (Sahota, 2011, p. 45). Imtiaz's recollection of Rizwan's humiliation parallels this earlier dialogue, describing how he watched 'with a kind of horror, as if you're watching a tower collapsing' (Sahota, 2011, p. 73). This scene neatly illustrates the exclusionary mechanisms of collective governmental strategies to improve multi-ethnic relations in Britain based on 'shared values' and 'common citizenship'. Instead of 'cohesive communities', Sahota provides an account of multicultural Britain centred on the internalisation of state practices that rely on the subjugation and abjection of an internal other.

The insistence on Imtiaz's Sheffield identity complicates a governmental discourse which associates Northern England with a monolithic, White working class. *Ours are the Streets* merges Sheffield local dialect terms (e.g. 'sempt' instead of 'seem') with Urdu, Punjabi, and Arabic, with each diary entry often closing with the affirmation 'ameen'. Phil O'Brien reads this dualism as marking the existence of a 'British Pakistani northern working class' (O'Brien, 2020, p. 139) through a kind of vernacular specificity. However, given the presence of an exclusory state nationalism elsewhere, I would argue that the presence of Sheffield dialect rejects an expanded Britishness as a mode of affiliation, aligning instead with a specifically localised, working-class Sheffield identity. This placed, working-class consciousness is reiterated in the symbolic significance of urban space – and specifically, the street – for establishing intersectional modes of belonging. As the novel indicates, the street becomes a site of both political contestation and reclamation against a state-sanctioned Britishness structured on assimilation. The novel articulates a Sheffield-based, intersectional, working-class identity that includes Muslims, echoing precisely Paul Gilroy's advocation for a widening of classed subjectivity 'so that it can be supplemented by additional categories which reflect different histories of subordination' (Gilroy, 2013, p. 7). For example, Imtiaz resents how his father must work long hours as a taxi driver, where he is frequently subjected to racism: 'Yesterday they took a leak in your taxi, last month they put a brick through your window. Maybe next they'll just burn the thing' (Sahota, 2011, p. 72). This reality, as Imtiaz tells us, is far from what Rizwan had hoped for his family when moving from Pakistan; the taxi driving was intended only to be a temporary source of income before moving on to something better but is now a cycle of extremely long hours and very little pay. Rizwan assures Imtiaz that 'we are doing it all for you' and 'it will all be worth it in the end' (Sahota, 2011, p. 69). Instead of the collective migrant story viewed by his father – demonstrated in his use of the pronoun 'we' - Imtiaz regards his father's immigration journey as a failure; he is unable to move away from their estate or earn enough money to send home, while Imtiaz's cousins boast of their holiday home in the suburbs of Lahore.

To return to the image of urban exclusion with which this chapter opened, *Ours are the Streets* articulates the transition of Sheffield's city streets from symbolic sites of possibility to dispossession. The limitations of assimilationism are catalysed in Rizwan's death, caused by a heart attack while chasing a fare-dodger down the streets of Sheffield. Imtiaz directs the retrospective narrative at his Abba:

> We were meant to become part of these streets. They were meant to be ours as much as anyone's. That's what you said you worked for, came for. Were it worth it, Abba? Because I sure as hell don't know, I used to just slam the door and stand with my back to it wondering, What end? Whose end? When is this fucking end? Because what's the point, man? What's the point in dragging your life across entire continents if by the time it's worth it you're already at the end? Ameen.
>
> (Sahota, 2011, p. 70)

The frequency of the possessive pronouns 'ours' and 'theirs' throughout the novel articulates this spatial and social division, configuring the street as a symbolic urban space of conflict and contestation, but also a potential place of collective reclamation – as Imtiaz tells his father, 'they were meant to be *ours*' (Sahota, 2011, p. 70). The anger marking Imtiaz's speech, conveyed through the repeated internal questioning of his father, alludes to a key critical narrative of the 2001 riots that explores how second generation migrants took to the streets to contest the status of their parents. Yasmin Hussain and Paul Bagguley, for example, describe how

> by the 1990s, a new generation of young Asians, born and bred in Britain, was coming of age in the northern towns, unwilling to accept the second-class status foisted on their elders. When racists came to their streets for a fight, they would meet violence with violence.
>
> (Hussain and Bagguley, 2005, p. 408)

Satnam Virdee similarly observes how the streets were often the designated space of far-Right activism of the National Front, who attempted to 'mark out and reclaim territory that they believed had been conceded to racialized minorities by strategically deploying graffiti, random violence and, increasingly, marches in ethnically diverse areas' (Virdee, 2014, p. 130). In this context, the street in *Ours are the Streets* is situated in a longer Northern regional history which articulates not only the complex intersection of race and class, but how options for citizenship and belonging for Muslims in Britain are contingent upon the performance of assimilation.

Despite the narrative's rootedness in Sheffield's cityscape, this local specificity is not a straightforward precondition for belonging. The novel attributes only a temporary 'authenticity' to these localised spatial coordinates, articulating how, as a second-generation Muslim, Imtiaz's existence is marked by precarity and vulnerability. The sections of the novel that take place prior to Imtiaz's visit to Pakistan are all set within locally particularised settings, moving between his home in Brightside, Becka's home in Meersbrook, the Leadmill, Students' Union bars, the High Street, the Peak District, Bramall Lane football stadium, and Meadowhall. In contradistinction to this local specificity, after Imtiaz visits Pakistan, Sheffield's reference points are empty as the city is devoid of all meaning. Late at night, Imtiaz looks out over the city and describes 'row after row of semi-detached houses, Toyotas parked out front, and I don't understand how these people can invest so much hope in those things' (Sahota, 2011, pp. 2–3). Rather than being a site of social interaction and belonging, Sheffield is merely a combination of geographic coordinates:

> It's amazing how quiet this city can get. Sometimes I can hear drunks making their way back from town. Sometimes a Paki bombs down the road in his souped-up wheels. But usually, like now, the city goes quiet and it all looks and feels as ghostly as an abandoned fairground. I can see across the whole city from here. It's like it's built on these huge great grey waves. Off to the right up ahead there's the floodlights poking up from Bramall Lane. On the other side, I can see Meadowhall with its shiny dome wrapped in some sort of dim halo.
>
> (Sahota, 2011, p. 29)

Sheffield's urban geography reflects the socio-economic deprivation resulting from deindustrialisation, emerging from a specific cultural and historical moment in Northern England. For Imtiaz, Sheffield ultimately represents a dead end, which, as Ana Cristina Mendes argues, offers 'no prospect of cosmopolitan self-reinvention' (Mendes, 2019, p. 57). Despite Imtiaz knowing these streets well, he experiences the city as an outsider, observing from the remove of his bedroom window. Imtiaz experiences the city only through absence as an 'abandoned fairground', with the grey, 'ghostly', inner-city spaces of deindustrialised districts like Highfield – the location of Bramhall Lane – contrasting with the lights of Meadowhall, but also against 'the brightness' of Pakistan, where Imtiaz has 'been shining' (Sahota, 2011, p. 283). The local specificity of *Ours are the Streets* weakens further upon Imtiaz's return from Pakistan, with Sheffield described as 'unreal'. As Imtiaz approaches his home, he describes how he

> stepped out of a fake car and went up the fake path and buzzed the fake doorbell, but it felt like only my arms and legs were working, the rest of me, all the important things inside, were refusing to take part
>
> (Sahota, 2011, p. 279)

This representation of Imtiaz's home in Sheffield contrasts sharply with Imtiaz's recollection of Pakistan, where he feels 'a great sense of solidness in the world' (Sahota, 2011, p. 258). Despite wishing he 'could just be like everyone else' and attempting to grasp a meaningful concept of citizenship for much of his life, for Imtiaz, existence in Sheffield is no more than an empty façade, aligning assimilation with both social and spatial exclusion.

Likewise, Pakistan forms only a partial counterpoint to Sheffield in the novel. Imtiaz describes how he feels at home in Pakistan when he looks across the village at night from the roof of his uncle's house, paralleling earlier scenes in which Imtiaz surveys Sheffield from his bedroom window:

> it might've been the most isolated place I've ever been, but I don't think I've ever felt more connected to the world. Not in the packed streets of Sheff or at uni, not in England really, where I always felt that even though there were all the rush and noise you could want, I weren't actually bumping up against life, instead just constantly moving out of its way.
>
> (Sahota, 2011, p. 203)

Imtiaz's psyche is marked by an opposition between his belonging in Pakistan versus his disenfranchisement in Sheffield, indicating an ideological difference between the narrator and the novel itself, which goes beyond such binaries. Indeed, Imtiaz's unreliable narration does not reflect his experiences of Pakistan elsewhere in the novel. During his time in Pakistan, Imtiaz is continually at pains to avoid being regarded a *valetiya* (foreigner) (Sahota, 2011, p. 116). Upon his arrival in Lahore, he is immediately stopped by airport security on suspicion of holding a fake passport and trips out to the nearest city are hindered because he is not fluent in Urdu, with the workers in the tourist area mistaking him for a 'Britisher'. Likewise, Imtiaz's uncle refers to England as 'your country', a battle that Imtiaz concedes that there is 'no point in fighting' (Sahota, 2011, p. 203). Imtiaz's cultural alienation in Pakistan is further emphasised when a soldier threatens to deport him, a situation Imtiaz eventually evades by supplying a fake name. Imtiaz himself describes himself as looking like an 'idiot tourist' and resents himself for being unable to fully grasp the intricacies of life in Lahore (Sahota, 2011, p. 104). The subtleties of social conventions frequently mark him as an outsider. Thanking his family for their prayers after his father's death, Imtiaz recognises this to be a faux pas; he makes a mental note 'that saying thank you weren't the done thing over here', with the exchange becoming a source of self-humiliation in the same way as the 'Asian Freshies' he mocks back in Sheffield (Sahota, 2011, p. 94). Imtiaz remains at the border of both territories, marked by cultural illiteracy in both England and Pakistan.

It is in the act of terrorism that Imtiaz's resistance ultimately finds political expression, turning to Islamic extremism as a political ideology that he associates with democratic participation. In a pre-meditated attack on Meadowhall as 'a chosen soldier' (Sahota, 2011, p. 56), Imtiaz attempts to reconfigure an urban public sphere, a site of political action for the 'failed citizens' of British multiculturalism. Defying the discourse of 'community cohesion' and 'managed diversity' underpinning political multiculturalism, Imtiaz's attack is a symptom of the desire to reconstitute himself and the members of his family as 'subjects of value' (Tyler, 2013, p. 214) in the public realm. Through an exploration of the 'national abjects' who reside as interiorisied others within the parameters of the state, we might, therefore, read Sahota's debut novel as reposing the political problem of citizenship as being 'no longer a question of national character but of how multiple identities receive equal recognition in a single constitutional form' (Rose, 1999, p. 176). This new relation between community, identity, and political subjectivity is exemplified in multiculturalism, and a set of political strategies which, as Nikolas Rose argues, 'construct the citizen in terms of adherence to a code which once again justifies itself by reference to something natural, given, obvious, uncontestable' (Rose, 1999, p. 192). In *Ours are the Streets*, this 'natural' or 'uncontestable' code is Britishness.

In terms of countering a hegemonic Britishness, however, the revolt at the centre of *Ours are the Streets* is stuck in a structural paradox. While terrorism provides the conditions for Imtiaz's resistance based on political action, the form that this act takes simultaneously performs the ideological work of the state and legitimizes the governmental 'management of diversity' based on the ongoing subjugation of an interiorised other. In this respect, the post-British possibilities that reside in *Ours are the Streets'* imaginative horizon remain in tension with both the divisive narrative of 'us' and 'them' and a state-led image of Northern England as a place in need of community cohesion. Although *Ours are the Streets* appears to enable a reconfiguration of abjection to what Imtiaz sees as a form of radical agency, the novel is unable to reconcile a participatory political subjectivity for Muslims with an ethical human ontology. The actuality of the attack is left open to question, but in any event the prospect of Imtiaz achieving individual agency within the boundaries of the state is far from reach.[8]

British Citizenship and the Neoliberal Migrant Narrative: *The Year of the Runaways*

There is a scene in *The Year of the Runaways* in which Randeep and Avtar, newly arrived in England, are sitting in Heathrow Airport in the middle of the concourse watching people depart. Having called a family contact to explore the possibilities of work, Randeep reflects how far they are – both geographically and practically speaking – from finding employment:

'There was only one [job],' Randeep said. 'It's too far.'
'Where?'

'He said Scotland.'

'How far's that?'

Randeep shrugged. Avtar walked over to the fag-holed timetable on the lamppost. *Birmingham. Bristol. Derby. Edinburgh. Glasgow. Gravesend. Leeds. Manchester. Newcastle. Wolverhampton.* But no Scotland.

'It's not on there,' he said, sitting back down.

'Because it's too far.'

'But if that's where the work is …'

(Sahota, 2015, p. 193)

Randeep and Avtar's inability to connect 'Glasgow' and 'Edinburgh' to their idea of a distant 'Scotland' communicates both their lack of knowledge regarding Britain's geography but also the symbolic emptiness of place, meaning little beyond the ability to provide capital. *The Year of the Runaways* is a novel concerned with place, exploring the navigation of both contrasting geographies of 'home' and 'exile', and the process of achieving agency and citizenship in England. Moving between several areas of England and India, the novel's spatial optic is global but it is also a locally particularised migrant story concerned with ordinariness and the micropolitics of everyday life in Sheffield. Frequent references to bus routes, street names, restaurants, takeaways, and convenience stores punctuate the narrative, and yet place in *The Year of the Runaways* appears to mean very little. Rather than being a place of familial roots, emotional ties, or self-fulfilment, the city functions as a site of economic possibility and neoliberal self-reinvention experienced only through the pursuit of work.

Unlike *Ours are the Streets*, *The Year of the Runaways* has attracted critical and popular attention as a conventional 'migrant story' and is often placed alongside canonical figures of literary multiculturalism. According to Janet Wilson:

> [t]he novel belongs to the established literary genre of migrant or diaspora fiction and is comparable to Monica Ali's *Brick Lane* (2003) and Zadie Smith's *White Teeth* (2000) in its referencing of both the homeland and the relocated community. As a familiar account of migrant hardship being overturned that gestures at the good luck migration story, it was acclaimed on publication and shortlisted for the Man Booker prize in 2015.
>
> (Wilson, 2017, n.p.)

In a literary economy in which 'regional novels' are rarely considered for mainstream literary prizes (cf. Fowler, 2008), and the fact that *The Year of the Runaus* was shortlisted for the Man Booker and likened to Smith and Ali is all the more surprising. However, the change in fortune between Sahota's debut and second novel might be attributed to the latter's adherence to a conventional 'migrant story' which is much more readily marketable in the way that Graham Huggan terms the 'postcolonial exotic' (Huggan, 2001).

Continuing the discussion of migration belonging and a state-led multicultural Britishness, my reading of *The Year of the Runaways* concerns what I describe as the novel's ambivalent relationship with the 'good luck migrant story'. In the remainder of this chapter, I argue that *The Year of the Runaways* largely undermines this narrative in favour of an ultimately unobtainable 'good life', a neoliberal agency project which is continually compromised by a state-governed concept of British citizenship. However, as we shall see, the novel appears to later abandon this project, resorting to a kind of muted, celebratory multiculturalism based on assimilationist ideology.

In *Cruel Optimism* (2011), Lauren Berlant suggests that, since the 1990s, the social-democratic promise of the post-Second World War period in the US and Europe has not been possible.[9] The result, as Berlant sees it, is a neoliberal present experienced through an affective concept of 'cruel optimism', a process marked by an attachment to, and fascination with, an increasing unobtainable and ultimately damaging pursuit of 'the good life' (Berlant, 2011, p. 1). According to Berlant, 'cruel optimism' is a way of understanding the attachments formed to fantasies of 'the good life' that are no longer sustainable when the promise of upward mobility has been replaced by an ongoing sense of crisis – a precarious present.[10] The ultimate unreachability of the promises individuals make to themselves leads to an experience of the present structured around the persistence of 'aspirational normativity' where the *project* of obtaining the objects of desire becomes a foundational reality in the absence of reaching the goal itself (Berlant, 2011, p. 164). In this context, the neoliberal present operates as 'a space of transition, not only between modes of production and modes of life, but between different animating, sustaining fantasies' (Berlant, 2011, p. 261). These 'fantasies' may take the form of multiple 'desires' that are not confined to work, including food, love, a political project, or a fantasy of 'the good life', all of which are associated with offering an improved quality of life. What is notable in Berlant's formulation is how attachment to these objects becomes 'cruel', with the pursuit of the object actively impeding the subject's 'flourishing' (Berlant, 2011, p. 1). In *The Year of the Runaways*, cruel optimism relates to a transnational class fantasy of 'the good life' based on the economic and social freedoms associated with migration to England, a neoliberal pursuit which informs all of the protagonists' life choices throughout the text. As we shall see, this optimism becomes 'cruel' through the continual suffering of austerity, homelessness, and a cycle of exploitative labour.

The cruel optimism inherent in state-sanctioned British citizenship is expressed through the pursuit of 'sustaining fantasies' about the habitation of domestic space and the nuclear family. As hallmarks of post-war capitalist culture in the UK and the US, the home and the family are fundamental to the perceived 'success' of migration in *The Year of the Runaways*, with the performance of nuclear domestic norms acting as a gateway to being recognised as British citizens. Throughout the novel, exclusion from British citizenship is encoded in and through varying rights to inhabiting domestic space. The urban architecture of Broomhall, a residential area in south-west Sheffield, reflects an entrenched socio-economic deprivation and fragmentation. Shortly after arriving in Sheffield, Randeep observes the vastness of Sheffield's train station, deciding that it 'must be a good city' before he is transported out of the city centre towards Broomhall and its 'narrow, boarded-up, wretched-looking streets' (Sahota, 2015, p. 201). Randeep's overcrowded shared house, provided by his boss so he can have all his staff in one place, encloses himself and his fellow workers from public view behind an 'overgrown front garden' where 'curtains were drawn haphazardly and giant cobwebs hammocked above the door', representing the invisible migrant labour fundamental to a global economy (Sahota, 2015, pp. 202–203) Inside, the rooms are packed with mattresses with 'grey crumpled sheets on them', and the wallpaper is 'torn in several places' (Sahota, 2015, p. 202). Contrary to the promise of 'the good life' that has brought the men to England, their dilapidated living conditions evoke the illusory promises of multicultural citizenship, falling short of its promise of offering 'a new improved way of being' (Berlant, 2011, p. 1). Despite Randeep's initial 'luck' of being provided with his own room, the luxury of space is short-lived; the house quickly becomes a space of abjection, where England's 'failed' citizens are hidden from society, eventually turning on one another in the battle for both work and living space.

The story of Randeep is the primary way in which the novel communicates a state-prescribed notion of migrant citizenship which relies on a domesticated loyalty to the nation-state. Randeep's citizenship in England has been secured through a visa-marriage to Narinder, a young Sikh woman from London, who moves to Sheffield to be closer to Randeep and lend credibility to their arrangement. Sahota establishes a link between the domestic sphere and citizenship that necessitates a collapse of the political and the personal, resulting in the creation of what Berlant terms an 'intimate public sphere' (Berlant, 1997, p. 4). Berlant describes the formation of an 'intimate citizenship' based on 'a rhetorical shift from a state-based and thus political identification with nationality to a culture-based concept of the nation as a site of integrated social membership' (Berlant, 1997, p. 3). Sexuality, reproduction, marriage, and family values are, according to Berlant, no longer private concerns but central to debates about nationality and come to define how citizens should act (Berlant, 1997, p. 8). Although Berlant is writing from a US perspective, the collapse of the public and private that she describes as the 'intimate public' is instructive for thinking through the politics of race in contemporary Britain. Indeed, the kind of domesticated citizenship identified by Berlant parallels political multiculturalism's emphasis on the internalisation of 'core national values' that are performed through social institutions such as marriage.

In this context, Narinder and Randeep's visa-marriage enacts a British 'intimate citizenship' (Berlant, 1997, p. 2), a state-managed blurring of private and public realms. Narinder believes it is her spiritual calling to marry Randeep and help him secure British citizenship. Despite her emotional coldness and insistence that the relationship is purely transactional, Randeep soon becomes invested in the idea of marriage and familial life. Traditional images of the family home become Randeep's object of attachment tied to the life he has promised himself upon arriving in England; this optimism is made clear in the note he leaves for Narinder before she moves into the flat he has rented for her, in which he offers to be of service 'day and night' and describes that flat as '*a new start for us both, maybe*' (Sahota, 2015, p. 9, original emphasis). Randeep's enactment of an intimate public sphere thus serves as a performance of the conditions of British citizenship through the domestic sphere of the family home, with his legal citizenship and settlement in England predicated upon his 'successful' marriage to Narinder. Finding that he is alone in the flat for the first time, Randeep begins to perform ordinary acts he associates with married cohabitation; he locates 'an onion and some potatoes in the fridge and start[s] dicing them up. He'd surprise her with a sabzi' (Sahota, 2015, p. 242). Randeep's association of success in the domestic sphere and British citizenship is reiterated by immigration officers who audit the authenticity of the marriage. The night before Narinder and Randeep's inspection,

> they hung up their wedding photos, and around the TV Narinder stood the holiday pictures Randeep had brought with him on one of his first visits. They littered the bathroom with more of his toiletries, incorporated his clothes into her wardrobe, and hid the suitcase under her bed. She bought a pack of gummed Post-it notes, too, which she wrote on and stuck to the fridge: *Back at 6 p.m. today. Can you put the rubbish out, please? Mummyji called.*
>
> (Sahota, 2015, p. 242)

This blurring of the public and the private locates a governed national citizenship premised on 'the home' and 'the family' insofar as legal residency is contingent upon the subject's successful performance of the social norms of domestication. The Post-it note discursively represents how state-regulatory citizenship based on 'personal acts and identities performed in the intimate domains of the quotidian' (Berlant, 1997, p. 4) has displaced democratic citizenship which presupposes acts of political agency. This version of citizenship which is based upon domestic ordinariness demonstrates how multicultural practices result in the projection of public politics into the private realm as a mode of racialised state surveillance.

The presence of immigration officers in Randeep and Narinder's 'family home' also indexes the intimate relationship between the public and the private. When the immigration officers question Randeep and Narinder's plans for the future, they assume a joint identity rooted in traditional notions of home and the nuclear family. Upon the officers' suggestion that they will be 'looking to build [their] own family soon', Randeep replies that

> the first thing we need to do is save up enough to buy a house. With a garden. Instead of renting. ... There are some very nice areas to the south of the city. Near the Peak District National Park. Those are good areas for schools, too. After that we can start thinking about children.
>
> (Sahota, 2015, p. 245)

Here, Randeep legitimises himself as an integrated citizen in the eyes of the state, aligning citizenship with the stereotypical conventions of domesticity and the practicalities of family life. The physical intrusion of the immigration officers in the home and subsequent interrogation of Randeep and Narinder about their personal lives enacts the collapsing of the boundaries between the public and domestic realms which reduces citizenship to the adherence of social norms under the policing of the state.

This legal, state-sanctioned citizenship echoes the formalisation of British identity under Thatcher's 1981 Nationality Act which, as Salman Rushdie puts it, effectively transformed citizenship into 'the gift of the government' (Rushdie, 2012, p. 417). Indeed, Randeep's intimidation by an immigration officer who becomes suspicious that Narinder has not taken Randeep's surname recalls precisely the kind of state surveillance initiated by the Act. Tyler pinpoints the Act as a watershed moment in terms of an explicit politics of state racism, observing that it was less about the constitutional rights of citizens and more about 'an immigration Act designed to define, limit and remove the entitlements to citizenship from British nationals in the commonwealth' thereby creating 'aliens' within the borders of 'a newly circumscribed nation-state' (Tyler, 2013, p. 54). Sahota's focus on the domestic as an intimate public sphere articulates the processes by which the Act rendered immigrants an 'invasion' of the nation, and in doing so located an Anglo-British identity 'in the moment of its vanishing, as whiteness, a command of the English language, and a certain kind of domestic space' (Baucom, 1999, p. 15). Similarly, Randeep's performance of citizenship through the familial domestic sphere enacts the state's intrusion into the private realm of migrant citizens couched within the language of integration and national values. Here, British citizenship does not enable political participation and individual agency, but results in an intensely governed existence secured by structures of state racism.

The affective structures of British citizenship in *The Year of the Runaways* also undermine a celebratory multicultural ideal through failed neoliberal projects of freedom and self-reinvention. The title of Chapter 11 – 'What Price Freedom' (Sahota, 2015, p. 379) – becomes the central question of the novel and its critique of the way that 'modern selves have become attached to the project of freedom' in the context of global economic migration (Rose, 1999, p. 262). As Rose explains, to be *'obliged to be free'*, he explains, is a form of government domination, containing individuals within a way of life based on the capacity to be free to choose (Rose, 1999, p. 87, original emphasis). In *The Year of the Runaways*, the pursuit of freedom tethers migrants to exploitative work and a cyclical process of socio-economic deprivation. While Randeep's legal citizenship forms an affective structure of cruel optimism wedded to state racism, Avtar's student visa and Tochi's status as an illegal immigrant only provide a gateway to a kind of employment that serves as an impasse in the pursuit of 'the good life'. Limited in the economies in which they can participate, the conditions of informal and unofficial work do not offer social or economic fulfilment, leaving both men stuck in an endless paradox of 'cruel', entrepreneurial optimism.

On his first day in England, Tochi takes a job pot-washing at a restaurant in London. Reflecting on his luck, he ponders that '[m]aybe it was true what they said about England. That this was where you could make something' (Sahota, 2015, p. 82). But despite what Tochi initially assumes to be good fortune, the exploitative conditions of his labour quickly materialise: he largely resides in the restaurant, is forced to sleep on the kitchen floor – despite the promise of a mattress – and is paid 'a tenth of what he'd expected' (Sahota, 2015, p. 83). Nevertheless, Tochi is convinced that saving enough money to return home is simply a matter of perseverance, after which 'he'd get there, *wherever there was*' (Sahota, 2015, p. 84, original emphasis). Tochi's unwavering optimism with regard to the possibility of a financially stable future articulates the persistence of 'aspirational normativity' (Berlant, 2011, p. 164) in the process of life-building. The absence of a clear end-goal even in Tochi's own psyche foregrounds the unlikelihood of achieving the aspirations that brought him to England in the first place, a futility which is reiterated in a later exchange with an older colleague in the restaurant:

> 'How long are you staying here?'
> 'I can leave now.'
> 'In England, I said.'
> 'Until I've earned enough.'
> 'Then you're a fool.'
>
> (Sahota, 2015, p. 89)

Warning against the cyclical traps of neoliberalism, the older man's comment identifies the process in which Tochi's optimistic temporal imaginary results in a repetition of actions, or 'sustaining fantasies' (Berlant, 2011, p. 2) that merely prolong survival or prevent the reality of defeat. The fact that Tochi believes that he 'can leave now' alludes to a false sense of freedom, as he rationalises his engagement in exploitative labour for little financial benefit on the basis that he can *choose*. Unlikely to achieve his financial goals, Tochi's optimism about his future reflects neoliberalism's 'refusal of futurity in an overwhelmingly productive present' (Berlant, 2011, p. 179).

Tochi's lack of spatial freedom in London further communicates the futility of this project. Most days Tochi stays in the restaurant, observing the world from the inside of the restaurant's window. The furthest away Tochi manages to walk is 'to the end of the street and around the corner ... He always paused outside a shop that sold homes' where he 'calculat[es] how long it might be before he could afford one' (Sahota, 2015, p. 86). Tochi's lack of spatial freedom and exclusion from the city articulates the social entrapment brought about by the aspirational desire to live 'the good life'. His migrant narrative is based a neoliberal temporal imaginary that simultaneously looks forward to 'getting ahead, to making it, *and* to a condition of stasis, of being able to *be somewhere* and to make a life, exercising existence as a fact, not a project' (Berlant, 2011, p. 179). Yet, in spite of his optimism, Tochi is both socially and spatially trapped; existing at an impasse, he only occasionally ventures outside to read property listings. Tochi's journey might therefore be read as part of a larger 'transnational class fantasy' (Berlant, 2011, p. 179) throughout Sahota's novel, which commonly structures the lives of migrants through their affective experiences of economic precarity.

In terms of optimistic attachments to the future, the idea of the self as project is central to Avtar's story. When Avtar arrives in England, he enrols on a 'Computing and Security Systems' course at the College of North-West London as a condition of his student visa. Sahota constructs a binary between a state-led 'official' narrative of migrant experience in England and the lived reality of migrant 'structural contingency' (Berlant, 2011, p. 11) experienced through financial precarity, casual work, insecure settlement, and continual class struggle. For example, during a break on the building site Avtar is working on in Leeds, he stops to read his college documentation – he reads the title 'Preparing You for Your Future', while all around him 'lunchtime talk was of the latest raids' (Sahota, 2015, p. 223). The snippet of motivational dialogue in his college folder exemplifies a neoliberal discourse of entrepreneurial self-reinvention supported by the British education system. This image sharply contrasts with Avtar's precarious reality sitting among industrial debris with his fellow migrant workers, all of whom are becoming increasingly worried about the possibility of police raids and subsequent deportation.

This disconnection between the 'official' migrant story and reality is continued, when, after failing his college exams, Avtar is beaten up by a loan shark, having fallen behind on loan repayments for his student visa. On his way back from London, he leaves the train at Leeds and observes the layout of the roads beneath him: 'Easy. It was all easy and yet he was still losing '

(Sahota, 2015, p. 420). Here, again, *The Year of the Runaways* returns to a successful citizenship which is achieved through spatial agency. At this point, Avtar rejects the 'good life'; he recalls a soundbite from his college folder: *"reaching beyond his dreams"* (Sahota, 2015, p. 420, original emphasis) and tears up his college work, throwing 'the white pieces into the air and watch[ing] them shower and drift' until they 'vanished' (Sahota, 2015, p. 420). The image of Avtar's college documents falling in snowflake-like shards to the ground symbolises the fragility and unsustainability of 'the good life' now that the promise of upward mobility has been replaced by precarity and an ongoing sense of crisis (Berlant, 2011, p. 3). This is a crisis which, as we have seen, is particularly acute for illegal immigrants and the 'failed citizens' of British multiculturalism.

Avtar's employment is also underpinned by the affective structures of the transnational class fantasy. Having shunned formal education for immediate employment, Avtar takes up casual work breaking down fatbergs in underground sewers. Avtar and the other workers 'wound tape around the tops of their boots so too much of the thicker shit wouldn't find its way in' when they enter the tunnel, noting that it was only 'two arm-widths across' with just 'enough room to stand' (Wacquant, 2008, pp. 382–383). Wading through human waste and battling what looked like 'a writhing ten-foot-maggot' underneath the surface of the city, Avtar's situation embodies the structures of inequality that Zygmunt Bauman describes as the 'fight for survival' characteristic of globalisation's migrant underclass (Bauman, 2004, p. 5). Both geographically and socially underground, Avtar and his colleagues are invisible citizens, whose ongoing precarity excludes them from the realm of everyday normality, becoming the 'wasted humans' (Bauman, 2004, p. 5) produced as the outgrowth of neoliberal modernity. Predicated on 'who performs best' (Sahota, 2015, p. 386), Avtar's exploitative hand-to-mouth employment reveals the pursuit of economic freedom to be a cyclical process of inescapability, an 'inevitable outcome of modernisation, and an inseparable accompaniment of modernity' (Bauman, 2004, p. 5). Here, the novel rejects the 'official' migrant narrative centred on optimistic attachment to England's self-actualising potential as a place of individual freedom. As Gurpreet, a fellow worker, tells Avtar: 'It makes you only care for yourself ... This life. It makes everything a competition' (Sahota, 2015, p. 225) – for all of these men, there is little room for imagining revolution or indeed any future beyond the scavenging present (Berlant, 2011, p. 179).

Like *Ours are the Streets*, Sheffield's deindustrialised city space also rejects a celebratory logic of multicultural Britishness in *The Year of the Runaways*, reiterating the unattainability of 'the good life'. *The Year of the Runaways* relies on a dialectic between social and spatial freedoms, evoking what Louïc Wacquant identifies as a *'dualisation of the social and physical structure of the metropolis'* (Wacquant, 2008, p. 25, original emphasis) that relies on structural violence. This duality between the social and the spatial emerges in the novel through persistent unemployment, resulting in relegation to decaying neighbourhoods on the periphery of the city, and heightened stigmatisation in daily life through intracultural discrimination. After being forced to leave the house he shares with his boss' other migrant workers, and realising he has no future with Narinder beyond their contractual arrangement, Randeep is homeless and unemployed. He begins sleeping in the Gurdwara where he is asked to leave after a few days and redirected to the outskirts of the city. An unnamed figure in the Guardwara pointedly mentions that '[m]ost of the young men like you come together under the old railway bridge near the city. The one on the river, by the new flats' (Sahota, 2015, p. 379). Here, the social and political abjection of illegal immigrants is inflected with internal prejudice, as Randeep takes on the status of the 'abject' non-citizen even within the Sikh community; finding a 'wide, bottle-green bridge' at the edge of the city, Randeep takes his place among three other figures 'all in shadow' (Sahota, 2015, p. 380). Despite being in England legally, socio-economic and residential precarity position Randeep outside the realm of active citizenship and prevent him from assuming any degree of individual agency.

Randeep's spatial disenfranchisement renders him a 'failed citizen' who is effectively detained 'within the polis as its interiorized other' and pushed to the peripheries of the city (Tyler, 2013, p. 62). The spatialisation of the precarious migrant underclass in *The Year of the Runaways* alludes to Wacquant's process of 'territorialised stigmatisation' (Wacquant, 2008, p. 250) that renders invisible those who are unable to perform within the accepted social norms of neoliberal agency. Randeep's socio-spatial marginality locates the ideological contours of British citizenship that are designed, as Tyler posits, to govern populations within the state by 'producing some subjects as successful citizens and others as variously precarious or failed' (Tyler, 2013, p. 62). Randeep's socio-economic precarity and marginalisation might, therefore, be read as a product of the neoliberal state and governmental approaches to race. Randeep becomes a 'demonised other' figure in both the Gurdwara and Sheffield, a human by-product of a state that needs an internalised other to maintain its legitimacy.

Randeep's status as a 'failed citizen' is reiterated through his psychological and spatial dislocation. Realising that he is the last man left under the bridge, Randeep breaks down, leading to him visiting a sex worker (a decision he immediately regrets) and, afterwards, falling into a river.[11] The narrative charts his psychological deterioration, describing how

> he didn't know where he was. He didn't know these roads. They weren't full of shoppers. They were grubbier, most of the windows painted over. Signs. Chaddesden. Mickleover. Burton-upon-Trent. His heart was thick in his chest. He didn't know where he was going. He didn't know his place. He didn't know this country.
>
> (Sahota, 2015, p. 460)

Sahota communicates Randeep's fragmented psyche through textual disjointedness, passages of frenzied emotional response, and disorientating local geographic markers. The combination of extramarital sex with a stranger and the reality of Randeep's precarity has made visible the affective structures behind his optimistic attachment to migrant life in England and produced a feeling of local and national unbelonging. The derelict landscapes of 'Chaddesden', 'Mickleover', and 'Burton-upon-Trent' are reduced to empty signs that heighten Randeep's socio-spatial disenfranchisement. So, while Wacquant suggests that stigmatised territories 'provide propitious terrain for reformulating "from below"' (Wacquant, 2008, p. 250), in *The Year of the Runaways* the promise of a politics of dissent does not materialise for migrant citizens. Instead, they occupy a paralysing liminality and become simultaneously trapped both outside and within the parameters of the British state.

Narinder experiences a similar socio-spatial alienation; despite being born in England, she is unable to reconcile her faith and culture as a Sikh woman of Indian descent with any degree of agency in England. Before moving to Sheffield, Narinder is a devout Sikh, 'the girl from God' (Sahota, 2015, p. 248), who volunteers at the Gurdwara daily and dutifully assumes the care of her father following her mother's death. However, Narinder befriends Savraj, a young sex worker who manipulates Narinder into giving her money to send to her family in India, initiating a change in her. Reflecting on the excitement of 'going into the world and seeking [Savraj] out' (Sahota, 2015, p. 263), Narinder gradually begins to challenge the patriarchal control of her brother and father; she rejects her arranged marriage, moves to Sheffield to marry Randeep, and subsequently becomes estranged from her family.

This familial exclusion leads to Narinder's existential crisis articulated through her navigation of space. After an awkward meeting in Leicester in which she requests the deferment of her arranged marriage, Narinder returns to Sheffield and begins to question her faith, having 'only the vague apprehension that she needed space, clarity, air' (Sahota, 2015, p. 323). Walking without direction, the novel charts Narinder's route

> through suburbs in the south of the city – Nether Edge, Millhouses, Totley – full of brooding Victorian houses under a thin summer moon. Near a church, she stopped and looked across the green depth of the country, at the vast spirit of those giant hills. Is that where He was hiding?
>
> (Sahota, 2015, p. 323)

Narinder's breakdown, coded through the notation of specific spatial coordinates, is a product of the linkage between spatial agency in the city and the identification of the self. This process is repeated towards the end of the novel, when Narinder avoids going home after work. Instead, she 'preferred sitting on her own by the window, letting the bus carry her through the city in the lovely pretence that she could stay sitting here forever, going round and round, observing' (Sahota, 2015, p. 448). The image of Narinder circling the city without purpose renders acutely visible her lack of political and social agency as attempts to carve out a life in Sheffield that she can reconcile with her family's aspirations. In the same way that Narinder resides on the peripheries of both English and Indian culture, she too circles the outskirts of the city – both geographically and temporally suspended at an impasse, and unable to take control of her future.

This chapter has argued that Sahota's Sheffield-based novels *Ours are the Streets* and *The Year of the Runaways* counter a state-led, racialised narrative of the urban North as a white, working-class monolith, instead redirecting conversations of racism and alienation towards British political practice at the turn of the millennium. To varying degrees, Sahota's novels represent critiques of the ideological thrust of state-national approaches to race that are informed by a commitment to locale. Through decentralised accounts of the relationship between ethnicity, place, and national belonging, these novels both destabilise London as the centre of literary multiculturalism and highlight the productive role that places within Northern England play in imagining multi-ethnic experience within England after Empire. Both *Ours are the Streets* and *The Year of the Runaways* complicate the view of Northern England as a place of racial prejudice, positioning the broader structures of the British state at the core of their protagonists' social disenfranchisement and lack of belonging. In doing so, Sahota's novels initiate a 'politics of location' resulting in the denaturalisation of Britishness within the category of literary multiculturalism. I want to end this chapter, however, by briefly discussing the epilogue of *The Year of the Runaways*, which offers narrative closure through a retreat to assimilation. Despite the novel's decentralised spatial optic and thematic concern with the possibility of civic agency for Muslims and Asian people in Sheffield, the epilogue constitutes an ideological retreat to the 'good luck migrant story' in alignment with a centralised, multicultural Britishness.

Set ten years later, the epilogue offers an optimistic conclusion that neatly ties up the various stories of Sahota's protagonists, who have since found happiness in becoming middle-class suburbanites: Avtar marries Randeep's sister, Lakhpreet, and is now living in his own home with his family; Randeep secures a white-collar managerial role, living in a studio flat independently near to the home he provides for his family, a 'modern semi with a neat stamp of a front garden' (Sahota, 2015, p. 460). This cosy domesticated citizenship marks the abandonment of earlier attempts to denaturalise Britishness and state-sanctioned notions of citizenship in favour of cultural assimilation. By the end of the novel Narinder also moves with a new sense of purpose, free to navigate space on a global scale. After attending her uncle's funeral, she 'changed her flights and flew to Thiruvananthapuram and from there took a coach to Kanyakumari. She remembered Tochi mentioning the place and came because she wanted to, and *because she could'* (Sahota, 2015, pp. 466–467 my emphasis). While in Kanyakumari, Narinder sees Tochi (who has since returned to India) with his wife and children, watching him from afar at a community theatre. Observing his contentedness, Narinder decides to catch a night-train to Cochin, continuing her path around India's cities. Given her new-found spatial agency, Narinder's journey operates within neoliberal definitions of the project of global freedom and the ability to imagine oneself as a 'solitary agent who can and must live the good life promised by capitalist culture' (Berlant, 2011, p. 167).

Rather than yielding to a straightforward celebratory cosmopolitan agenda, the novel's U-turn towards tropes of the 'successful' migrant narrative might also be read as possessing a greater degree of scepticism towards the future of race relations in England than it might at first appear. Melissa Kennedy reads the 'improbable leaps of fortune' that have necessarily transpired to enable *The Year of the Runaways'* epilogue as an indication 'on the part of creative discourse ... to think a clear path through the economic motivations and steps required to move from developing-world illegal immigrant to developed world middle-class mortgage-holder' (Kennedy, 2017, p. 289). Yet, I would argue that this unexpected sea change represents a reversion to a politically bankrupt assimilationist idealism that enacts the narrative impossibility of alternatives to state-sanctioned notions of citizenship. Just as the prospect of Imtiaz's ultimate act of violence against his oppression never materialises in *Ours are the Streets*, the concluding lapse into a 'happy ending' in *The Year of the Runaways* operates within the state-supporting integrationist narrative purported by multiculturalism. Taken together, the delimited imaginative horizons of these two texts stage not only the abjection and suffering that accompanies state-sanctioned notions of citizenship and belonging in multicultural Britain but also the difficulty of locating an alternative. The need for a viable alternative to the British centralised state form that emerges in Sahota's novels is, as the following chapters attest, an urgent concern within Northern England's twenty-first-century literary imagination.

Notes

1 See Paul Bagguley and Yasmin Hussain's critique of this association in (2004) *Riotous Citizens: Ethnic Conflict in Multicultural Britain*. Abingdon: Routledge.
2 Nadeem Aslam's *Maps for Lost Lovers* also explores racial hostility towards Pakistani communities in an unnamed fictional town (nicknamed 'Dasht-e-Tanhaii', or 'The Desert of Loneliness' by locals) in Northern England during the mid-1990s. See Nadeem Aslam (2004) *Maps for Lost Lovers*. Faber and Faber: London.
3 Arjun Kundnani traces the state surveillance and subsequent demonisation of Muslims in the twenty-first-century public imaginary in both the UK and the US. See Kundnani (2014) *The Muslims are Coming!: Islamophobia, Extremism, and the War on Terror*. London: Verso.
4 See, for example, John McLeod's (2004) *Postcolonial London*. London: Routledge, John Clement Ball's (2004) *Imagining London: Postcolonial Fiction and the*

Transnational Metropolis. Toronto: University of Toronto Press, and Michael Perfect's (2014) *Contemporary Fictions of Multiculturalism: Diversity and the Millennial London Novel.* Basingstoke: Palgrave Macmillan.

5   After the post-war ethnonationalism of Enoch Powell and Margaret Thatcher, there was a reluctance to engage with the idea of a progressive Englishness from those on the cultural Left, calling instead for a revision of Britishness. Paul Gilroy's call to 'put the black in the Union Jack' (2013) demonstrates the way in which England and Englishness existed only as a reactionary ethnonationalism. Gilroy's scepticism towards a post-imperial, civic English nationalism is also echoed by Stuart Hall, who describes Englishness as 'closed', 'exclusive', and 'regressive' (Hall, 1996, p. 446). In his influential 'New Ethnicities' lecture, Hall proposes a 'non-coercive and a more diverse' understanding of ethnicity set explicitly against 'the hegemonic conception of "Englishness" which, under Thatcherism, stabilizes so much of the dominant political and cultural discourses' (Hall, 1996, p. 446). In a later interview however, Hall concedes that 'Englishness is something we need to talk about' but it remains opposed to 'radical appropriation' (Derbyshire, 2012).

6   See, for example, the White Paper 'Secure Borders, Safe Haven: Integration with Diversity in Modern Britain'. February 2002. Available at: https://assets.publish ing.service.gov.uk/government/uploads/system/uploads/attachment_data/file/ 250926/cm5387.pdf [accessed 10 September 2020].

7   This governmental 'othering' of Muslims was reinvigorated following the 2005 London bombings, and other recent terror attacks across Europe, including the Manchester Arena bombing in May 2017.

8   It is not confirmed whether the attack actually goes ahead, but it is unlikely. The novel ends with Imtiaz's emotional breakdown, asking his dead father to sit with him as he goes to sleep, prior to which Imtiaz has informed Becka of his plans.

9   Berlant identifies a range of social promises that are fraying in a neoliberal and precarious present, including upward mobility, job security, and what she describes as 'lively, durable intimacy' (Berlant, 2011, p. 3).

10 See especially, 'After the Good Life, an Impasse: Time Out, Human Resources, and the Precarious Present' in Berlant (2011) *Cruel Optimism.* Durham, NC: Duke University Press, pp. 191–222.

11 We never know whether Randeep jumps or accidentally falls into the river. He reveals to another figure under the bridge that he himself cannot be certain: 'All he remembered was staggering along the towpath, suitcase heavy in his hand, seeing their faces. And then someone was pulling him out' (Sahota, 2015, pp. 406–407).

2 Post-British England and the Rural North

The 'Great British Summer' of 2012 remains a clear manifestation of London-centred Anglo-Britishness. London's thoroughfares were adorned with the Union Jack in celebration of Queen Elizabeth II's Diamond Jubilee, while at home, 27.3 million members of the public tuned in to watch the capital host the Olympic Games (BBC Media Centre, 2012). The latter saw Danny Boyle stage 'Isles of Wonder', a vision of British history and culture that was simultaneously inclusive and diverse. The spectacle featured multiple cultural and national references, from Dizzee Rascal, Rowan Atkinson, and the Sex Pistols to tributes to the National Health Service, the suffragette movement, and ethnically diverse cricket teams. Central to this display of cultural heterogeneity was the idea that Britain was an open, diverse, and yet timeless multi-national formation. This continuity was captured in the cameo of Queen Elizabeth II alongside Daniel Craig playing James Bond, in a peculiar bridging of an archaic institution of Britain's class system and the modern-day nation. However, the monarch was not the only imperial formation to take centre stage during the opening ceremony. Boyle's 'narrative of the nation' began in pre-industrial England, presenting a rural panorama of lush, green pastures and peasants dancing happily around maypoles. Titled 'England's Green and Pleasant Land', this bucolic image was set against a choral adaptation of William Blake's 'Jerusalem' – a hymn taken to be England's unofficial national anthem – and positioned England's rural idyll as a communal part of British history around which viewers were invited to unite. Shortly afterwards, the approach of beating drums signalled the threat of the Industrial Revolution, disrupting Boyle's pre-modern pastoral vision. In the advent of urban modernity, these images of elegiac Englishness were contrasted – and ultimately subsumed – by the dominance of industrial Britain, conveyed by the appearance of machinery as the green turf was literally ripped up on stage.

Boyle's production embodied the paradox of the relationship between England and Britain (encapsulated in the term 'Anglo-Britain'), an association in which the former is both universal and perpetually negated.[1] The opening saw Jerusalem take on a universalising role for the four nations in a distinctively Anglo-centric focus, relying on the conflation between England

DOI: 10.4324/9781003388722-4

and Britain. This elision of England under Britain was apparent in the bold patriotic displays enjoyed by Scotland, Wales, and Northern Ireland, compared to the performance of the pastoral as a stand-in for England, while the Industrial Revolution stood as the crucible for the emergence of British urban modernity. The violent stripping away of the English pastoral veneer to make way for the transformation of Britain via the industrial age reinforced this alignment of England with a mythological and unchanging rural tradition.[2] In their reading of the opening ceremony, Claire Westall and Michael Gardiner note how '[t]he British Empire was seen to erase England and the industrialist spoke for – and instead of – both the imperial and domestic other as capital and empire built the British state' in an elision that 'deflect[ed] the need to ask pressing constitutional questions' (Westall and Gardiner, 2013, p. 2). In terms of constitutional questions, the Olympics Games' opening ceremony made clear that a key a blocker to England's political actualisation has been the imperial construction of Englishness. A primary location of this cultural Englishness is the countryside, which has circulated the imperial iconography of the English pastoral.

The constitutional questions raised by the Olympic Games opening ceremony are central to the recent rural novels of Sarah Hall. Cumbria's rural landscape is the site on which political debates are played out, from conflicting regional and national priorities and the complexities of devolved political powers to the overthrowing of the British government. In contrast to Boyle's staging of rural England in London, *Haweswater* (Hall, 2002), *The Carhullan Army* (Hall, 2007), and *The Wolf Border* (Hall, 2015) complicate England's association with the pastoral and attempt to disentangle the nation from its imperial form. More specifically, Hall's novels explore the relationship between England and Britain and position the North-West as a privileged site from which to imagine a post-British future for England. This location is politically significant. Cumbria's proximity to Hadrian's Wall and 'the debatable lands' alludes to historical territorial conflicts in Britain, while the roots of English regionalism today have been primarily found in the North-East, an area which has played a disproportionate role in the debate about regional devolution in England. By examining constitutional questions posed in three of Hall's novels, this chapter explores how in *Haweswater*, *The Carhullan Army*, and *The Wolf Border* the 'wild places' of Cumbria's uplands pull against the idea of an idyllic English pastoral. My argument here is that Hall's attempt to disentangle rural space and the literary pastoral suggests a political future for England beyond the Union.

Before turning to Hall's fiction, however, it is important to note that England's association with the pastoral has a long history. The Olympic Games is one of many contemporary manifestations of the most celebrated and lasting evocation of England as the 'green and pleasant land' coined by William Blake in his verse in 1804. Yet, the founding of an entire national consciousness on Blakean elegies of England had implications for the nation's own status: where in the constitutional functioning of the British Union did Englishness have its place beyond a mythical principle? This question is not new. In his influential study, *Out of Place: Englishness, Empire and the Locations of Identity*, Ian Baucom explores the ways in which 'struggles to control the idea of Englishness over the past 150 years have largely been struggles over places endowed with the capacity to evoke a sense of the nation's essential continuity over time' (Baucom, 1999, p. 4). Baucom proposes that the English countryside has functioned as a simultaneously symbolic and material space which has been understood as a synecdoche of the nation's consciousness during and after Empire (Baucom, 1999, p. 4); in turn, this image constructs, maintains, and circulates myths of a unified national identity in place of a codified, *political* identity (Baucom, 1999, p. 4). In this context, the pastoral idyll has been crucial in the framing of England as a cultural, mythological space, rather than as a bounded territory with its own jurisdiction.

Critical debates regarding the political status of England emerge from a particular context of debate regarding the future of the Union. The constitutional instability Nairn observed in *The Break-Up of Britain* (1977) was set to materialise twenty years later, leading to New Labour proposing the devolution of Scotland, Wales, and London in 1997. Westminster's concessions during the 1990s did not end the debate about the tenability of the Union; Nairn's study continued to influence a whole generation of scholarship on the future of the British state, and where England might fit within this new constitutional arrangement.[3] After 1997, England became less 'the gaping hole' in the devolution question and increasingly took centre stage in the debate about what it meant to be English in the wake of Britain's perceived imminent break-up (Hazell, 2000, p. 1). But what makes England such a peculiar case is the easy slippage that is often noticed in the relationship between England and Britain and encapsulated in the term 'Anglo-Britain'. The fact that they are essentially 'two sides of the same coin' is precisely what makes conceiving of England-without-Britain – or Britain-without-England – just short of an impossibility (Kumar, 2015, p. 4). As Boyle's display demonstrated, the pastoral idyll functions as a cultural registration of English identity that secures the suppression of a civic, political Englishness.

Pastoralism and the English Rural Novel

Constructions of a timeless, imaginary 'old England' have a long literary lineage. A particularly important staging post in the literary development of a mythological English pastoral is the 1920s and 1930s, when the rural novel reached its heyday (cf. Head, 2017). H.V. Morton's *In Search of England* (1927) presents a nostalgic version of rural England which, in turn, 'helped establish and, importantly, perpetuate, the myth of England as a prelapsarian, pastoral country, famed for its rolling hills and pastures green' (Berberich, 2015, p. 159), while the development of new mass printing technologies 'saw the rise of memoirs and periodicals that focused on England's countryside' (Bluemel, 2019, p. 161). As Bluemel explains, 'everything from novels to travel guides to picture books and pamphlets exhorted readers to head out of cities, into the countryside, if not to a villa, then to a garden suburb or weekend retreat' (Bluemel, 2019, p. 161). This mythological construction of the English countryside retains contemporary cultural currency today; it is monetised in the heritage industry and subject to nostalgic celebration in period dramas in aristocratic rural settings typically taking place within the English country home. ITV's *Upstairs Downstairs* (1971) and *Brideshead Revisited* (1981) are two of the most famed cultural examples of the cult of the countryside in English television series. More recently, *Downton Abbey* (2010–) has epitomised a Conservative 'National Trust' projection of England and English rural space.[4]

This idealised pastoral 'tradition' has largely been associated with the South of England. For instance, Peter Mandler describes Englishness as it came to be represented in late nineteenth-century literature as '[n]ostalgic, deferential and rural' (Mandler, 1997, p. 155). In these accounts, he suggests, Englishness 'identifies the squirearchical village of Southern or "Deep" England as the template on which the national character had been formed and thus the ideal towards which it must inevitably return' (Mandler, 1997, p. 155). Criticising the tendency to view Englishness as characterised by 'cultural stagnation' and 'rural nostalgia', Mandler argues that Englishness has functioned as a generalised, stretchy, cultural 'template' and incorrectly been associated with the South of England (Mandler, 1997, pp. 155–156).

One historical example of the political mobilisations of this template of Englishness is former Prime Minister Stanley Baldwin's 1924 speech to members of the English patriotic group, the Royal Society of St George. Baldwin projected a deeply nostalgic and celebratory evocation of England as Arcadia, describing the sounds of England as 'the tinkle of the hammer on the anvil in the country smithy' and 'the corncake on a dewy morning' (Baldwin cited in BBC News, 1997). The toast promoted an exclusionary image of rural space that entirely elided Wales, Scotland, and Northern Ireland, and was rooted only in the South of England. Baldwin's use of the Southern pastoral as the *de facto* image of England offers a very obvious historical illustration of the mobilisation of this 'stretchy' pastoral idyll for a political agenda that emerged at the same time as the regional-rural novel reached its prime in the 1930s. Contrary to the idea that the pastoral idyll is found exclusively in the South of England, in literary culture, 'the English rural tradition embraces a much wider geographical range, and strikes repeatedly discordant notes in its treatment of place and national consciousness' (Head, 2017, p. 13).[5]

English pastoralism was more overtly encoded in popular culture than in the rural novel. The literary treatment of the pastoral has always been complex and self-conscious. Thomas Gray's *Elegy Written in a Country*

Churchyard (1751) provided a model for exploring the English countryside during the second half of the eighteenth century, and early twentieth-century rural writing is equally punctuated with images of inequality, hardship, and exploitation. As Bluemel puts it regarding the rural tradition of H.E. Bates and Winifred Holtby, these writers 'do powerful cultural and aesthetic work contesting the South-East England rural ideal maintained by a 1930s print culture fixated on thatched roofs, village greens, and hedgerows' (Bluemel, 2019, p. 163). Rural writing has often been highly self-reflexive, epitomised by Stella Gibbons' satirical caricature of the 'simplicities' of rural life in opposition to the city in *Cold Comfort Farm* (1932). Moreover, Emily Brontë's *Wuthering Heights* (1847) established a 'Northern' literary genre of rural writing that pulls against a pastoral engagement with the countryside, but which simultaneously instilled a 'Southern' misconception of the violent, 'untamed', rural Northern landscape.[6]

Terry Gifford's *Pastoral* (1999) identifies the ongoing cultural purchase of idealised evocations of the English countryside, setting out four forms of the pastoral. First, a literary device relying on a process of retreat and return; second, any literature that describes the countryside with explicit contrast to the urban; third, a pejorative use of the term 'pastoral' that signals scepticism towards an oversimplified and idealistic pastoral vision, and fourth, a form 'neutrally descriptive of literature concerned with a life of pastoral farming practices in raising grazing animals' (Gifford, 1999, pp. 1–2). These versions of the pastoral are overlapping and can occur simultaneously, but Gifford attributes his third iteration to the English pastoral idyll. In contrast to the idealising tendencies of the pastoral, post-pastoral literature 'possesses acute awareness of the culturally loaded language we use about the country, accepting responsibility for our relationship with nature and its dilemmas' (Gifford, 2012, p. 45). Yet, the post-pastoral is inherently different from the notion of anti-pastoral, which entirely rejects celebration of the land, serving as a kind of reconciliatory 'bridge' between the pastoral and anti-pastoral. Gifford's summary of the post-pastoral is worth quoting at length here:

> What is needed is a new term to refer to literature that is aware of the anti-pastoral and of the conventional illusions upon which Arcadia is premised, but which finds a language to outflank those dangers with a vision of accommodated humans, at home in the very world they thought themselves alienated from by their possession of language. Such a term should enable 'a mature environmental aesthetics' to sift the 'sentimental pastoral' from the 'complex pastoral' in a way which takes account of the urgent need for responsibility and, indeed, advocacy for the welfare of Arden, informed by our current and updated best judgements of what that should be.
>
> (Gifford, 1999, p. 151)

In the light of Gifford's definition, the literary form of the post-pastoral has constitutional implications in the context of Britain, where the rural idyll has served as a cultural construction of a mythological Englishness. Unlike the imperial English pastoral, Gifford's post-pastoral would render visible the ideologies of the 'sentimental pastoral' and enable an environmentally conscious politics of England as a place.

While the anti-pastoral mode was established long before the twenty-first century, there is a gradually intensifying post-pastoral consciousness in contemporary depictions of rural life across Northern England. Ross Raisin's *God's Own Country* (2008), Andrew Michael Hurley's *The Loney* (2014), Jenn Ashworth's *Fell* (2016), Naomi Booth's *Sealed* (2017), and the novels of Ben Myers (2012, 2014, 2016, 2017, 2019), all align various landscapes across the North of England with a distinct suppression of the pastoral mode. These texts separate their rural environments from the idealising tendencies of the pastoral, presenting instead gothic, unsentimental accounts of Lancashire and the Yorkshire Moors. Raisin's novel, for example, is told from the perspective of nineteen-year-old Sam Marsdyke, who is forced to work on his family farm instead of attending the local school.[7] Raisin's rural portrait explores the isolation of family farming and the narrator's troubled adolescence, juxtaposed against the city incomers looking for postcard views of Goathland's rural landscape - the site of ITV television series *Heartbeat* (1992–2010). Similarly, Myers' representation of rural Yorkshire consciously eschews an idealised pastoral mode, depicting the countryside as an inherently violent space. The prologue to his first novel, *Pig Iron* (2012), references the artist Francis Bacon, whose paintings are known for their visceral, raw imagery and blurring of the human-animal distinction: 'Even within the most beautiful landscape, in the trees, under the leaves the insects are eating away at each other; violence is a part of life' (Bacon cited in Myers, 2017, n.p.). Myers' anti-pastoral drive is particularly pronounced in his historical novel, *The Gallows Pole* (2017), which fictionalises the story of David Hartley and the Crag Vale Coiners in the eighteenth century. This pre-industrial history of the rural North configures the Calder Valley as a gothic space of criminal enterprise, territorial violence, and regional myth.[8] What is therefore notable about these texts is that they position North Yorkshire's rural topography as a site of wilderness that resists human influence; their depictions of the land are visceral and decidedly unromantic, often the setting for acts of violence and the renegotiation of power. These novels provide evidence of a wider literary trend in which Northern England has functioned as a fertile site for creative expressions of rural life which draw attention to the artificiality of the pastoral.

Within this emerging post-pastoral Northern literary imaginary, Hall's novels map the ideological contours of the English pastoral and place constitutional questions within a distinctively regional frame. Competing claims to rural space in *Haweswater, The Carhullan Army*, and *The Wolf Border* intersect with tensions between region and nation, including the depriveleging of rural-regional priorities under the British state's industrial vision and entrenched class system. Hall's rural tragedy, *Haweswater*, fictionalises the historical deliberate flooding of Mardale's agricultural community. In 1935, Mardale Green was submerged to create a reservoir supplying water to Manchester as the figurehead of Britain's modern industrial revolution. *Haweswater* embodies a tension which is characteristic of rural-regional fiction, between attachment to older ways of life and the recognition that change is inevitable. This realisation is brought into stark focus in Isaac Lightburn's untimely death at the end of the novel. Returning to the site of the lost village, his drowned body in the reservoir becomes an emblem for the irreconcilability of local priorities with the unceasing forward momentum of twentieth-century British urban modernity. *The Carhullan Army* amplifies this disconnection between region and nation. Set in an unspecified but recognisable future, the novel imagines the end of Britain as a consequence of economic collapse and global warming, with the flooding of the River Thames destroying London and the Houses of Parliament. In Hall's vision, the historical institutions of the British state have been abandoned and replaced by a newly formed totalitarian government body termed 'The Authority' (Hall, 2007, p. 15). Escape from this controlled society is possible for the protagonist only by undertaking a treacherous journey to a feminist ecotopia in a mountainous area of North-West England, where a regionalist movement to challenge The Authority is in the making. The political energies of Cumbria that emerge in *The Carhullan Army* find a more historical expression in *The Wolf Border*. Set against the political backdrop of the 2014 Scottish Independence referendum, the novel centres on an ecological conservation project in the fictional Annerdale estate that will see wolves reintroduced into England for the first time in 300 years. These parallel constitutional and ecological preoccupations merge as the narrative progresses, with the central plot of wolf reintegration becoming entangled with Scotland's secession from Britain and, as Hall imagines it, the ensuing dissolution of the Union.[9]

Contrary to Anna Cottrell's assertion that Hall's preference for the regional is 'hardly new or daring' (Cottrell, 2017, p. 682), I suggest that Hall's fiction frequently positions Cumbria as a privileged site from which to stage post-British politics and evoke the prospect of an independent England. This chapter identifies a preoccupation throughout *Haweswater*, *The Carhullan Army*, and *The Wolf Border* with the two narratives of devolution in England that we saw in the Introduction. Returning to Robert Hazell's observation that there is both a 'UK version, about rebalancing England's place in the Union post-devolution' and 'an English version, about decentralising the government of England' (Hazell, 2000, p. 221), this chapter focuses on the relationship between the two, suggesting that these texts are concerned with the possibility – or rather, the impossibility – of effective regional government in England while the nation remains part of the Union. *Haweswater*, *The Carhullan Army*, and *The Wolf Border* offer an emerging vision of post-British autonomy for England that is never fully realised. Equivocating between a commitment to the disruptive politics of rural wilderness and pastoral retreat, the post-British potential of these novels is

undermined by the pastoral structures that maintain a mythological Englishness and its suppression under 'Anglo-Britain'. Hall's focus on rural
Cumbria thus indexes a contained regionalism emerging from the North-
West which enacts precisely political devolution's limited constitutional
charge.

Region and Nation

Hall's reworking of the pastoral country-city oppositions articulates the
dislocation between regional and national priorities. *Haweswater*, Hall's
debut, foregrounds the tensions between region and nation that she returns
to in her more recent work, but the prospect of a post-British England
remains far from reach. In contrast to the organised political dissent of *The
Carhullan Army*, *Haweswater*'s Cumbrian village is unable to pose a viable
threat to Britain's industrial vision, with regional unrest only ever amount-
ing to mere 'rumblings' (Hall, 2002, p. 91) among the community. Upon
hearing of plans to flood the village, a local farmer reflects that 'Parliament
was a long way south, and seldom this far-reaching. But its law was
final' (Hall, 2002, p. 53). Aligned with the priorities of Westminster, the
dam project sits uncomfortably alongside the agricultural priorities of the
region and its residents. The novel's contemplation on the enduring
sovereignty of British institutions points to the lack of democratic participation in England and indicates the difficulties of imagining an alternative
to the jurisdiction of the centralised state. Samuel Lightburn's unsuccessful
attempt to foment discontent within the local community underlines the
limits of current forms of parliamentary democracy; he waits for 'the mul-
titude of voices that did not come' (Hall, 2002, p. 53), hinting at a democratic deficit in the area. *Haweswater*'s central conflict concerns a socio-
economic and political division between the native Cumbrian community
and Manchester City Waterworks (MCW). The asymmetrical power relations between Mardale's locals and the semi-fictional corporation functions
as a parallel to the uneven development characteristic of British urban
modernity, enacting the disjuncture between both regional and state-national
priorities as well as an intra-regional division between metropolitan and
non-metropolitan communities.

    Haweswater's opening scenes foreground the contrast between Mardale's
small-scale local economy and the nation's burgeoning industrialisation; the
area 'consisted mostly of tenant farmers' with the land 'devoted to the
grazing of sheep, cattle and mountain ponies' and 'a little agriculture where
the soil was deep enough' (Hall, 2002, p. 29). Here, the rural North-West is
a place of isolation far removed from the workings of modernity, where the
villagers '[live] independently from the rest of the country, almost separate
from the world' (Hall, 2002, p. 37). Detached from the industrial developments of larger cities, Mardale's residents live as part of a localised micro-
economy of 'exchange and barter, with the swapping of produce as it was

needed ... carrots for eggs, smoked ham for cigarettes or tobacco, apples for the occasional postage stamp' (Hall, 2002, pp. 37–38). While the novel suggests that Northern England's industrial cities like Manchester have recovered from the First World War, in rural Cumbria, 'there is not much recovery yet. Tenancies do not fall from trees in this part of the country, especially now' (Hall, 2002, p. 108).

The building of the Haweswater Reservoir is the central antagonism around which these competing regional and national priorities are staged. The construction entails the expropriation of the village and the evacuation of Mardale's rural community, with their small-scale agricultural ecosystem deemed insignificant compared to larger, industrial projects in cities like Manchester. As Michael Woods explains, the rural is always understood to be part of a wider national economy, society, or environment with 'the state in capitalist societies [making] decisions impacting on rural economies in line with this imperative' (Woods, 2010, p. 232). This submission of regional-rural communities under the dominance of a metropolitan-oriented state project is a recurrent preoccupation throughout Hall's work, emerging most forcefully in *Haweswater*. For example, the reservoir is characterised as benefitting 'the country entire' while it will disrupt only the local community, embodying a political centralism that relies on the ongoing marginalisation of Northern regional-rural locales. The central opposition between MCW and Mardale's residents articulates these asymmetrical power relations. In the novel, MCW representative, Jack Liggett, symbolises a hegemonic, external 'other' figure in this division. Jack's presence in the village is initially perceived as accidental, with locals noting how 'he could not be in the right place, must have somehow become dislodged from his metropolitan setting' (Hall, 2002, p. 44). At this stage, Jack is perceived as an imposing outsider whose 'foreignness' is made conspicuous from the moment of his arrival at Mardale:

> He was dressed for dinner, or a dance, like an unusual, exotic bird, its silk and sheen foreign in the cold landscape. The artist thought to himself that the man was not lost. He had come to the valley as a man would enter a room to receive a guest – territorially, impossibly possessive, and with charm, politeness, with a tip of a hat, a warmly shaken hand. He, the stranger, assuming control.
>
> (Hall, 2002, p. 44)

Jack's territorial authority signifies a national hierarchy that neglects regional-rural priorities; as Daniel Lea puts it, Jack's 'rationality [is] based on national rather than local duty' (Lea, 2017, p. 158). Here, and elsewhere in the novel, Jack's role in the reservoir construction serves as a reminder of the insignificance of Northern rural communities to a national project focused on urban industrial development.

Jack's concern with possessing a golden eagle buttresses this dominating position. Upon his arrival in the village, Jack makes a bet with a local poacher to capture and kill a golden eagle so that he can display the bird in his home 'as a proletarian prize' (Hall, 2002, p. 200), affronting his privi-leged colleagues at MCW. Jack ruminates that the bird 'was no Indian tiger, no polished ivory tusk, it was not another country usurped, or the spoils of exotic adventure. It was indigenous, a symbol of the beauty of the islands, the hub of the empire' (Hall, 2002, p. 199). The bird's native status registers MCW's expropriation of the village, framing the development of the reser-voir within the language of colonialism. This association is also reflected in the structural function of the eagle as a trigger for *Haweswater*'s first tra-gedy – Jack's death. Later in the novel, when Jack has fallen in love with Janet, the poacher presents him with the bird as agreed. Faced with an ethical dilemma between his former extrinsic view of the place and his new internal vision, Jack seeks atonement by returning the bird to its nest. Here, the golden eagle's regional credentials – a protected species which can now be found only in remote parts of Scotland and the Northern English uplands – encode Cumbria's oppression under the larger territorial grasp of the cen-tralised British state form.[10] Although Jack's view of the bird is detached from 'exotic adventure' (Hall, 2002, p. 199), his enlistment of a local poacher to capture and kill the bird on his behalf emphasises his disconnection from the region. At this point, he is framed as an outsider, unfamiliar with the intricacies of the region and its native species. Jack's inability to recognise his role in the marginalisation of Mardale's community reinforces his status as an outsider. Just as the Indian tiger is a symbol of British imperial conquest, so too is Jack's desire for the golden eagle as a class-inflected trophy signifying his seizing – and subsequent obliteration – of Cumbrian territory.

Haweswater's insistence on Cumbrian dialect – a formal device absent elsewhere in Hall's novels – also communicates the corporation's close relationship to what is represented as a Westminster-inspired wave of industrialisation. The use of dialect can be observed most clearly during exchanges between Jack and the local community: 'yor t' fella that's gonna mek lake bigga' / 'Yes I am' (Hall, 2002, p. 81). In staging an opposition between Standard English and regional dialect, *Haweswater* gestures towards the cultural and political chasm between Jack as a symbol of state-led modernisation and Mardale's rural-regional community. This linguistic division works to establish the complex hierarchal structures that designate Northern England as the nation's 'other', defined against hegemonic metro-politan modernity. Reciting the process of reservoir construction, Jack views the locals' concerns as little more than a nostalgic reluctance to engage in modernisation, speaking to the locals in 'another tongue, or in abstracts far removed from the life of these men and women. His purpose was incon-ceivable' (Hall, 2002, p. 42). The perceived untranslatability of the dam project to the locals in the passage drives a wedge between 'national interest' and its metropolitan discourse of development and the 'parochial border towns' (Hall, 2002, p. 43) of Cumbria, with the latter marked by stasis and political inertia.

It is notable, however, that Hall's fiction after *Haweswater* retreats from the use of dialect and a delimited regional mode while retaining an insistence on local identity markers. In *The Carhullan Army*, for example, one of the first things Sister notices about Jackie is her accent sounding like 'the country's rural equivalent [of her own]' (Hall, 2007, p. 78). Similarly, in *The Wolf Border*, when Rachel returns to Cumbria after a period of living in the US, Pennington's secretary questions her authenticity: 'You're local? I don't hear an accent' (Hall, 2015, p. 11). Yet what distinguishes these accounts from *Haweswater*, even as they appear superficially to echo many of that novel's preoccupations and engage with a similar setting, is that their central concerns of climate change and animal conservation are inherently global while at the same time experienced within a local frame. Janet Lightburn recognises that she is 'in a place too remote to fall prey to political or industrial assembling. ... Now she has had to alter her vision. She must look with new eyes' (Hall, 2015, p. 112). It appears that Hall's fiction also 'alters' its vision. The politically inert Cumbria of *Haweswater* gives way to a much more politically activated regionalism in *The Carhullan Army* and *The Wolf Border*. In both novels, *Haweswater*'s 'placed' regional voice is situated within wider national and global shifts.

The 'devolutionary' thrust of *The Carhullan Army*, for example, is registered much more explicitly. Here, Cumbria's mountain regions are depicted as post-British spaces operating outside state jurisdiction, with the political 'rumblings' of *Haweswater* evolving into plans to overthrow the centralised government. The novel's exploration of the relationship between region and nation takes place within a distinctively global frame; Britain is now a diminished colony dependent on American paternalism, whose constitutional collapse has coincided with planetary environmental crisis. In a continuation of *Haweswater*'s motif of water, *The Carhullan Army* sees the flooding of London's River Thames and destruction of the Houses of Parliament. The material destruction of the Houses of Parliament in the novel parallels the disintegration of the British political system. *The Carhullan Army*'s fragmented structure and epistolary narrative formally register this constitutional collapse; the narrative unfolds retrospectively in a series of confessional records recovered after Sister is captured by The Authority, with some records marked 'complete' and others 'partially corrupted' or 'data lost' (Hall, 2007, n.p.). Emilie Walezak suggests that the records of the interrogation, in which Sister details her life at Carhullan, signify 'the destruction of a familiar national identity from the near past' while also being an attempt to 'resist dissolution' (Walezak, 2019, p. 69) of Cumbria's regional identity under the centralised military government. The narrative style of *The Carhullan Army* does more than encode regional-national tensions, however. In offering an individual narrative in opposition to the state, Sister's records offer a 'devolved' method of telling a defiantly regional story that eschews national affiliation, with the fragmentary narrative style symbolising the break-up of the British multi-national bloc.

Yet, in this novel, the end of Britain has not led to an egalitarian regional English federalism. Instead, political power has simply been re-centralised in a series of local bodies under the wider surveillance of 'The Authority'. Sister describes how '[t]here was no verification of what the structure of government really looked like now, whether it was impenetrable, or whether it had vanished altogether, and in its place something else existed' (Hall, 2007, p. 39). When Sister arrives at Carhullan, she is told that 'London's finished. We're no longer the region we were … we're back to being a country of local regimes' (Hall, 2007, p. 104). But this is no radical region-alism. Hall indicates that a kind of despotic regionalism has transpired; in the novel's fictional setting of Rith (a play on former Cumbrian capital, Penrith) there are strict surveillance measures with the land divided into 'zones' that 'do not allow for transference' (Hall, 2007, p. 15), binding people to their regions at the time of governmental collapse. Sister describes how '[a]nyone living beyond the designated sectors was considered autono-mous, alien' and were 'no longer part of the recognised nation. The Authority simply called them Unofficials' (Hall, 2007, p. 15). The division of Rith's population into 'official' and 'unofficial' categories is a last-ditch attempt at governmental control, extending also to the closure of the public realm and the loss of the civic. 'The Authority' is described as 'an affront to the rights of the public', with the regime led by 'power hungry' Powell (Hall, 2007, p. 26), who has suspended general elections, bound people to their zones to prevent public protests, and created a militarised police force.

The Carhullan Army's concern with Britain's constitutional organisation also pertains to the relationship between England – both symbolic-pastoral and national – and Britain. References to a 'distorted' image of England under Britishness mark representations of Cumbria's ruined countryside:

> People from the South had once bought retirement homes here, under the blue shadow of its fells. After the fuel crisis it had been left to its own devices, and slowly it must have emptied like all the others, before the orders were finally given to evacuate. On the wall of one cottage someone had written the words Rule Britannia in red and white paint. They had tried to draw the Cross of St George but it looked distorted, bent out of shape. I couldn't tell if it was an act of vandalism or one last loyal statement from the proprietor before leaving.
>
> (Hall, 2007, p. 22)

Sister recalls how people from the South of England had used Cumbria as a site of retreat, pointing both to the association of Englishness with the rural landscape and a distinctively Anglo-Britishness. The painting of 'Rule Brit-annia' in red and white, and the failed attempt at painting the St George's flag, exemplify a slippage between England and Britain. Sister's inability to discern whether the 'distorted' St George's Cross was a final display of national allegiance, or one of vandalism, registers the slipperiness of exactly what constitutes England. This concern with England following the collapse of Britain is evidenced elsewhere in the novel, underlining the cultural functioning of England in the former Union. Locals reflect that 'of all the English traditions to have been compromised, the weather was the saddest', drawing attention to England's existence in a cultural capacity (Hall, 2007, p. 6). To varying degrees, both *Haweswater* and *The Carhullan Army* position Cumbria as a privileged site to render visible the contradictions inherent in Anglo-Britain and imagine the end of the unitary British state form.

Contested Territories

Cumbria's history as a contested territory in the Union provides the contextual foundations for the constitutional questions explored in Hall's fiction. *Haweswater* frequently references Cumbria's historical status as a borderland between England and Scotland, inviting parallels between the region's political history and the present conflict in the novel. For example, one of Jack's walks near the village takes him towards 'the old Roman route' (Hall, 2002, p. 149), a reference to the Roman Conquest which is later paralleled when the army arrive to destroy Mardale, which is described as 'a phantom sighting of Roman legionaries, marching south from Hadrian's Wall' (Hall, 2002, p. 219). Similarly, following the construction of the new Burnbanks village to house the MCW employees, the village's 'rebirth' is framed as taking place among 'the old border myths and long-ago frictions of the area' (Hall, 2002, p. 219). In this way, *Haweswater* situates the flooding of the village in 1936 as part of a longer history of territorial conflict in which Cumbria has been a key territory of political contestation in the Union's history, positioning the area as an appropriate site from which to stage contemporary constitutional questions. Further, given that the novel was published just five years after the devolution of Scotland, Wales, Northern Ireland, and London, *Haweswater* prophetically echoes recent claims for devolved governance from the North-West.

The idea of a politically activated Cumbria is what underpins *The Carhullan Army*. Sister depicts Carhullan as a strategic geopolitical location with roots that lie in the Ancient Britons and the Romans.

> It was, and had always been, removed from the faulted municipal world. It sat in the bields, the sheltered lull before the final ascent of the High Street range. There was a panoramic view point for miles. The Romans knew it and they raised a fort there that Carhullan's byes and pens were later built around. And before the Centurions, the Britons had a site nearby; five weather-pitted standing stones which leant awkwardly towards each other, west of the paddocks. The Five Pins they were called.
>
> (Hall, 2007, pp. 54–55)

The remaining standing stones testify to Cumbria's status as a former Celtic Kingdom, while the presence of a Roman fort 'heralds proleptically the final siege of The Authority headquarters in Rith when the women fighters occupy the medieval defensive castle of Rith that Hall relocates on top of Beacon Hill' (Walezak, 2019, p. 69). These recurrent depictions of the region as a conflicted borderland with Scotland and the border reivers situates the antagonism between Carhullan's army and The Authority as part of a history of national conflict. The novel presents Cumbria's past and the topographical features of its landscape as particularly well suited to territorial battle, framing the area's rural landscape as a place of political possibility.

These constitutional reference points are placed within contemporary debates regarding British devolution in *The Wolf Border*. The novel foregrounds the potential for a post-British England in establishing a counterpoint between Northern England and the devolved nation of Scotland. The positioning of *The Wolf Border*'s ecological narrative against the backdrop of the Scottish Independence referendum is not a mere geographic coincidence, but works productively to highlight the inequalities. inherent in Anglo-Britain. Rachel's initial reservations about the rewilding project concern its location in England, a country that she considers to be 'particularly owned' (Hall, 2015, p. 29). Meanwhile, the opposite is happening across the border, where land is being de-privatised and returned to public hands:

> [Rachel] is aware of the reform plans across the border – public acquisition of private land, recalibration of resources – a notion that must make the likes of Thomas Pennington more than a little uncomfortable. The BBC is full of debate about independence and the forthcoming referendum; she's been surprised by how close the polls are, how troublesome the matter is proving for Westminster.
>
> (Hall, 2015, p. 26)

In Scotland, the hierarchies of land ownership that have characterised the British class system since feudalism are being readily dismantled as the nation prepares to rebuild itself anew, presenting post-British Scotland as an increasingly egalitarian civic space compared to England. Hall's reference to the BBC in this scene functions as a comment on the ideological construction of Britishness. The corporation has long occupied a position in the national imagination as a cultural symbol of the Union which has helped to define Britain-as-nation and thus become part of Britain's unwritten constitution (cf. Gardiner and Westall, 2016).

Intertextual references to the Scottish literary renaissance also appear throughout *The Wolf Border*, establishing Scotland as a 'radical' counterpoint to England. Prior to a healthcare appointment, Rachel listens to a radio station on which Scotland's First Minister is

[g]oaded, accused of being racist, an economic dunce, but he maintained optimism, Scotland was, is, and will be a beacon of social enlightenment. He quotes one of the country's premier writers: work as in the early days of a better nation.

(Hall, 2015, p. 102)

The writer in question here is Alasdair Gray, whose fiction forms a significant contribution to the revival of Scottish literary nationalism; his dystopian novel, *Lanark* (1981), was 'significantly supported by a wave of left-leaning nationalist journals … including *Cencrastus, New Edinburgh Review*, and *Radical Scotland*' (Gardiner, 2012, p. 120). This intertextual reference gestures towards literature's potential to accelerate a devolved national consciousness in lieu of political devolution, indicating an awareness of the relationship between literary and political forms of devolution.[11] Indeed, the relationship between literary and political devolution in Scotland is coded architecturally, with Gray's quotation written on Holyrood's Canongate Wall. In *The Wolf Border*, the 'early days of a better nation' refers to Scotland but may also speak to a potential independent England. Rachel's hope that 'the country as a whole will one day rewild, whatever its manmade divisions created at the ballot box' (Hall, 2015, p. 234) indicates a vision of Scotland progressing towards a post-British nationhood and evokes the potential for England's own political 'rewilding'. *The Wolf Border*'s rewilding project thus stands as an allegory for a post-British politics of England located in the North West. Yet, it is important to note that the novel distinguishes between cultural and political forms of devolution. *The Wolf Border* highlights cultural devolution's inadequacy to yield a political praxis that transcends British state structures, simply substituting legislative power for a cultural civic nationalism. This ambivalence echoes the now commonplace assertion that 'in the absence of elected political authority [in pre-devolutionary Scotland], the task of representing the nation has been repeatedly devolved to its writers' (Whyte, 1998, p. 284). The process of cultural devolution Whyte outlines here emerges in Hall's work; her fiction tends to a similar task for England, speaking from a region with a particular historical relationship with Scotland and which has been defined by longstanding socio-economic and political marginalisation.

The Wolf Border does not present Scotland's secession from Britain as straightforwardly utopian, however. Even as the nation gains independence, its future remains exclusively discussed by 'grey-haired' retirees and 'the district's rich' (Hall, 2015, p. 95), which suggests that independence from Britain may simply result in a lateral redistribution of power between two pre-existing political elites. *The Wolf Border*'s imaginative political horizon for Scotland is marked by antiquated British hierarchies in which matters of 'the World Heritage status bid, new speed limits on the lakes, the Scottish polls [and] the wolf-project' (Hall, 2015, p. 95) remain uncomfortably upper-class affairs. The end of the novel communicates a similar pessimism when the future of the wolves is negotiated at Holyrood, a state-mandated institution signifying only a lateral transfer of power. As such, *The Wolf Border* presents a version of state-led devolution which manifests itself more as a reshuffling of local power rather than 'instigating a complete social rethink' (Gardiner, 2007, p. 46). While the novel goes as far as imagining a post-British Scotland, it offers only a guarded prognosis for progressive politics in a country still dominated by class interests and the institutional remnants of the British state.

Contingent (Post-)Pastorals

In terms of approaches to the land, Hall's novels are marked by what I describe as a contingent post-pastoralism. While the uses of the land prioritised in *Haweswater* (small-scale agriculture), *The Carhullan Army* (environmental sustainability), and *The Wolf Border* (rewilding) create the conditions for deconstructing the pastoral idyll, approaches to rural space in all three novels overlay multiple pastoral and post-pastoral modes. For example, *Haweswater*'s opening scenes appear to commit to the post-pastoral. The novel presents Mardale's rural territory in terms of its agricultural use value; the village is not a place of rural retreat, but of home and work for tenant farmers and 'a little agriculture where the soil was deep enough' (Hall, 2002, p. 29). The novel viscerally describes the reality of farming practices, puncturing any association of space with an image of a 'green and pleasant land'. In *Haweswater*, Janet's intricate familiarity with agricultural practices emphasises their cruelty; her knowledge spans from understanding how to 'pry open the mouth of an unorphaned lamb to introduce milk through a fake teat' to the most efficient ways to kill live-stock, 'the point on the side of a head to place the rifle barrel, exact inches from an eye, where the bullet will meet the least resistance' (Hall, 2002, p. 22). As the narrative voice reminds us, 'there are no miracles in this dale' (Hall, 2002, p. 6).

Haweswater's blurring of the boundary between the human and the non-human reinforces this post-pastoral thrust. The novel opens during Ella Lightburn's labour as she gives birth to Janet, a process which is 'beyond animal' (Hall, 2002, p. 5). This scene foregrounds *Haweswater*'s collapsing of the hierarchy between humans and the land, with Janet's birth likened to the slaughtering of animals on the farm; Ella's groans are described as 'the torrid calls of the cattle and sheep in their herds when their time came, a stuck bellow, a panicked bleat' (Hall, 2002, p. 6). This description antici-pates Janet's close relationship with the farm that comes to define her life and death in the novel, while also evoking another characteristic Gifford attributes to the post-pastoral, that '[w]hat is happening in us is paralleled in external nature' and 'our inner human nature can be understood in rela-tion to external nature' (Gifford, 1999, p. 156). As the novel progresses, Janet comes to symbolise this struggle to separate ideas of nature and culture and of humankind and the land. When Janet is older, her father reflects that she 'terrorises the old notions ... There are no absolutes to be found in the blood on her wrists, and under her nails. She has feral qualities not belonging to either sex' (Hall, 2002, p. 73). The fact that Janet does not conform to the expected gender roles of the 1930s parallels her rejection of the 'old notions' of the rural as an idyllic space; just as Janet is described as possessing 'feral' qualities, so too, does Cumbria's landscape.

Janet's affair with Jack reiterates these 'feral qualities'. Their sexual encounters reaffirm Hall's blurring of the human and non-human, both in their instinctual physicality and the way in which Janet approaches Jack as a predator pursuing its prey;

> [h]e did not know that she was more aware of his movements within the valley than he was of hers. That the direction of her walks was dependent on first pinpointing his location or hearing word of where he had been.
>
> (Hall, 2002, p. 119)

The violence of the encounters themselves reiterates this visceral animalism: 'there were always injuries. Bruises as she struggled to leave him' and '[p]ieces of her hair torn out when she demanded he leave' (Hall, 2002, p. 120). Jack and Janet's bodily struggles articulate the coming together of two contradictory approaches to the land as Hall 'makes use of the staple fictional convention of the union of opposites' (Head, 2020, p. 356). While Jack is initially presented as an outsider due to his association with MCW, later, we learn of his familiarity with Cumbria's landscape, complicating the rural conventions of the threat of the 'outsider'. It is revealed that Jack previously visited the area as a child and knew the fells intimately 'to the point of being able to climb Helvellyn at night' (Head, 2020, p. 356).

Jack's attitude towards his relationship with Janet also demonstrates a complex pastoralism. Aligning sexual pleasure and the recuperative effects of the land on his psyche, Jack reflects that 'the fulfilment of a high climb and the sensuality of [Janet's] body ... brought a level of contentment beyond any he had reached in the past. The two at once seemed to offer a spiritual answer' (Hall, 2002, p. 147). Jack's alignment of the female body with 'nature' and the mythical properties he attributes to the combination of these acts exemplifies the colonial impulses that undercut the narrative's post-pastoral vision. Yet, his relationship with Janet does to some extent alter Jack's approach to the reservoir project and his predisposition to the Mardale community; he transitions from being '[o]ne of those classless types who believes that [the countryside] is about scenery and escape' to being allowed 'free passage. As if he, too, now belonged in part to the region' (Hall, 2002, p. 149; p. 180). Jack's relationship with Janet initiates a trans-formation of his character and his subsequent reframing in the novel – he transitions from being described as a figure of metropolitan dominance and hegemony to possessing an intimate knowledge of Cumbria's landscape. The novel appears to distinguish between pastoral and post-pastoral approaches to the region's rural space, between Jack's territorial bravado and anthropocentric pastoral position and Janet's intimate but nevertheless anti-pastoral affinity with the land established through farming practices.

Haweswater's most explicit, self-conscious engagement with the pastoral idyll resides in the character of Paul Levell, a landscape painter who refuses to include the human form in his work, instead 'push[ing] the limits of Lakeland geological existence' (Hall, 2002, p. 39).[12] Levell represents a complication in *Haweswater*'s post-pastoral vision as it encompasses both the farmer and the artist's view of the landscape. Yet, despite being a landscape painter, Levell's non-human depictions of Mardale are post-pastoral in that they insist on viewing the landscape as a 'wilderness' free from human interference and cultivation, a form of what Head describes as 'impersonal modernism' (Head, 2020, p. 358):

> Humans were, without exception, banished from the bleak, natural scenes, as if unable to survive or simply not welcome in the wilderness created by Levell's brush save for a suggestive form in a rock, a women's back surfacing in the river as a stepping stone.
>
> (Hall, 2002, p. 38)

Levell's village portraiture represents a counterpoint to William Wordsworth's poetry, whose representations of the Lake District have been appropriated in popular culture and turned the region into a national artefact. The force of the Wordsworthian Lake District has cultural purchase today. Known as 'Wordsworth's County', the area's tourism centres on the National Trust's Wordsworth House, encouraging an experience of the grounds as they were described in his poems. Scott Hess notes that Wordsworth's influence has seen the Lake District presented as 'an aesthetic sphere, dominated by the arts in general and poets in particular' (Hess, 2012, p. 13), referencing Wordsworth's influence on the construction of the national park. This appropriation of the countryside was decidedly pastoral, a popular misreading of Wordsworth's often anti-pastoral poetry which has augmented a 'tradition' of 'aesthetic leisure and spirituality, separated from everyday work, subsistence, and economic activity' (Hess, 2012, p. 15). In the character of Levell, then, Hall reworks a key figure in the ways in which depictions of rural space are often appropriated as part of the pastoral idyll in the English cultural imagination.

The Carhullan Army's environmental consciousness continues Hall's deconstruction of the pastoral idyll. This novel disassociates the rural landscape and pastoralism through the potential of Northern England's mountainous landscape, suggesting a synergy between rural wilderness and political autonomy for the region. *The Carhullan Army* represents an explicit attempt to harness Cumbria's wilderness as a tool against governmental structures. Despite occupying the space once known as the Lake District, Carhullan is far from a place of rural retreat. Upon her arrival, Sister is kept in a metal tank and subject to physical and psychological torture, a process performed for a second time when she joins Carhullan's army as a test of her commitment to overthrowing The Authority. This distinctively unsentimental regime extends to all aspects of existence on the farm: material goods are markedly absent, clothing is functional, dietary intake is dependent on energy expenditure and bodily protection against the weather (with butter added to meals in the winter), and days are filled with militarised exercise or tending to the farm. The characterisation of Carhullan's leader, Jackie Nixon, reiterates this hardened quality:

> She was always depicted formidably; hard-cast, like granite. People in the region were wary even of her name. old as it was – stock of ironmongers, masons, and the bowmen of the North. In Rith it was issued like superstition from the mouths of those discussing her and her girls. 'Jackie Nixon,' they said. 'She's one of the Border Nixons. They were the ones who went out with bulldogs to meet the reivers'.
>
> (Hall, 2007, p. 49)

Jackie is presented as part of a distinctively Northern place-myth, deeply rooted in the region's history, and the driving force behind Cumbria's post-British potential. Having rejected the jurisdiction of The Authority, she is now 'formidably' *of* the region, whose 'hard-cast' character is intricately tied to Cumbria's former role in the nation's historical territorial conflicts.

Cumbria's mountainous landscape appears to hold political potential in its wildness. In contrast to the pastoral idyll associated with the South, the supposed 'wild places' of the North hold the possibility of 'independent communities', with Sister reflecting that '[s]omething durable and extra-ordinary could be created in these mountains' (Hall, 2007, p. 55). Upon her arrival at Carhullan, Sister notes the changes in the landscape: 'I could feel it already, that I was entering her country, her domain. *It was a raw landscape, verging on wilderness*' (Hall, 2007, p. 50 my emphasis). Here, the novel registers socio-political transitions in Cumbria's material terrain. Any notion of a bucolic rural idyll is literally punctured as 'the rock was beginning to show through the grassland' (Hall, 2007, p. 50), signalling Sister's transition from the control of The Authority to Carhullan. *The Carhullan Army* frequently positions the wilderness of Northern England's rural landscape as a fertile site for the staging of post-British politics; Carhullan is located in 'the disputed lands. They have never been settled. And those who live in them have never surrendered to anyone's control' (Hall, 2007, p. 195). The novel explicitly ties Carhullan's project to a democratic form in which current centralised governmental structures are no longer visible – as Jackie reminds us '[r]evolutions always begin in the mountain regions. It's the fate of such places' (Hall, 2007, p. 195). The prospect of ongoing pressure for radical governmental reform is confirmed on the novel's final page in Sister's defiant assertion that she does not 'recognise the jurisdiction of this government' (Hall, 2007, p. 207), ending on an emphatic rejection of the British institutional system.

However, *The Carhullan Army*'s post-pastoral vision is not sustained, and, like *Haweswater*, the novel overlays pastoral and post-pastoral modes. Hall forecloses the political potential of *The Carhullan Army* in the novel's return to the idealising tendencies of pastoral approaches to the landscape. Despite the initial rejection of pastoral sentimentalism at Carhullan, as the novel progresses, a focus on the transformative effects of the rural emerges: '"There's nothing like this place for rehabilitation,"' Sister is told, '"It's working with the land that does it. Getting back to basics"' (Hall, 2007, p. 131). Sister, too, reflects that she had often thought of the landscape as 'a place of beauty and escape'; even after her treacherous journey to the farm, she finds the landscape ' more beautiful than ever' (Hall, 2007, pp. 174–175). Later, Sister's post-pastoral expectations of rural wilderness are often undermined. When she arrives at Carhullan, Sister notes that, in contrast to '[a]fter the austere expanse of the fells' during her trek, 'the farmland seemed peculiarly cultivated' (Hall, 2007, p. 65). Here, the novel foregrounds the contradictions and complexities of the pastoral mode; even in Carhullan, the landscape is not free from human influence and cannot be considered 'wilderness'.

These complexities also register structurally. Like *Haweswater*, *The Carhullan Army* relies on the inherent pastoral opposition between the country and the city. Sister's move to Carhullan is essentially one of rural retreat from the corruption she perceives taking place in England's urban spaces; her initial journey to from Rith to Carhullan, followed by her later return, enacts what Gifford described as 'the ancient pastoral impulse of retreat to a rural landscape and return to the city' (Gifford, 2012, p. 44). Considering the complexity of the novel's engagement with the pastoral, Deborah Lilley suggests that 'the novel begins to shift the pastoral into new forms. Sister's understanding of the landscape is newly tempered by her anti-pastoral experiences, which supplement, rather than overcome, the pastoral vision with which she came to it' (Lilley, 2016, p. 67). Despite the novel's commitment to the disruptive politics of Northern rural wilderness, the novel cannot be considered entirely post-pastoral. Rather, it equivocates between pastoral and post-pastoral impulses, reflecting an ambivalence towards the possibility of overthrowing centralised state structures and decoupling England from the pastoral. These paradoxes develop alongside Sister's realisation that Carhullan is far from an egalitarian utopia or a radical redistribution of power compared to that of The Authority. Jackie's reign is supported by social inequalities, with Carhullan reliant on a 'system of control' and a strict 'hierarchy' (Hall, 2007, p. 84). This limited renegotiation of power indicates a scepticism towards the prospect of regional devolution, presenting a regional democratic form in which one unequal system of control has simply been replaced by another. In this sense, *The Carhullan Army* offers only an emerging vision of post-British autonomy for England that is tentative and never fully realised. There are, however, signals that this project remains open-ended. Right before the seizing of Rith, Jackie mentions that Cumbria is 'still missing a big predator in the chain' (Hall, 2007, p. 184) and she would like to see wolves back in England, anticipating the political function of wolves in *The Wolf Border*.

If *The Carhullan Army* initiates a post-British vision for the North-West, it is in *The Wolf Border* that these politics find their most successful post-pastoral outlet. *The Wolf Border* dismantles elegiac images of the country-side in England; Chapter 1 is titled 'Old Country', the novel's first gesture to an ideological construction of Englishness characterised by artistic engagements with the rural landscape. At the beginning of her project with Pennington, Rachel becomes frustrated that 'people here don't care about the country in any deep way, they just want nice walks, nice views, and a tea room' (Hall, 2015, p. 35). In contrast, Rachel possesses a local affiliation with the land rooted in her childhood memories. Upon her return from America, Rachel realises that 'England is unreal, a forgotten version, with only a few pieces of evidence left to validate it' (Hall, 2015, p. 23). This musing aligns the landscape with a pastoral version of Englishness, yet, when Hall evokes the landscape on a micro scale, it is much more vivid and ecologically conscious. When Rachel returns to Cumbria, she quickly becomes reacquainted with the 'spruce and sagebrush, the rancid vegetable smell of the paper mill downriver from the Reservation. Cumbria's sig-nature aroma is immediately recognisable: upland pheromones' (Hall, 2015, p. 9). Rachel's sensorial familiarity decouples the landscape from the mythical rural and reframes it in localised terms through the notation of specific reference points. Hall's prioritisation of a local connection to Cum-bria's topography – a characteristic of Rachel's role on the wolf-project – signals the landscape's demythologisation and England's own counter-pas-toral return as it becomes geographically rooted and 'placed'. The kind of 'grounded ecology' the wolf-project represents is opposed by groups who reinforce the country's 'green and pleasant land' as a synecdoche of a national consciousness. When Rachel attempts to answer the public's ques-tions, the protesters sing a song 'written to the tune of Jerusalem' (Hall, 2015, p. 154). This performative ode to a mythical version of Englishness alludes to Blakean elegies of the pastoral idyll and, in drawing on a hymn frequently co-opted as England's unofficial national anthem, elevates rural space beyond a material and placed reality.

The material fact of the wolves in *The Wolf Border* also establishes con-nections between the novel's rewilding project and a post-British vision of Eng-land. Counterposing fantasises of the pastoral imaginary, the physical presence of wolves on the Annerdale estate initiates a post-pastoral reconfiguration of English rural space as the land becomes used for an environmental cause, rather than being reduced to a national iconography or object of aesthetic contempla-tion. The novel's epigraph, for example, communicates the bind between the wolves and a kind of decentralised politics: '*Susiraja* (Finnish) – Literally 'wolf border': the boundary between the capital region and the rest of the country. The name suggests everything outside the border is wilderness' (Hall, 2015, n.p.). Here, the wolf-project highlights the disconnection between Westminster – a symbol of Anglo-British hegemony – and what is tellingly described as 'the rest of the country'. As such, the novel's title translates into a case for decentralised politics in England emerging from a space of wilderness, a landscape Hall often attributes to Cumbria in particular and Northern England as a whole.

The project of rewilding in *The Wolf Border* thus necessitates a post-pastoral commitment to English rural space. Graham Huggan's explanation of the ecological value of rewilding is particularly instructive for reading the wolf-project in post-pastoral terms:

> Rewilding is not the romantic idea of restoring [natural ecosystems] to their putatively original state, which is recognised by practitioners as illusory; rather, it reflects the pragmatic need to boost their in-built capacity for regeneration, such as by performing reintroduction experiments that might encourage natural ecological processes to start.
>
> (Huggan, 2016, p. 169)

The Wolf Border was published in an emphatically post-pastoral moment in Britain in which there was a societal focus on ecological conservation and rewilding. There are, for instance, parallels to be drawn between the novel's fictional Annerdale estate where the wolf enclosure is located and Paul Lister's Alladale Wilderness Reserve in the Caledonian Forest.[13] In the novel, the highly political project of rewilding contains the potential to bypass regional and, as the wolves make clear, national lines of demarcation. The transgressive politics of rewilding disregard humanmade territorial divisions and, in *The Wolf Border*, expose the ways these divisions serve to reinforce regional inequality. In this sense, the novel's concern with rewilding maps onto its post-British project.

The literary function of the wolves in *The Wolf Border* also encodes an ambivalence towards the possibility of achieving a post-British England; they are overdetermined spatial metaphors whose symbolic purpose becomes increasingly slippery. The wolf has long been used as a literary device for exploring human, political, social, and environmental preoccupations. The figure of the wolf, as Karen Jones points out, is often 'a symbol of ecological vitality located in the wilderness' (Jones, 2011, p. 202): because of its biological proximity to the domestic dog, the wolf is a suitable device for navigating the porous boundary between civilisation and 'the wild'.[14] Likewise, in *The Wolf Border*, the wolves are indifferent to the human-made boundaries of North/South and wilderness/civilisation. The novel's intent focus on the physicality of the wolves dismantles the illusory mechanisms of the pastoral idyll. The wolves and their rewilding demonstrate a post-pastoral commitment to presenting 'the fact of an animal, not the myth' (Hall, 2015, p. 35). Described by Rachel as creatures of 'geographic success' (Hall, 2015, p. 35), the physical presence of wolves on the Annerdale estate in *The Wolf Border* symbolises the momentum for constitutional change. The material fact of the wolves punctures the pastoral throughout the text. What Rachel finds most fascinating about the wolves is their physical attributes, their 'extraordinary jaw' and 'small, clever, yellow eyes', an animal 'perfectly made' (Hall, 2015, pp. 7, 253, 3). Yet, the novel avoids reducing the wolves to myth, rendering their entire journey visible: from their arrival from the US and the delivery of the pups, to their paw prints in the ground following their escape. Upon the birth of the new wolf pups, Rachel reflects that '[t]hey become almost like mascots for exactly what no one is sure, a beleaguered England, an England no longer associated with Scotland's great natural resources' (Hall, 2015, p. 326). Explicitly lent to a national England, the concurrent narratives of the birth of the wolves and the birth of an independent Scotland collide.

This is not the only function of the wolves in the novel, however. Although here the wolves appear to signify the prospect of 'rewilding' England as a politically autonomous nation, they are later deployed as cultural symbols and pet projects for political figures. This shift is clearly visible in a passage in which the novel draws attention to the way the centralised state form has accelerated regional inequality within England. As the Scottish polls tip towards a majority Yes-vote, Sylvia remarks that she 'would like to see a shift to more regional power, too ... A lot of Cumbria's needs are not London's or Cornwall's. My concern is what happens in England if they go' (Hall, 2015, p. 179). Sylvia's comment attributes the uneven distribution of political and financial resources throughout England to its precarious position within an increasingly unstable Union. The difficulty of imagining an independent England in the novel is partially due to a democratic deficit: Rachel quickly becomes aware that 'regardless of democracy, the greater schemes are led by the upper echelons' (Hall, 2015, p. 25). Rachel's musing characterises the 'English Question' as national only insofar as it is regional, suggesting that the discussion that surrounds the break-up of Britain must also address political, financial, and social inequality in regions within England. Nonetheless, despite Sylvia's acknowledgement of these implications, it is not long before any potential regional grumblings are pacified. Rachel notes how '[t]here's been no more trouble around the fence periphery', a beneficial outcome for England's prime minister, who, after the Scottish Yes-vote is 'desperate for good press, progressive politics – especially in the regions where there is growing agitation for devolved powers – and the project qualifies' (Hall, 2015, p. 260). Here, the symbolic value of the wolf project is harnessed by political figures for their own self-legitimising agenda – in this case, for preventing increased momentum for regional devolution in England.

So, while previously the wolves symbolised the potential for a post-British England, here they are seen to potentially become part of a *state* project.

The slipperiness of the wolves throughout the novel indicates an ambivalence towards the possibility of achieving a post-British England, especially one that may be attuned to regional inequality throughout the nation. The wolves' various symbolic functions ultimately remain unresolved, suggesting a reading of the wolves and their rewilding in *The Wolf Border* as manifestations of the novel's inability to overcome the ideological stranglehold of Britain and the pastoral.

Freedom and Enclosure

The Wolf Border's critique of British state dominance also concerns the competing regional and national tensions implicit within the bureaucratic regulation and increasing privatisation of rural space.[15] Since the 1800s, land enclosure in England has been a politics of social class. E.P. Thompson observed in 1963 that enclosure represents a form of 'class robbery' and has been used as a method of social discipline for 'the village poor' (Thompson, 1963, p. 195). As he puts it, the privatisation of land through enclosure 'became a matter of public-spirited policy for the gentleman to remove cottages from the commons, reduce his laborers to dependence, pare away at supplementary earnings, drive out the small holder' (Thompson, 1963, p. 219). The private ownership of what had previously been publicly owned land drives *The Wolf Border*'s exploration of the tensions between region and nation, as Hall locates these questions within a longer history in which land was a central component of the British class system. When the novel rewinds to Rachel's childhood, she recalls an experience of rural space that is clearly demarcated and owned. In contrast to a pastoral idyll, she remembers instead a 'fence built tall and seriously, up into the trees. The wire is thick and heavy, knotted into diamond-shaped holes' (Hall, 2015, p. 5). In this sense, the uneasy tension between freedom and enclosure as part of the rewilding project operates within the politics of private and public space and their intersection with inequalities between region and nation.

The entire project depends upon Pennington's impulse, whose hegemonic dominance underscores the way ownership of and control over rural space is intrinsically political: his vast ownership of immense land signifies the hierarchies of an anachronistic British class system. Pennington's privatisation of common land for the wolf enclosure emblematises the lasting power of Britain's land-owning political elite and conveys Hall's pessimism about the possibility of achieving an egalitarian post-British England. As Williams has already argued, enclosure of the commons facilitates the 'steady concentration of power in the hands of the landowners' which in turn represents 'a conscious national system and interest in the constitution of landowners as a political class' (Williams, 2016, p. 147). More recently, the nature writer Kathleen Jamie has argued that while previously 'the wild land was a working place, whether you were a hunter-gatherer, a crofter, a miner … now it seems it is being claimed by the educated middle classes on spiritual quests' (Jamie, 2008). Indeed, the class dynamics that underpin both Scottish Independence and the wolf project in *The Wolf Border* are a comment on the hierarchies implicit in the management of British rural space via conservation charities and interest groups. The John Muir Trust, for example, now owns eight estates in Scotland under the remit of protecting and managing 'wild' land. *The Wolf Border*'s class-inflected rewilding project certainly reflects the moral complexities of the way ecological developments are imbricated in socio-economic relations; the project has essentially been made possible because of the processes of privatisation and privilege identified by Williams and Jamie respectively. It is driven by the wealth of Britain's aristocracy, described by Rachel as a member of the 'ebullient, boyish elite' (Hall, 2015, p. 15) who 'owns almost one fifth of her home country' (Hall, 2015, p. 3). She remains unimpressed by Pennington's expansive estate and attitude towards his 'latest environmental venture' (Hall, 2015, p. 15), an experiment enabled as a result of his manipulation of the Game Enclosure Bill.

In centring the wolves' rewilding on privately owned and cultivated territory, the novel deconstructs ideas of the rural 'wild', recognising the very idea of 'wilderness' as an impossible necessity. Rachel's return to Annerdale as an adult illustrates this paradox. Rachel reflects that 'she did not know it [as a child], but in reality it was a kempt place, cultivated, even the high grassland over the fells was manmade. Though it formed her notions of beauty, true wilderness lay elsewhere' (Hall, 2015, p. 29). Rachel realises that her childhood landscape has always been subject to constant human influence and regulation; it is by no means 'wild'. Her dissonance highlights the way experiences of the English landscape are contingent on modernity's innate separation from the countryside, an association she is forced to reject when she returns to Cumbria years later. In *Deep Ecology* (1985) Bill Devall and George Sessions pinpoint wilderness as fundamental to a new ecological consciousness, defining it as 'a landscape or ecosystem that has been minimally disrupted by the intervention of humans, especially the destructive technology of modern societies' (Devall and Sessions, 1985, p. 10). Both 'wild' enough to accommodate the wolves, yet simultaneously governed by human interests, *The Wolf Border*'s ambivalent landscape locates the contradictions embedded within notions of 'rewilding' and 'wilderness' and thus presents Hall's partial prognosis for imagining a post-British re-inscription of rural space.

Governing interests over land in *The Wolf Border* primarily pertain to Pennington as the inherited legal owner of Annerdale. Referring to the Cumbrian village of the same name, Pennington's surname is a literal translation of the economisation of private land, deriving from the Old English words 'Penny' (a tribute due on the land) and 'tun' (enclosure or settlement). Significant ideological divisions between Pennington and Rachel characterise the entire wolf project. While Rachel's ecological and professional commitment to the wolves is clear, she is never able to fully appraise the project due to 'the hegemony, the unsettling feeling of imbalance' (Hall, 2015, p. 29) she recognises between herself, Pennington, and his loyal gamekeeper, Michael. In particular, the freighted relationship between Rachel and Michael – and the position he occupies in the social hierarchy of land management – reflects both the gendered and class-based inequalities that have long facilitated the maintenance of a British land-owning elite.

> [Michael] is not happy about being replaced in the chain of command. [F]or now [Rachel] holds the lateral position, perhaps even a higher position. Certainly [he is] not happy about the reconstitution of Annerdale, with its new apex predator. She represents dire competition, beyond his experience.
>
> (Hall, 2015, p. 117)

Michael is an anachronistic symbol of aristocratic ruralism, a stark opposition to Rachel's progressive approach to the land. He is proud of his position on the estate enabled by its 'old orders' (Hall, 2015, p. 117), opposing both the redistribution of power that the wolf project represents socially and the material threat of the wolves. After all, the working relationship forged by the fathers of both Michael and Pennington secured the former's continued role on the estate – his claim to the landscape is 'all in the blood' (Hall, 2015, p. 94). Rachel's entry into Pennington's employ thus signifies the breakdown of this social order centred on inherited wealth. Rachel herself reflects that Annerdale is 'a realm so antiquated it seems impossible that it has survived reformist centuries' (Hall, 2015, p. 281). Here, the reconstitution of Annerdale refers to the end of a current social arrangement in the politics of land ownership and the emergence of a new system in which Michael's position is compromised; the reality that his legitimacy on the estate survives only as long as Pennington underwrites it is made starkly clear. In this sense, Michael's social standing on the estate is bound up in Hall's wider exploration of the class relations and wider capitalistic ideologies that underwrite rural land management. Beyond *Haweswater*, farmers barely feature in Hall's fiction and, in *The Wolf Border*, Pennington's concern with the rural landscape does not extend to farming purposes, but to monetising the aesthetic value of the land in a bid for World Heritage status.

In this way, *The Wolf Border* demonstrates how modern conservation strategies have gone hand in hand with the maintenance of neo-feudalist class relations and served the maintenance of the interests of a land-owning class. The fact that Rachel has been conscripted into a role left vacant by Michael's marginalisation means that her role cannot be considered straightforwardly progressive. Although Rachel's presence at Annerdale hints at the destabilisation of old class hierarchies based on ancestral lineage, she ultimately replaces Michael in an already existing chain of command that serves Pennington. Rachel herself 'begins to feel a little uncomfortable, part of the machinery of segregation, which always enables the elite' (Hall, 2015, p. 281). So, as much as Michael's resistance to the rewilding project indicates a desire for the continuation of archaic class relations linked to the separation of English rural space and modernity, the social hierarchies of the rewilding project pose an ideological problem to the wolves' status as symbols of England's progressive future.

The wolves' association with governing structures further complicates their symbolic disruptive potential in the novel. In contrast to Rachel's local and professional credentials as a zoologist, Pennington possesses a colonial paternalism towards the land and the rewilding project; for him, the wolves are little more than an ecological experiment, a 'hope-and-glory' (Hall, 2015, p. 56) project key to recreating 'the British soul' (Hall, 2015, p. 80). Rachel's uneasiness about her living arrangements, and the above-average pay, gesture towards Pennington's social and professional dominance over her as the native expert. Rachel continually tries, but ultimately fails, to reconstitute their power relations and 'get to know the system' so that she may ascertain 'where she herself fits into it' (Hall, 2015, p. 84). Pennington's orchestration of the wolves' early release from their enclosure highlights Rachel's lack of agency. The very fact that the Earl of Annerdale still owns his estate signifies his absolute authority and foreshadows his ability to evade accountability over the eventual fate of the wolves. The wolves are taken first to a managed estate owned by a member of the political elite skilled at manipulating the powers at Westminster, and their impromptu release speaks of his vast power. Pennington's ability to override Rachel's decisions and dismantle the wolf-project 'as he wishes' (Hall, 2015, p. 414) is analogous to the limited political autonomy offered by state-managed devolution, in which the British state always retains its political grasp. The fate of the wolves is ultimately uncertain and becomes tied up in the Scottish Prime Minister's project of rebuilding the nation. As Rachel herself notes, 'not much has really changed ... now our free Caledonian cousins may actually have to put theory into practice' (Hall, 2015, p. 413). While there are endless renegotiations of power in the novel, the wolves remain subject to ongoing management, even as they cross the border and enter the territory of a newly independent Scotland.

Despite the outcome of the referendum, *The Wolf Border* imagines Anglo-Britain's ongoing cultural grip on the national imagination of England and, to some degree, Scotland. Rachel's forced administration of the wolves' invasive sterilisation, a treatment she believes is 'the price of partial freedom' (Hall, 2015, p. 339), communicates the reality that the rewilding will always remain governed. Indeed, it is possible to read *The Wolf Border* as a critique of devolution as it occurs within the institutions of the British state. Given the wolves' pacification under human influence and the rewilding's eventual outcome as the prime minister's token gesture towards upholding Scotland's new environmental policy, freedom from governing structures is only ever partial, a process of containment and pacification, rather than a radical redistribution of power. The wolves' planned relocation to Ben Nevis, one of Scotland's most iconic cultural symbols, also indicates a contained, partial freedom. The culmination of the rewilding project thus signals a retreat of *The Wolf Border*'s post-pastoral vision for English rural space, ending instead with an image of a commodified national iconography in Scotland. The nation's most cultivated 'wild spot' (Hall, 2015, p. 430) functions here as a mirror image of Annerdale: host to 125,000 walkers a year, Ben Nevis is hardly 'wild'.

It is useful at this point to return to Jackie's assertion in *The Carhullan Army* that everything radical happens 'in the mountain regions' (Hall, 2007, p. 195). While in Hall's previous novel the mountains provide a space for radical political change, *The Wolf Border*'s mountain regions are instead subject to fierce regulation. Pennington's interference in the project of Scottish independence and excitement that the wolves will become 'a new icon for a new nation' implies that the figure of the wolf will once again be reduced to its symbolic value, an 'icon' (Hall, 2015, p. 423) realigned with historic and geographic myth. In this sense, Britain's continuing domination, its anachronistic class system, and institutional remnants prevent the novel from achieving the post-British potential it initially imagined. The project's fatality is suggested for a final time when a lorry driver hits one of the stray wolves. The driver has bought into the Scottish Prime Minister's political appropriation of the wolves and wanted them to make it to Nevis, 'he was for them, a Yes voter' (Hall, 2015, p. 430). The syntactic ambiguity in this line enables the 'Yes' to take on a dual significance, referring to both his outlook on the wolves' reintegration and his voting choices in the referendum. What is more, the fact that the wolf subsequently dies as a result of the collision indicates that the idea of rewilding has always been a fantasy, suggesting a pessimism about the realisation of post-British potential either side of the border.

Alternative Unions

There is, then, a limited degree of post-British potential to be found in the representation of Cumbria in *The Wolf Border*. However, by way of conclusion, I want to examine one of the ironies of this novel which captures the complexities of Hall's post-pastoral vision. I have suggested that Rachel's professional narrative in many ways facilitates a post-pastoral understanding of England and English rural space; however, Rachel's personal narrative exists in conflict with this project insofar as the novel tends towards the pastoral mode when she forges emotional attachments. The landscape bears heavily on Rachel's emotional ties to both Alexander and his daughter, Chloe, and in the development of her familial reunion with Lawrence. While at the novel's outset Rachel does not form emotional or geographic ties, she undergoes a personal transformation in which the 'uncivilised spirit' (Lea, 2017, p. 154) characteristic of Hall's protagonists becomes tamed. This process of 'taming' occurs in Rachel's shift in attitude towards romantic relationships. Initially emotionally detached, her relationships with men generally end after they have had sex, and consequently, 'she has never really made it past the first argument with a man' (Hall, 2015, p. 218). Her matter-of-fact approach towards sexual partners is aligned with her treatment of the land: it is raw, visceral, and inherently unromantic. She describes kissing as 'one of evolution's stranger necessities' (Hall, 2015, p. 40) in the same way her role as a conservationist enables her to see through Pennington's sentimentality towards the land. However, her developing relationship with Alexander and her unplanned pregnancy initiate a transformation of her character towards forms of place-bound emotional attachment. Rachel's attraction to Alexander is not instinctual. She does not immediately find him attractive and in contrast to her previous brief sexual exchanges, she gradually transitions from sex as power – from knowing someone will 'want to fuck' a woman 'like her' (Hall, 2015, p. 39) – to sex as an emotionally invested act that enables her to dwell in place. When Rachel finds herself pregnant after an uncharacteristically vanilla one-night stand with her friend, Kyle, she tells her GP that she does not have relationships, 'just sex' (Hall, 2015, p. 81). Yet, Rachel's pregnancy instigates a softening of her approach to relationships as she moves away from what Cottrell describes as 'fierce aloofness' (Cottrell, 2017, p. 683) towards a desire for placed attachments.

Rachel's reunion with Lawrence – primarily achieved during walks through the countryside and watching the wolves in their enclosure – similarly evokes these pastoral tendencies. During their awkward first meeting, the potential sighting of the wolves breaks the tension in Lawrence and Rachel's reunion; Lawrence is 'taken by the exoticism' of Rachel's job and, when they reach the top of Blencathra, Rachel 'suddenly feels moved' (Hall, 2015, pp. 125–126) to be with him. The unexpected emotional connection with her brother is tied to the catharsis that attends their freely roaming the rural landscape. Later, when they walk through the land surrounding the enclosure, Lawrence 'occasionally glanc[es] over, with a possessive tenderness, as if she might stumble' (Hall, 2015, p. 162). The stability of the landscape affords Rachel the vulnerability to establish the emotional connection to Lawrence she never had as a child. This impasse in *The Wolf Border*'s post-pastoral representation of the rural is also emphasised in Annerdale's restorative role during Lawrence's recovery from addiction. Upon the breakdown of his marriage, Lawrence is exiled from the domestic sphere and the landscape becomes a place of retreat and recovery. When Lawrence is discharged from a brief stay in e hospital, he is prescribed 'recuperation and isolation in the countryside' in which Rachel's cottage 'will be a sanatorium' (Hall, 2015, p. 317). The novel emphatically represents the landscape as bearing restorative qualities; it enables Lawrence to undergo a process of convalescence so that he may 're-enter the world' (Hall, 2015, p. 354) after he has become re-domesticated. Both Rachel and Lawrence's 'rewilding' therefore results in the process of taming as the novel grapples with the contradictions embedded within notions of rewilding and wilderness. Significantly, these passages necessitate a temporary abandonment of the novel's political project in favour of Hall's characters' personal narrative; they emphasise 'fertility, resilience, beauty, and unthreatened stability in nature' (Gifford, 2012, p. 49), qualities that Gifford attributes to the 'idealising' tendency of the pastoral mode.

It is thus in the refusal to neatly reconcile competing versions of the pastoral and post-pastoral that *The Wolf Border* engages with the complexities of imagining a post-British England. Ultimately, the novel is unable to resolve its own counteracting impulses towards pastoral retreat and a post-pastoral representation of rural space. Like *Haweswater* and *The Carhullan Army*, *The Wolf Border* also appears to operate within the 'mature environmental aesthetics' Gifford attributes to the post-pastoral. These aesthetics 'go beyond the closed circuit of pastoral and anti-pastoral to achieve a vision of an integrated natural world that includes the human' (Gifford, 1999, p. 148). We might consider these texts part of this movement that attempts to define a pastoral that avoids the traps of idealism in seeking to find a discourse that celebrates and takes responsibility for nature without false consciousness. In this sense, *Haweswater, The Carhullan Army*, and *The Wolf Border* offer only a *disruption* of the pastoral mode, reflecting the deeply entrenched social and political barriers to a post-British England as much as a political urgency for change.

Given the outcome of a referendum that took place the year following *The Wolf Border*'s publication, the dissolution of Britain that Hall's work often imagines seems increasingly possible. Hall's critique of the centralised state form and vision of an independent Scotland is even more prescient in the context of the UK's vote to terminate its membership of the EU in 2016. This outcome brought existing geographic, political, and socio-economic divisions throughout the archipelago into unprecedented public prominence and called into question once again the tenability of a union between the four nations that comprise the UK. Variations in support for leaving the EU and governmental uncertainty have already led to further strain on Britain's constitutional integrity. In the media, the Leave vote was perceived as more to do with England's internal divisions than with European relations, replayed as a revolt against Westminster's political elite by a disenfranchised, working-class, English population located beyond the parameters of the M25. Rachel's reflection at the close of *The Wolf Border* that there is potential to change 'the fabric of British politics, state definitions ... if people want it badly enough, if they are tired and hopeful' (Hall, 2015, p. 423) takes on a new significance in a post-Brexit-vote context. If, as a consequence of Britain's deepening constitutional fissures, there lies the potential for the emergence of a national England, placing literary politics beyond London is all the more urgent.

Notes

1 See, for example, Anthony Barnett, 'The Fire and the Games. How London's Olympic Opening Confronted Corporate Values'. *Open Democracy*, 30 July 2012. Available at: http://www. opendemocracy.net/ourkingdom/anthony-barnett/fire-and-

games-how-london%E2% 80%99s-olympic-opening-confronted-corporate-values [accessed 17 September 2020] and Aaron Bastani, 'Olympic Britishness and the Crisis of Identity', *Open Democracy*, 3 August 2012. Available at: https://www.opendem ocracy.net/en/opendemocracyuk/olympic-britishness-and-crisis-of-identity [accessed 18 September 2020].

2 Boyle has also acknowledged that pre-industrial England was not all 'green and pleasant', but '[t]his is the countryside we all believe existed once.' See London Organising Committee of the Olympic Games and Paralympic Games (LOCOG) (2012), *London 2012 Olympic Games Opening Ceremony Media Guide*. London: LOCOG), p. 19. Available at: www.london2012.com/mm/Document/Documents/ Publications/01/30/43/40/OPENINGCEREMONYGUIDE_English.pdf [accessed 13 May 2020].

3 For an elaboration of this conversation, see 'Brexit and the Two English Questions' in the Introduction to this book.

4 See Katherine Byrne (2014) 'Adapting Heritage: Class and Conservatism in *Downton Abbey*', *Rethinking History*, 18 (3) (2014), 311–327.

5 See William Cobbett's *Rural Rides* (1830) for an early example of English rural writing focused on the reality of agricultural decline and rural poverty in the South of England.

6 While Brontë's text is characterised by rural violence, it's worth noting that the novel has always functioned entirely separately in the cultural sphere. Despite its anti-pastoral approach to the rural landscape, the novel has occupied the literary forefront of the 'cult of the countryside': West Yorkshire remains widely regarded as the 'Brontë Country' and the literary heritage of the Brontë's is the motor force behind Howarth's tourist industry.

7 A notable filmic comparison is Francis Lee's *God's Own Country* (2017) for its account of the hardships of sheep farming in Yorkshire.

8 See also Fiona Mozley's *Elmet* (2017) and Sarah Moss's *Ghost Wall* (2018) in Chapter 4.

9 Hall has revealed that she intended *The Wolf Border* to be a state-of-the-nation novel, indicating a wider exploration of twenty-first-century Britain than has previously been the case in her work. See Ruppin (2017) 'Sarah Hall, Foyles'. Available at: https://www.foyles.co.uk/sarah-hall (accessed: 17 September 2020).

10 For more on the conservation of the golden eagle in Cumbria, see https://www. cumbriawildlifetrust.org.uk/wildlife-explorer/birds/birds-prey/golden-eagle.
The reference to the golden eagle in *Haweswater* also foregrounds a preoccupation with wildlife conservation and the national park, concerns that Hall returns to in *The Wolf Border*.

11 See, most recently, Scott Hames (2018) *The Literary Politics of Scottish Devolution: Voice, Class, Nation*. Edinburgh: Edinburgh University Press, and Cairns Craig (2018) *The Wealth of the Nation: Scotland, Culture, Independence*. Edinburgh: Edinburgh University Press.

12 Given the focus of Hall's later work, it's worth noting that the surname 'Levell' is derived from the Norman French word *lou*, meaning 'wolf'.

13 See https://alladale.com.

14 The figure of the wolf is bound up in rural images of wild Northern landscapes, particularly North America, alluded to in Rachel's initial work with wolves in Idaho.

15 In literary culture, enclosure is perhaps most famously associated with the poet John Clare, whose Lake District poetry was marked by regional and ecological sensibilities which opposed parliamentary enclosure in the early nineteenth century.

Part II
Revolt

3 Brexit England and the Deindustrial North

On 4 February 2016, the front page of the *Daily Mail* asked: 'WHO WILL SPEAK FOR ENGLAND?' (*The Daily Mail*, 2016). Printed in bold capital letters, the headline was a call to arms, demanding that the English public choose between becoming a self-governing nation or remaining under the stranglehold of European administration:

> Are we to be a self-governing nation, free in this age of mass migration to control our borders, strike trade agreements with whomever we choose [...]? Or will our liberty, security and prosperity be better assured by submitting to a statist, unelected bureaucracy in Brussels ...?
>
> (*The Daily Mail*, 2016)

Despite what the *Daily Mail*'s rhetorical claims implied, voting 'Leave' alone would never deliver self-governance for England. However, this is of little importance, given that the editors were not referring to England alone. The editorial notes that 'of course, by "England"... we mean the whole of the United Kingdom' (*The Daily Mail*, 2016), adopting a view that England is interchangeable not only with Britain but with the entire UK. Unknowingly, the *Daily Mail*'s call for sovereignty neatly captured what Tom Nairn described as the 'English enigma' (Nairn, 1977, p. 293) – that is, the way that England is so often a stand in for the entire UK despite the absence of its own national parliament. The problem, as Anthony Barnett writes, is that the constitutional suppression of England 'lies at the heart of Theresa May's project for Brexit Britain (Barnett, 2017, p. 115). Rather than pertaining solely to Britain's relationship with Europe, Brexit was in many ways a *national* event. The outcome of the referendum, and its ensuing political fallout, signalled a deepening of existing constitutional fissures throughout the UK and threw the spotlight on England's place in the Union in particular. One narrative of the referendum positioned Brexit as a UKanian nationalist project that sought to realign the UK's place in the global order with England at the fore. After all, of the UK's component nations, England voted most decisively for Brexit. Scotland voted to remain by 62 per cent to 38 per cent, Northern Ireland voted to remain by 55.8 per cent to 47.5 per cent, while Wales only very narrowly voted to leave by 52.5 to 47.5 per cent (Ashcroft, 2016). It is

DOI: 10.4324/9781003388722-6

no surprise, then, that critical attempts to understand the implications of the referendum have turned to its largest leave-voting constituency, a territorial unit with no parliamentary basis.

At the same time, the aftermath of the vote saw governmental efforts to contain this politicised Englishness. During Theresa May's first speech as prime minister, she attempted to assure the Party of her commitment to constitutional stability in light of the vote to terminate membership of the EU:

> [b]ecause we voted in the referendum as one United Kingdom, we will negotiate as one United Kingdom, and we will leave the European Union as one United Kingdom. There is no opt-out from Brexit. I will never allow divisive nationalists to undermine the precious Union between the four nations of the United Kingdom.
>
> (May, 2016b)

May harnessed a Unionist discourse in an attempt to quash serious conversations about English national political representation. Although English nationalism is not singled out, the pretext of the post-referendum British politics and the preoccupation with 'England's Brexit' undoubtedly influenced the content of May's speech. The idea that the multiple and contrasting nations of the UK voted 'as one' is, of course, a falsity and little more than a last-ditch attempt to maintain Britain's integrity as it comes under increasing scrutiny. What is more, despite the acknowledgement of the four nations of the UK here, it is worth noting that the remainder of the speech was dedicated to the Party's vision of a 'Global Britain' after Brexit. This policy became the lifeblood of the Conservative Party as the complications of removing Britain from the EU played out and was later renewed by Boris Johnson's promise to 'unleash Britain's potential'. In this sense, May's concern with the threat of nationalism appeared to pertain to the integrity of the British archipelago, rather than the entire UK. In any case, a Westminster-located Britishness dominated political practice both before and after the referendum. As we have seen in the preceding two chapters, a Union based on notions of 'stability' and 'continuity' has been crucial in the postcolonial imagination of Britain as it attempts to reassert itself after the breakdown of Empire, the establishment of devolved institutions in 1997, and, now, following the Brexit vote.[1] However, given the constitutional fractures revealed by Westminster's negotiations with Europe and the devolved nations, and the disunity with which the UK – and indeed, England itself – voted in the referendum, there remains the question of what a post-Brexit Britain may look like, or whether it might exist at all.

Writing Brexit: From State-of-the-Nation to Place

Literary culture has turned to the question of post-Brexit Britain and England's place within it. Britain's transition period since 2017 has witnessed what Joe Kennedy calls a new iteration of the condition of England novel (Kennedy, 2017) with writers seeking to explore Brexit as symptomatic of a working-class, insular English nationalism. Bruno Vincent's *Five on Brexit Island* (2016), Sam Byers' *Perfidious Albion* (2018) and Ian McEwan's *The Cockroach* (2019) offer pessimistic visions of Brexit-era Englishness, while Fiona Shaw's *Outwalkers* (2018) utilises dystopian allegory as a narrative centred on the securitisation of territorial borders. Shaw's young-adult *Bildungsroman* imagines a future of constitutional rupture and governmental surveillance that encloses England from the rest of Britain and the wider world. In this novel, Englishness emerges as a staunchly protectionist nationalism with the narrative punctuated by the refrain of government vans playing: 'Our English shores stand clean and proud, Our English shores stand clean and proud' (Shaw, 2018, p. 24). *Autumn* (2016), the first novel in Ali Smith's 'Seasonal Quartet' (2017, 2019, 2020), also conveys a metropolitan desire to escape from England and retreat to the Remain-voting nations of the UK:

> All across the country, people looked up Google: what is EU? All across the country people looked up Google: move to Scotland. All across the country, people looked up Google: Irish passport applications. ... All across the country, everything changed overnight.
>
> (Smith, 2017, p. 59)

Smith's England is both a fragmentary and deeply divided place marked by geographic, political, socio-economic, and cultural fault lines. It is only the unlikely connection between Elisabeth Demand – a university lecturer in her thirties – and 101-year-old Daniel Gluck that offers a glimpse of a society unmarred by social and territorial borders.

While these writers offer broad, state-of-the-nation explorations of England which are characterised by a protectionist hostility to inward migration, literary culture has equally turned to England's margins. To return to the two English Questions introduced at the outset of this book, the literary concern with a national England has developed in parallel to a renewed interest in England's own regional inequalities. Post-Brexit literary culture has explored regional and national English Questions within in an opposition between a *localised* Englishness and a London-centred *global* Britishness. Amanda Craig's *Lie of the Land* (2017), Kenneth Steven's *2020* (2017), Douglas Board's *Time of Lies* (2017), Jonathan Coe's *Middle England* (2018), and Sarah Moss' *Ghost Wall* (2018) and *Summerwater* (2021) all seek to explain Brexit by returning to England's socio-economic and geographical margins. This polarisation between an inward-looking – and often, Northern English – regionalism and an outward-facing Britishness is a duality which, as we shall see in Chapter 4, is a contemporary evolution of the North–South divide and all its class-inflected connotations. These novels index Brexit's two geopolitical and socio-economic English narratives: a

'Little England' whose identity is distinct from Britain and yoked to the rise of working-class, anti-immigration sentiment, and a governmental narrative of 'Global Britain', which is routinely associated with a metropolitan, liberal elite.

There are, however, limitations to the political and literary tendency to associate the Leave vote with the working class. As Lisa Mckenzie points out:

> temporarily framing working-class politics, identity and culture around 'Brexit' and consequently dismissing the outcome as irrational or xeno-phobic betrays a lack of sociological understanding of the long-term progression of narratives and markers of class as a social and long-itudinal formation over generations.
>
> (Mckenzie, 2017, p. 268)

Brexit has been marked by a monolithic class discourse which treats 'the working class' as a singular demographic, eliding nuances of contemporary class formation as well as its intersection with race, age, and geography. This is not least because the referendum itself hinged on a linguistic binary of 'yes/no', but also because this opposition precludes nuanced and evolving manifestations of class that are bound up in a history of uneven develop-ment and structural inequalities. Brexit was not an exclusively working-class 'revolt' as has often been suggested. Indeed, what is too often missing from accounts that seek to explain the referendum result is the fact that the wealthy, land-owning rich were a largely Leave-voting demographic (The Electoral Commission, 2019). As Phil O'Brien points out, 'the clammer [sic] to point the finger at an imagined working class' elides the reality that 'the Leave campaign was not only orchestrated by those wedded to the ideology of neoliberalism but was also able to mobilise a broad-based coalition of voters which is much more wide-ranging than the "left behind"' (O'Brien, 2018, p. 15). Despite England's Eastern coastal towns, affluent areas in the Southern shires, and parts of rural England reliant on agribusiness also being majority Leave-voting demographics, the Eng-lish nationalism associated with the Leave vote was readily attributed to the post-imperial nostalgia of an English working class, broadly located somewhere in 'the North'.[2]

Anthony Barnett's analysis of the vote identifies this manoeuvre, noting that 'the London media rushed to the North of England, to see if Brexit could be blamed on the lumpen working class missing out on the benefits of economic growth' therefore placing 'all the weight of reporting onto a mythological real country with authentically poor health' (Barnett, 2017, p. 107). Likewise, writ-ing shortly after the referendum, Zadie Smith notes how London was often labelled an 'outward-looking city … so different from these narrow xeno-phobic places up north' (Smith, 2018, p. 27). Smith's comment suggests a per-sistent London exceptionalism which casts the North as both insular and inherently 'local'. Smith herself admits she 'wanted [this account] to be true', but she concedes that Brexit revealed the 'deep fractures in British society' that must be acknowledged, 'between north and south, between the social classes, between Londoners and everyone else' (Smith, 2018, p. 27).

This chapter focuses on literary engagement with the North after the EU Referendum, taking Brexit as a watershed moment for the relationship between Northern England and the wider nation. In particular, it examines Anthony Cartwright's *The Cut* (2017) and Adam Thorpe's *Missing Fay* (2017) whose responses to the referendum are instructive for assessing the place of the North in the twenty-first-century national consciousness. Not only do these texts explore the relationship between 'Northernness', deindustrialisation, and class, they index a link between literary constructions of the North and the 'Little Englandism' that was perceived to lie behind England's vote in favour of exiting the EU. The analysis that follows thus examines how Thorpe and Cartwright engage with – and partially replicate – a dominant polarity within Brexit discourse: a specifically English, inward-looking North versus an outward-facing, London-centred Britishness.

The Cut explores how 'the local' became associated with a reactionary form of 'Northern', deindustrial nostalgia in the context of Brexit. One of the earliest examples of 'BrexLit' (Shaw, 2021), *The Cut* was commissioned as a response to the referendum by Peirene Press – a publisher specialising in 'European novellas' – and given the task of 'building a fictional bridge between the two Britains that opposed each other on referendum day' (Cartwright, 2017, n.p.). The form of the novel echoes Brexit's overarching narrative of division. Arranged in alternating chapters titled 'Before' and 'After', *The Cut* tells the gradually merging stories of film-maker Grace Trevithick – an embodiment of London-based cognitive labour – and Cairo Jukes, a precariously employed manual labourer who is symbolic of the so-called 'left behind' working class. *The Cut*'s narrative structure and thematic concerns rely on these binary oppositions; the text follows Grace's exchanges with Cairo and his family in the weeks leading up to the referendum, with the aim of better understanding the voting choices of England's 'ordinary people' (Cartwright, 2017, p. 22). Told from their contrasting perspectives, the narrative captures a political discourse in which the deindustrial North and metropolitan London became competing, incompatible ideologies of class and geography.

During the same year, Adam Thorpe published his crime-thriller-cum-Brexit-novel, *Missing Fay*. Set in Lincolnshire – the highest Leave-voting county in England – this localised exploration of Englishness takes the form of a 'whodunnit' narrative, with the disappearance of fourteen-year-old Fay interwoven with the lives of Lincoln's residents.[3] The non-linear narrative unfolds in vignettes focusing on several individuals with some connection to Fay. Notably, Fay continues to inhabit the narrative after she goes missing, forming a point of connection between multiple characters, and implicating them in her case. The reader first encounters Fay in David's story, in which he becomes increasingly distracted by her 'MISSING' poster while on a family holiday in rural Lincolnshire. Fay is also connected to Sheena, who supervises Fay's work experience placement and is one of the last people to see her before she goes missing. Elsewhere, Fay inhabits the novel as a spectral presence. Bookshop owner, Mike, becomes psychologically haunted by Fay and believes that one of his books is possessed by her spirit, while former steelworker, Howard, glimpses Fay in a local park and mistakes her for the ghost of his own daughter who went missing several years earlier. Cosmina, a healthcare assistant from Romania, possesses vital information regarding Fay's fate, while Chris, a television producer turned postulant Trappist monk, encounters Fay in a prophetic vision in his sleep. Utilising the generic conventions of crime fiction, Fay's mobilisation as a spectral presence maps a localised social network emerging from each character's role in Fay's disappearance and addresses the need for collective responsibility in a socially divided present.

Missing Fay was not the only novel published in the year after the Brexit vote to centre on the disappearance of a young girl in England. Thorpe's novel has been readily compared to McGregor's Derbyshire-based *Reservoir 13* (2017), which similarly utilises the central crime – the disappearance of Rebecca Shaw – as a way in which to explore the intricacies of place.[4] In McGregor's novel, the thirteen-year-old goes missing while she and her family are on holiday in a village in the Peak District; the narrative unfolds through a series of local efforts to find her.[5] Both *Reservoir 13* and *Missing Fay* are emphatically local English crime novels, flowing between the perspectives of their characters and their everyday lives. They are less concerned with police procedures – in *Missing Fay*, police presence is virtually non-existent – and more about the places in which they are based and the everyday lives of their communities. Contrary to typical crime narratives, the project of locating Fay or Rebecca does not drive the plot, as their disappearance only serves as a necessary conduit for the exploration of urgent contemporary social concerns. Shaw describes *Reservoir 13* as a 'rejuvenated state-of-the-nation novel' that reveals 'the breakdown in communication that led to an emergent "Little Englander" mentality' (Shaw, 2018, p. 21). Shaw's observation recalls *Missing Fay*'s focus on a small English town and the multi-vocal narrative told by the town's residents and visitors. However, further to the 'Little England' narrative, in both novels, this placed, English 'rejuvenation' of the state-of-the-nation novel also articulates a fraying of the relationship between England and Britain that demands further critical investigation. Thorpe captures England's overdetermination in the twenty-first-century cultural imagination. While the novel rarely mentions the word 'England' directly, there are frequent references to a *cultural* Englishness: the idealised 'grassy villages' of a mythological English pastoral; the ethnonationalist connotations of the St George's flag; growing hostility towards Europe's democratic influence; and references to England as a territory under threat by immigration.

This overdetermination is achieved considerably in both novels with recourse to shifting modes of nostalgia. While the original coinage – combining the Greek for 'return to home' (*nostos*) and pain (*algos*) – relates to a profound longing that produced physical and psychological effects, nostalgia has since become displaced from its medical origins. As Tammy Clewell finds, by the eighteenth century, 'nostalgia ceased to be regarded in pathological terms, it assumed a temporal form [and ...] came to name ... an emotional longing for a lost time' (Clewell, 2005, p. 5). The term has long-standing links with literary regionalism.[6] As Dominic Head points out, there is a tradition in the English regional novel to tie nostalgia to a specific form of working-class culture, with 'the more overtly political element of this regional consciousness, rooted in the recognition of economic hardship, [...] it has the plight of the working classes at its heart' (Head, 2017, p. 129). At the same time, however, the regional novel's political consciousness is often limited by 'the problem of the backward look' (Head, 2017, p. 129), which avoids 'the inevitable onward march of progress' and weakens nostalgia's potential to confront the challenges of the present. As Stuart Tannock suggests, 'hostility towards nostalgia is fuelled in particular by the recurrent co-option of nostalgia by conservative, reactionary politics', but such critiques risk conflating nostalgia with 'the desire for a stable, traditional, and hierarchised society' (Tannock, 1995, p. 455). Akin to Tannock, Alistair Bonnett suggests that the past can provide a radical intervention in debates about the present, arguing that 'the difficulty of dealing with sudden and massive social change' is precisely the condition of nostalgia 'in its distinctly modern form' (Bonnett, 2010, p. 19). For Bonnett, 'nostalgia exists within and against modernity and is integral to the radical imagination' (Bonnett, 2010, p. 19) rather than acting as a barrier to it.

So, then, we might say that nostalgia is often stuck in a dichotomy in which it is seen as either necessarily reactionary or as a politicised response to profound social upheaval. Svetlana Boym's influential study, *The Future of Nostalgia* (2001) is helpful here for its distinction between 'restorative' and 'reflective' nostalgia. Restorative nostalgia is seen to be reactionary in that it signals a return to 'the original stasis', whereas reflective nostalgia is forward-looking, suggesting 'new flexibility' and emphasising 'social memory' (Boym, 2001, pp. xviii, 49). Boym explains that while restorative nostalgia prioritises *nostos*, and proposes to rebuild the lost home, reflective nostalgia dwells in *algia* (Boym, 2001, p. 45). Restorative nostalgia often manifests itself in complete reconstructions of monuments of the past, while reflective nostalgia lingers on ruins, cherishing 'shattered fragments of memory'; the former is limited by its idealising tendencies, viewing the past as 'a perfect snapshot' (Boym, 2001, p. 49).

Boym's modes of restorative and reflective nostalgia offer a critical framework for thinking through the literary implications of yoking the North together with a class-inflected, restorative nostalgia during Brexit. In their respective engagements with a deindustrial, 'left behind' North, both *The Cut* and *Missing Fay* resist a neat distinction between reflective and restorative nostalgia. Instead, they oscillate between a reactionary – or 'restorative' – engagement with the past that reinforces the mythology of the North–South divide while simultaneously deploying a radical – or reflective – nostalgia that mobilises the place-based history to highlight the need for democratic alternatives to the present. Put another way, while the excavation of place-based history in these novels functions as a 'devolutionary' praxis to prioritise the concerns of their respective locales, undercutting this potential is a return to a mode of restorative nostalgia that reinforces a set of class-inflected stereotypes that the texts otherwise aim to challenge. Ultimately, then, these novels articulate the limits of nostalgia as a form of devolutionary aesthetics in Brexit literature that engages with 'the North'.

While focusing on two novels published in 2017, this chapter's approach to Brexit literature extends to works published prior to the EU Referendum in 2016 and to texts which are not driven by this sole political rupture. Brexit was a product of decades of structural inequalities and uneven development throughout Britain, and cannot be fully understood in isolation. John McLeod adopts a similar position, pointing out that, like the milieu it represents, 'Brexit fiction, too, is nothing new' (McLeod, 2020b, p. 609). Indeed, there are several texts which might be productively approached as anticipating the social and political conditions that drove Brexit. Zadie Smith's *NW* (2012), Jonathan Coe's *Number 11* (2015) and John Lanchester's *Capital* (2015) are frequently cited in analyses of Brexit literature published prior to the referendum. Furthermore, while this chapter focuses on Cartwright's commissioned response to the referendum result, his earlier novels might productively be considered Brexit literature. *Heartland* (2009), *How I Killed Margaret Thatcher* (2012), and *Iron Towns* (2016) all explore the implications of deindustrialisation, working-class disaffection, and the socio-economic shifts of Thatcherism. In a similar vein, as we will see in the next chapter, Fiona Mozley's *Elmet* (2017) and Sarah Moss' *Ghost Wall* (2018) historicise several socio-economic and geographic inequalities underpinning the referendum within a longer narrative of Northern England's marginalisation.

In the same vein, I am deliberately using the term 'deindustrial' rather than the more commonly used 'post-industrial'. While 'post-industrial' indicates a completed development consigned to the past, 'deindustrial' acknowledges the ongoing effects of the decline of Britain's industrial economy, and the continued presence of the altered socio-economic relations it produced. My approach informed by Phil O'Brien's work on what he terms the 'deindustrial novel', where he proposes that the prefix 'post' 'suggests a clear break between before and after and a sense of finality' and is at risk of contributing to the notion of 'a post-class society' (O'Brien, 2018, p. 232). Both *The Cut* and *Missing Fay* approach deindustrialisation as an ongoing process which structures twenty-first-century working-class life, and so I echo O'Brien in deploying the terms 'deindustrial' and 'deindustrialisation' throughout this book.

Class Politics of 'Little England': Adam Thorpe's *Missing Fay*

Missing Fay is set across a range of micro-geographies within Lincolnshire, from its struggling coastal towns and deindustrialised rural fringe to its demonised council estates and gentrified streets lined with boutiques for wealthy residents and tourists. While Lincolnshire is rarely considered to be part of Northern England, *Missing Fay* attests to the ways in which a discursive construction of the North exists in the political and public psyche. The novel invokes a broader Brexit discourse in which a discursive construction of 'the North' became an ideological shorthand for a range of socio-economic and cultural class assumptions that transcended geographic parameters. Lincolnshire returned one of the highest majority leave votes in the UK at 69.9 per cent, and consequently became synonymous with a working-class leave-voting 'North' in the media. The day after the referendum, *The Independent* published an article titled 'Why the North of England Will Regret Voting for Brexit', singling out several areas including Yorkshire and the Humber, Hartlepool, Blackpool, and North-East Lincolnshire as 'summari[sing] the feeling: the North wants out' (Major, 2016). *Missing Fay* writes back to this dominant narrative that pitted two constructed poles of 'North' and 'South' in opposition with one another, demonstrating that Lincolnshire itself is highly divided along socio-economic, cultural, and political lines.

Nowhere is this dynamic clearer than in the novel's first vignette, which establishes a view of Lincolnshire as part of a reactionary 'North' when tourists visit the area from London. *Missing Fay* opens on the story of David and Lisa Milligan, who come to represent the cosmopolitan outlook of 'Remain', while Cleethorpes and its residents are framed within an iconography of the North as a reactionary regional backwater and the 'left behind' of the Leave camp. The remote spatial setting of this scene characterises the area as a place of regional stasis, set on a run-down beach just off a 'very straight and very depressing coastal road' (Thorpe, 2017, p. 3), where David, Lisa and their children are taking an increasingly vexed family holiday. Eco-keen David and Lisa have left England's capital city in search of the unspoiled natural beauty of the rural landscape, having decided on the Lincolnshire coast after a recommendation from a friend based in the trendy London suburb of Muswell Hill. Lisa's friend describes Lincolnshire as 'authentically mysterious and eerily unknown' (Thorpe, 2017, p. 8), foregrounding the localisation of England and framing the nation's non-metropolitan spaces in terms of their 'authentic' disconnection from modernity.

In contrast to Lincolnshire's localised character, the Millingtons are global citizens. As Australian and New Zealand expats living in London, they possess a portable, cosmopolitan citizenship communicated through several references to multi-national organisations and the climate crisis. The first word spoken by David and Lisa's six-year-old child is 'fracking' (Thorpe, 2017, p. 1) and David is employed at Ecoforce, a multi-national association dedicated to environmental sustainability. David, however, retreats to Lincolnshire, under the impression that it is 'the land time forgot' (Thorpe, 2017, p. 8). Condemning his children's attachment to technology, he remarks: 'That's what we'll be doing the moment the climate apocalypse happens. We won't even lift our heads from those tiny screens' (Thorpe, 2017, p. 25). David's yearning for the simplicity and authenticity he associates with the English landscape is what Boym would call 'restorative nostalgia', but it does not materialise in the novel; his children remain fixated on technology and the availability of fast-food chains, while even the supposed backwater of Lincolnshire's coastal landscape is now altered by invasive mass corporatisation. The presence of remnants of global trade also prevents the convalescence of David's rural retreat: 'Why did he leave New Zealand in the first place? To be more connected, less out in the planetary wop-wops? Connected with what? The great liberal-capitalist highway lined with fuckin Macca's and KFCs?' (Thorpe, 2017, p. 25).

The residue of global modernity has infiltrated even the most remote areas of England, altering David's experience of an idealised version of rural England. Pressing his toes into the sands of the beach, David ruminates on his altered coastal surroundings. He tries to 'picture himself as a hominid walking here a million years back, with a very simple life pattern, with straightforward thoughts and feelings and finely tuned sense receptors' but is prevented from accessing this pre-modern vision due to 'a huge bright-blue shipping container in his sight line, dumped for no discernible purpose in front of the concrete seawall' (Thorpe, 2017, p. 2). The shipping container marking Lincoln's seemingly remote coastline embodies materially both the omnipresence and reach of contemporary global capitalism, just as the concrete seawall shatters the illusion of a natural landscape unmarked by human influence. At this point in the novel, David's nostalgia appears to be a symptom of 'a new understanding of time and space' (Boym, 2001, p. 12) divided into the local and the universal. While his life in London and employment at Ecoforce speaks to an affiliation with the global, his retreat to Lincolnshire's coastline 'looks backward' and communicates a 'yearn[ing] for the particular' (Boym, 2001, p. 11).

David's illusion of Lincolnshire as an area of unspoilt 'natural' beauty is further negotiated by the presence of tourism. Thorpe uses irony as part of a wider satirical critique of how the relative isolation of coastal areas and their nearby towns are both fetishised and condemned externally. David becomes frustrated at the presence of 'static caravans and bungalows' occupying the coastline, having overlooked how, in his view, 'coastal towns are basically run-down housing estates with amusements' (Thorpe, 2017, p. 3). Even when David reaches the coast itself, he condemns the landscape's desolation: 'Lincolnshire spreads out behind him, as flat and featureless as the Outback. He'd go insane if he had to live there' (Thorpe, 2017, p. 25). Lincoln's residents also worsen the trip, with the tense parochial exchanges that

David encounters in the town signifying the insular 'Little Englandism' that was perceived to be behind the Leave vote:

> David's mouth is a tense coil of rope … The pasty, bored-looking and mostly fat folk seated outside the café are watching him, as Brits do. Not minding their own business. Stickybeaking into private matters neighbourhood fucking watchfulness. He glares back and they turn their heads away.
>
> (Thorpe, 2017, p. 18)

David views Lincoln as a town marked by isolation. Despite the lack of physical borders in this episode, the residents' 'neighbourhood watchfulness' parallels a contracted, insular nationalism concerned with territorial boundaries, emblematising the desire to 'pull up the drawbridge' (Virdee and McGeever, 2018, p. 1811) that was associated with the Leave campaign. This perceived insular localism also communicates internal social divisions throughout England. David's inability to reconcile the idealised Lincolnshire coast of his liberal imagination and the bleak, socio-economic realities of the place foregrounds a moral paradox in the trip. His longing for a remote English landscape and simultaneous disdain for the area's decline articulates an irony in the metropolitan desire to escape 'modernity' by retreating to England's socio-economic margins. Unaware of his privilege, David fails to acknowledge how, for many deindustrialised coastal towns, tourism remains their primary source of income. His trip is underpinned by the same kind of polarity that dominated Brexit discourse: a class-inflected opposition between London-based cosmopolitanism and England's non-metropolitan peripheries.

Furthermore, the parochialism that David observes of Lincoln's locals embodies a key facet of Brexit which conveyed EU membership as 'a direct catalyst for rising immigration and the erosion of parliamentary sovereignty' (Shaw, 2018, p. 27). Both *Missing Fay* and *The Cut* frame hostility towards inward migration within a distinct set of socio-economic and geographic correlations associated with a deindustrial, white working class.[7] Thorpe locates the novel in 2012, right in the middle of the eight years between the 2007–2008 global financial crisis and the Brexit referendum. This temporal setting and frequent references to the recession invite a reading of Brexit as the culmination of years of structural decline in England's non-metropolitan peripheries. Satnam Virdee and Brendan McGeever pinpoint the recession as accelerating the development of a particularly reactionary and hostile Englishness:

> This racialising nationalism has borne a particularly defensive character since the 2008 crisis. It is defined not by imperial prowess or superiority, but by a deep sense of loss of prestige; a retreat from the damaging impact of a globalised world that is no longer recognisable, no longer

"British". The decline of empire, then, has not led to the overcoming of the English imperial complex, but its retraction into a defensive exclusionary imaginary: we are under siege, it is time to pull up the drawbridge.

(Virdee and McGeever, 2018, p. 1811)

The anti-immigration sentiment captured in Thorpe's novel echoes Paul Gilroy's diagnosis of a resurgent 'postcolonial melancholia' (Gilroy, 2005). However, this 'defensive exclusory imaginary' can also be read as a response to regional uneven development and the spatial biases of a metropolitan-orientated national project. For example, *Missing Fay*'s focus on Lincoln's local specifics and the ordinary lives of its inhabitants communicates how the town has been unable to recover from the processes of deindustrialisation: struggling retailers, run-down social housing estates, and working men's clubs in which former labourers return to the community forged through manual labour all punctuate the narrative. In contrast to the Millingtons' global orientation, Lincoln is a place of socio-economic decline and rising anti-immigration sentiment. This opening chapter works to establish a narrative of opposition between the global orientation of cosmopolites like the Millingtons and Lincoln's supposed cultural insularity.

In a similar vein, *Missing Fay* situates Brexit within a class-inflected history of regional uneven development in England. Much of the narrative depicts gatherings in the style of working men's clubs, all of which are characterised by restorative nostalgia. Former steelworker, Howard, reflects that he and his friends are 'feller[s] of habit' and that 'their annual Monopoly pub crawl [has become] a shadow of its former self' (Thorpe, 2017, p. 51), echoing an attachment to the past that results in stasis and cyclicality in an unsatisfactory present. At the same time, these meetings are pervaded by Euroscepticism emerging from an anxiety that England is under threat: 'We're all as one in Europe: he's looked it up, and in January 2014 – in less than two years – Romanians won't even have to have a work permit. They'll be a proper part of the family' (Thorpe, 2017, p. 193). Later, we see an explicit juxtaposition of Europe and Englishness in a lament of 'European mollycoddling' shortly followed by a description of the 'St George's flag streaked here and there with bird muck' (Thorpe, 2017, p. 63). This brief reference to the absence of English parliamentary autonomy also forebodes the political restructuring that occurred following Scotland's decision against secession from the UK in 2014. In his first speech after the Scottish Independence referendum result, then Prime Minister David Cameron made the case for England to have its own independence in the form of English Votes for English Laws (EVEL). Thomas Docherty proposes that EVEL

is at the very core of Brexit and informs the "decision" to secede from the ECJ (European Court of Justice]; and its source lies in a speech that stirred up a sense of resentment among the English whose troubles – it was alleged – stem from the fact that they were supposedly not making their own laws, while the Scots, Welsh and Irish had all "taken control" of their lives.

(Docherty, 2017, p. 186)

This hostility towards supranational bureaucratic influence and immigration extends beyond Europe. A conversation between former British Steel workers in a working men's club further intensifies this English ethnonationalism:

> 'Christ, another four for the Pakis,' says Don, making him jump.
> 'Too many Pakis, too many runs,' says Ian.
> Gary crosses his stretched legs at the ankles. 'There aren't too many of them over our way, over here, though. Are they? Mostly doctors or teachers or summat.'
> 'We don't want 'em,' says Don. 'Not on top of the Polacks and whatnot. Romanians. Any minute now.'

(Thorpe, 2017, p. 71)

This anti-immigration sentiment is presented as a working-class response to the perceived weakening of England viewed as an island nation; repeated references to 'too many' immigrants frame England as a territory that has, in the opinion of these men, reached its limits. When Howard mentions Cosmina, a Romanian nursing home assistant caring for his mother, he notes how '[h]is mates don't want to know. There are always exceptions, they say. Stolen someone's job, she has. Someone native' (Thorpe, 2017, p. 58). Thorpe's location of working-class debates concerning English sovereignty in the spatial setting of a local pub gestures towards Nigel Farage's campaign throughout the EU Referendum in which he 'extolled the virtues of UKIP as "the people's party"' (Block and Negrine, 2017, p. 185). Farage was frequently pictured with a pint in hand, performing a 'pint, fag and cheeky grin routine' (Robinson, 2015, p. 9) in an ideological manoeuvre to present himself as an 'ordinary' man 'of the people' that was crucial to the credibility of his anti-elitist stance. Farage's drink of choice was often a pint of bitter, a drink which is heavily associated with 'Northern', working-class masculinity, especially the counties of Yorkshire and Lancashire (Spracklen, Laurencic, and Kenyon, 2013). The scene thus echoes a classed regional stereotype which was harnessed in Brexit media and political discourse, while also demonstrating the intersection of class and geography during the referendum.[8]

A narrow version of Englishness was a central component of UKIP's rise during the 2015 General Election and was later replayed leading up to the Brexit referendum. The Party's provocative poster featured a long stream of migrants at the Croatian-Slovenian border under the slogan 'Breaking Point' and was intended to be the first of a series of adverts to be released by UKIP each day until polling day. Emblematic of the far right's populist strategy, the poster aimed to target a disenfranchised working class and anxieties

surrounding further socio-economic decline using inward migration as a
scapegoat. At the same time, UKIP's campaign more broadly relied upon an
'island myth' of the state-nation as a colonial power and developed into a
Euroscepticism and racist resentment inseparable from restorative post-
imperial nostalgia.[9] Becoming synonymous with the Leave campaign, the
poster constructed a homogenous migrant figure as both a security threat to
Britain as an island nation and 'an economic threat to the domestic working
class' (Virdee and McGeever, 2018, p. 1806); this was, of course, in addition
to the bureaucratic stranglehold of Brussels which was also positioned as a
threat to British sovereignty.

Missing Fay appears attuned to this populist narrative, identifying resistance
to immigration in the years leading up to the referendum. Sheena reflects on
Lincoln's urban development and demographic diversification:

> Lincoln isn't quite as local these days. *Burgeoning* is how the estate
> agent Damon now puts it in his flash corner window at the top of the
> hill where the old record shop used to be: *burgeoning* blah blah in its
> *sylvan setting between fen and wold*. Quite the poet. Burgeoning with
> foreigners, that's for sure.
>
> (Thorpe, 2017, p. 131, original emphasis)

Sheena's internal monologue reveals a binary opposition between inward
immigration and the English local in which outsiders are seen as a territorial
threat to the nation-state. This perceived erasure of a 'local' English culture
is a product of anxieties surrounding the socio-economic implications of
immigration, and augments a set of regional and class archetypes associated
with the Leave vote, particularly UKIP's 'breaking point' discourse. Here,
the novel's approach to English political autonomy subscribes to Brexit's
polarising logic which was premised on the synonymity of class and region.

These Lincoln inhabitants experience England as a nation whose culture
and political sovereignty are compromised by inward migration and EU
bureaucracy respectively, but Englishness is an alienating presence throughout
Cosmina's narrative. Cosmina describes how the nation

> stretch[es] all about her, with its English trees and birds and grasses in
> which English insects crawl and spin and hum and jump. The English
> river swirls past and English fish rest as if dazed by the sunlight in its
> current.
>
> (Thorpe, 2017, p. 88)

Cosmina's description articulates a mythological Englishness residing in the
rural landscape, and the emphasis on 'English' in particular foregrounds her
status as an outsider. This is a landscape dissimilar to that of Romania,
whose geographic contours and small-scale local agriculture are contrasted
with England's 'monotonous fields' of globalised agriculture and migrant

labour. Here, there are 'no horses pulling ploughs or wagons', and 'no locals work in them' (Thorpe, 2017, p. 85). For Cosmina, England is conspicuous as an alienating presence. She notes how 'people in England are always chatty and smiling when they aren't drunk or in their cars – when something turns them into scowling monsters' (Thorpe, 2017, p. 70) or in the milky cups of tea 'just the way English people want them', a 'secret recipe [Cosmina] hasn't yet found' (Thorpe, 2017, p. 90). These subtle notations locate an exclusionary Englishness based on social codes that Cosmina is unable to grasp; they characterise her experience in Lincoln and coalesce to reinforce her isolation and nostalgia for the familiarity of her family home in Romania.

While *Missing Fay* associates Lincoln with an insular localism, the novel also frames Northern England within a globalised labour economy. The frequent presence of migrant labour in the novel rejects the idea that England's socio-economic margins are disconnected from the workings of globalisation. For instance, when Cosmina is sacked from her job as a healthcare assistant, her friend encourages her to apply for work at a global fish-processing firm, promising her accelerated upward progression:

> Madalina wants her to come to Grimsby, where there is skilled work available in the fish-processing factories or the chilled-food plants. Madalina is already assistant team leader in 2 Sisters Food Group after only one year. Better, she claims, than being a healthcare assistant. You could join 2 Sisters Food Group and rise to manager status, buy a house with a garden after a few years, with Romania properly in the EU so no permanent-residence problems.
>
> (Thorpe, 2017, p. 89)

The scene reflects a migrant narrative similar to that which we saw in Chapter 1, whereby migration to England promises economic return if one works hard enough, while locating England's supposed regional backwaters within a supranational economy. Here, Grimsby represents England's port towns, whose local economy formerly relied on the fishing industry; significantly, these areas were majority Leave-voting geographies and are often associated with industrial decline.[10] In the globalised present, the fishing economies of these towns are now dominated by low-paid labour in factories, packing food for supermarket chains. 2 Sisters Food Group – a large corporation that includes Five Star Fish – supplies retail giants like Iceland and Morrisons, further emphasising how localised trade has been deprivileged in favour of large-scale production methods and alienated migrant labour. Within this supranational context, *Missing Fay* also registers how increased geographic mobility has gone together with a migration system that views immigrants only in terms of their productive value. As Cosmina reflects, 'no one here could care less that she is already a graduate, except that it has allowed her into the country in the first place. She is useful, that's all' (Thorpe, 2017, p. 81). *Missing Fay* thus presents a specifically working-class version of local Englishness associated with 'Little England' and hostility towards immigration.

At the same time, however, the novel also locates a conflicting version of Englishness as a commodified, middle-class culture, echoing the Green Conservatism advocated under David Cameron's coalition government. Lincoln's Old Town works as an architectural image of 'quintessential' English culture. Lincoln's Cathedral, Lincoln Castle, and Steep Hill are highly commercial tourist sites that welcome thousands of visitors each year. *Missing Fay* intervenes in discourses of Englishness as a commodified culture, with much of the action taking place near Steep Hill. For example, Sheena's childrenswear shop, Mother Hubbard, is merely decorative. The boutique is housed in a sixteenth-century cottage with sea-saw walls and floors, functioning as an architectural metaphor for a paradigmatic English heritage; it caters for exclusively middle-class sensibilities, 'drawing the sort of mum who drives a silver Lexus RX and whose budget cares for itself' (Thorpe, 2017, p. 127). Located on Totterhill, Mother Hubbard trades alongside various other independently owned, 'hipster', bijou shops catering for Lincoln's wealthy residents' or tourists' tastes. Not 'the illustrious Steep Hill itself, but its neglected sister. ... "I'm at the posh end,' Sheila jokes, 'we talk different up there". Not all together a joke, in Lincoln' (Thorpe, 2017, p. 127). Rather than making purchases, tourists stop outside and take pictures of the building because it is 'old and typically English' (Thorpe, 2017, p. 246).

Mother Hubbard's cultural value resides in its association with a 'quaint', middle-class Englishness, recalling what Joe Kennedy has described as the 'aestheticisation of national identity' which masks a 'sociologically spectral' political Englishness. England has, as Kennedy explains,

> been made tasteful by a middle-class and basically middlebrow literary and musical and decorative culture that leans not only on the patriotic penchants nestled in the left-leaning figures like Orwell, but on the Anglocentric turn within criticism, fiction, poetry, travel writing and memoir over, roughly, the last decade ... if the middle classes, the argument seems to run, can demonstrate their patriotism through an optimistic traditionalism, the 'sociologically spectral' might be appeased in time.
>
> (Kennedy, 2013)

Chapter 2 demonstrated how the pastoral literary mode has contributed to a placeless cultural Englishness and served as a bulwark for the British state against a *political* Englishness. In a similar vein, Kennedy argues that middle-class appropriation of pastoral England in popular culture became 'a cornerstone of austerity politics' (Kennedy, 2013) under David Cameron, with Green Toryism helping to reduce Englishness to a bricolage of cultural signifiers, demonstrated in the popularity of *The Great British Bake Off* TV series and heritage apparel. This association between middlebrow cultural constructions of English heritage breaks down in the novel. Contrary to its quaint exterior, Mother Hubbard is far from 'quintessentially' English or exclusively 'local'; its formerly handmade fabrics have been switched to 'sweatshop machine-operators in China' (Thorpe, 2017, p. 128), presenting a version of the nation reliant on globalisation's uneven development and is less 'gentle England' than it is corporate and exploitative.

The artifice and exclusions inherent in this commodified cultural Englishness are acutely visible in the novel, with Fay's working-class narrative pitted against Sheena's middle-class sensibilities. Just as the novel imagines a parochial Englishness that is compromised by migration, the 'quintessential Englishness' of Lincoln's Old Town is threatened by an *internal* social other. As I noted in Chapter 1 in relation to racialised internal others, Imogen Tyler's 'social abjection' describes the way the neoliberal state relies on the maintenance of interiorised 'others' who are demonised and exist as scapegoats to harness support for political agendas (Tyler, 2013, p. 10). An abjectifying discourse that demonises the working class characterises Fay's relationship with Sheena, who moves between disdain for Fay and a kind of gestural, tokenistic affection; she enjoys 'the irony' of having a child from 'gutter level England' in her upmarket clothing store, noting that her customers will 'probably think the girl's a shoplifter at first' (Thorpe, 2017, p. 144). The dissonance between Fay and Mother Hubbard's demographic locates conflicting poles of Englishness that occur simultaneously in Lincoln: a middle-class and highly commodified genteel England and the 'gutter level', working-class England. While Sheena eventually develops a somewhat maternal affection for Fay, her attempts to help her are largely self-validating gestures. There always remains a distance between the two, with Sheena approaching Fay as an object of fascination 'outside the domain of the social proper' (Tyler, 2013, p. 161).

Class barriers between Fay and Sheena are also spatially encoded in Lincoln's urban architecture. Fay's residential estate is entirely 'other' to the image of 'quintessential Englishness' represented by Sheena's Totter Hill boutique:

> The girl lives in the Ermine, on the west side, which is the rougher half of the council estate up on the northern edge of the city, when you'd expect the rough half to be the east. As a matter of fact, edge isn't the right term because the estate is pretty much the North of Lincoln. Sheena has never more than skirted it. Parts of the city are no-go, or no-go for faint-hearted law-abiding types like herself.
>
> (Thorpe, 2017, p. 133)

Told at this point from Sheena's perspective, the passage neatly articulates the spatialisation of class relations in which occupants of state housing are demonised. Fay inhabits a kind of 'abject border zone' (Tyler, 2013, p. 160) that is geographically and socially far removed from the 'well-to-do' residents of the town. Fay's occupation of the Ermine estate limits her access to categories of morality and respectability. The demonisation of the council estate is a product of socio-political shifts during the 1990s and early 2000s, with the widespread association of the council estate with social problems attributed to New Labour's meritocratic discourse of Britain as a 'classless society'. This period ushered in a new era of class politics in Britain when the council estate signified 'the moral boundaries of the nation-state' in an intensification of Thatcher's 'configuration of the spaces as barracks for the poor' (Tyler, 2013, p. 160).[11] In his examination of urban space after Thatcher, Andrew Burke comments that

> the spaces [of council estates] are routinely associated in the popular imagination as the sites of, and symbols for, the major social problems of contemporary Britain (crime, poverty, anti-social behaviour), but such identification, by politicians and media especially, frequently serves as a cover for anti-working-class and anti-immigrant sentiment.
>
> (Burke, 2007, p. 176)

The social stigma Burke describes here reached its peak during and after Thatcher's assault on council estates that effectively labelled its residents as the 'enemy within' and positioned them as 'other' within the public consciousness.[12] Further to their overdetermined class connotations, the spaces of the council estate functioned as a microcosm for broader patterns of uneven development. As Burke suggests, they 'dramatise[d] the connections between local conditions of existence on the peripheries of contemporary British culture and the national, even global, political decisions and conditions that [gave] rise to them' (Burke, 2007, p. 176). The disconnection between Fay and the 'well to do' residents of the town foregrounds how Brexit merely activated a set of pre-existing social cleavages that are too complex to be reduced to a set of rhetorical polarities: 'Leave' versus 'Remain, 'poor' versus 'rich', 'North' versus 'South'.

Fay's inability to access the category of 'victim' in the novel reaffirms this class dynamic, as she comes to signify the human potential wasted by the political neglect of working-class communities and deindustrial towns. Fay is rarely perceived as an innocent victim or considered outside of class stereotypes. The only character in the novel who does not view her as at least partially responsible for her disappearance is David, who misreads Fay as a '[n]ice middle-class English girl' (Thorpe, 2017, p. 6) due to Sheena's oakwood beams in the background of Fay's 'MISSING' poster. Reflecting on the possibility of his own child going missing, David's reaction is markedly more sympathetic than characters in the novel who are Lincoln locals. For instance, Mike's reaction to Fay's 'MISSING' poster does not extend to viewing her beyond her socio-economic circumstances. He notes how some posters have been taken down, 'presumably as more details have emerged of the girl's home life, her truancy, her being caught shoplifting in a community supermarket on the day of her disappearance and a string of similar offences' (Thorpe, 2017, p. 190). It is not until Fay is read as middle class that she becomes a victim of a crime, rather than perceived as a criminal herself.

The relationship between Fay's class status and her ability to access victimhood illustrates a process of social abjection. As the daughter of a family in receipt of state support, Fay functions in the novel as a scapegoat for structural inequalities, becoming a victim of meritocracy as a 'key ideological term in the reproduction of neoliberal culture' (Littler, 2013, p. 69). This meritocratic vision underpins Mike's rejection of the idea of social inequality and the prospect of Fay's limited opportunities. He laments that social disadvantage is simply 'a myth …. Like the myth of impoverishment. Free school, free healthcare, free transport to school, free council house, free school trips, just about everything' (Thorpe, 2017, p. 150). Mike's logic embodies an ideology central to neoliberalism which ignores the realities of structural inequality and places all blame on a demonised working-class 'abject'. In Mike's account, the problem is inequality, but inequality produced *by* members of the working class, capturing the irony of a contemporary class discourse that demonises the poor (cf. Jones, 2011). The referendum saw a tidal wave of political and media rhetoric that cast Leave voters as members of a scapegoated working class, resulting in 'social abjection' (Tyler, 2013, p. 4). Fay's disappearance acts as a form of symbolic class violence against a stigmatised other. Here, class stigma goes hand in hand with a restorative nostalgia for an idealised and socially conservative English past, providing moralising markers of a divided present.

Missing Fay's central crime emphasises the social exclusions inherent in appropriations of 'quintessential Englishness', but it also warns against restorative nostalgia for a mythological national past. As we saw in the previous chapter, wolves are inhabiting England's literary margins. In Thorpe's novel, they are never explicitly seen but become a continually radiating presence indicating Fay's fate in the form of frequent allusions to *Little Red Riding Hood*: Fay attends a stage adaptation of the tale, featuring 'a bloke with a stupid wolf face what wouldn't stay on' (Thorpe, 2017, p. 45), and later, Cosmina has a nightmare about a demonic wolf. She recalls the story told by her mother when Cosmina was a child, in which a wolf 'persuaded three young goats to let him into their house' and 'the mother returns to find blood splashed on the walls and the heads of the two eldest children lying on the window sill' (Thorpe, 2017, pp. 87–88). Cosmina's version of the tale allegorises the anxieties surrounding immigration during the referendum, representing the threat of the 'outsider' penetrating the family home.

However, while here the wolves appear to signify the threat of a migrant 'other', becoming a scapegoat for a range of socio-economic and geopolitical concerns, elsewhere in the novel the wolves are explicitly associated with – and contrasted against – pastoral England.[13] Just as in *The Wolf Border*, the figure of the wolf cuts through the pastoral idyll as a cultural symbol of Englishness. This political function is explicitly registered in *Missing Fay* when David remarks that his adaptation of *Little Red Riding Hood* 'defend [s] the wolf from the usual pastoralist propaganda' (Thorpe, 2017, p. 40), explicitly positioning the wolf in opposition to pastoral myth. Furthermore, references to *Little Red Riding Hood* also warn against the dangers of a restorative nostalgia attached to a mythological or 'fairy-tale' idea of Englishness. For example, Cosmina's attachment to an idealised version of England prevents her from passing on key information that might help find Fay. Cosmina finds a torn red coat in a nearby woodland that looks like the one Fay was wearing on the day of her disappearance; Cosmina initially mistakes the item of clothing for 'a sheep torn apart by a wolf' (Thorpe, 2017, p. 77) but afterwards contemplates the probability of it belonging to a girl she recently saw on a 'MISSING' poster. In addition to this sacrificial imagery, the coat is now brown from dirt, but was 'once red' (Thorpe, 2017, p. 77), reworking the archetype of female victimhood central to *Little Red Riding Hood*.[14] While Cosmina notes the similarity of the coat – and the coincidence of its location – she eventually dismisses the evidence, rejecting the possibility of wolves in 'gentle England' (Thorpe, 2017, p. 128). Just like Fay, the wolves remain a moralising spectral presence cautioning against mythological attachment to an imagined nation and communicating the need for collective social responsibility.

Nostalgia and the Deindustrial 'North': Anthony Cartwright's *The Cut*

The preceding discussion of *Missing Fay* has begun to map the regional dimensions of Brexit's 'English Question'. Having set out the multiple, conflicting versions of Englishness in Thorpe's exploration of pre-Brexit England, the second part of this chapter concentrates directly on this regional correlate by turning to Anthony Cartwright's *The Cut*. By examining the symbolic role of deindustrialised space, class politics, and nostalgia in Cartwright's Brexit novel, I suggest that *The Cut* offers an ambivalent engagement with nostalgia as a form of place-based, working-class politics. In centring regional divisions between 'North' and 'South' at the centre of the narrative, Cartwright maps the ways in which a mythological – and geographically stretchy – version of 'the North' became synonymous with the Leave vote, bringing with it a whole nexus of overdetermined class connotations. The book critiques a dominant narrative in Brexit's political discourse in which the North was reified as a localised antithesis to a global Britishness that, it seemed, was located in London. In Cartwright's narrative, the North is more of a socio-economic category, whose cultural representation operates within specific, class-inflected characteristics, rather than a precisely defined geographical territory. Hazeldine suggests that

> what most binds the North together is industrial tradition plus political discontent—but it shows up across the whole gamut of socio-economic indicators: output, jobs, incomes, house prices, education, life expectancy.

The aggregated statistics point to a fissure running east to west between the Humber and Severn estuaries, stranding the northern regions, the West Midlands except Warwickshire and the East Midland counties of Derbyshire and Nottinghamshire in the zone of relative economic disadvantage.

(Hazeldine, 2017, p. 54)

Just as Hazeldine proposes that mainstream understandings of 'the North' are based more on socio-economic and political indicators than geography, Grace's documentary is premised upon a 'discursive, cultural version of the North in which 'class and region have become ... elided' (Russell and Wagg, 2004, p. x). Writing in a similar vein, Doreen Massey proposes thinking relationally about the spatialisation of capitalist production, maintaining that 'questions of geography in the United Kingdom reflect not just the formal relations of production, but wider questions of politics, power and social class' (Massey, 1984, p. 295). Taking the view that places are not simply physical locations but 'articulations of social relations', I read Cartwright's engagement with 'the North' less in terms of precise territorial boundaries. Instead, this chapter is interested in how *The Cut* pinpoints Brexit as a moment which generated the evolution of the North–South divide, with a geographically imprecise, imagined 'North' mobilised in political discourse via the euphemism of England's 'left behind' (Massey, 1994, p. 22).

We can see this dynamic most clearly in Grace's documentary project, which embodies the intranational relations between an ambiguously defined deindustrial 'North' and an equally constructed 'South' of England. Although Cartwright locates the novel in Dudley, a small town in the Midlands, Grace is described as travelling 'North' to speak to Leave voters – and views Dudley as very much part of the North – in a way that indicates how the region operates in the national imagination. Key to this geographical is socio-economic class division. *The Cut*'s use of regional dialect establishes how socio-economic configurations of class operate within broader regional power dynamics. Cairo's regional vernacular – of 'yer', 'yow', 'doh', and 'we'm' (Cartwright, 2017, pp. 10, 18, 24, 40) – is juxtaposed with Grace's Standard English, demonstrating the asymmetries between the two. *The Cut* initially articulates the 'invisible veil' (Cartwright, 2017, p. 19) between them linguistically. When Cairo's interview with Grace is broadcast on the television, 'they put subtitles over his words, translated into his own language, and sometimes they did not. But there he was, playing on some endless loop, making sense and not making sense at all' (Cartwright, 2017, p. 21). The image of Cairo watching himself in a programme on television in which his regional dialect has been translated demonstrates a class manoeuvre in which the working-class subject is unable to speak. Instead, Cairo's words are appropriated and effectively given back to him by a middle-class narrator to be broadcast to the nation.

The scene's suppression of Cairo's local idiom embodies the way '[t]he othering of the North operates within a specific set of power relations, in which the North is subordinated to a London and South-East centric locus of national economic, governmental, media and cultural power' (Phillips, 2017, pp. 150–151). The way Cairo's words are, as Mike Savage puts it, 'moralised through the lens of the dominant London worldview' (Savage, 2015, p. 263) is analogous to Westminster's political stranglehold within the constitutional organisation of the Union. In devolutionary Britain, even though power has been devolved to local governments, subnational jurisdiction is easily overridden by, and subordinate to, Westminster. Cairo's inability to represent himself is continued throughout the novel, as voice becomes an allegory for regional political autonomy and representation.

The decentralising potential of regional dialect has already been identified in Cartwright's work. O'Brien pinpoints a 'Dudley demotic' as a recurring aesthetic in Cartwright's novels, noting how they

> merge a form of Standard English with an explicit urban and industrial working-class Dudley accent and dialect. Quotation marks, separating the language of the characters from the authorial third-person narrator, are never used. This collapses the distance between the two and positions the narrative voice closer to the subjective experiences of the novel's working-class characters, presenting them as equivalents.
>
> (O'Brien, 2018, p. 233)

O'Brien's suggestion that Cartwright's deployment of regional dialect resists dominant class structures certainly holds true. However, the radical potential of *The Cut*'s regional dialect can also be problematised in ways that reveal an ambivalent engagement with dialect as a radical working-class praxis. On the one hand, the novel's idiom operates as a counterpoint to Grace's documentary in which Cairo takes authorial ownership of his experience; this authorial refocusing is devolutionary in the spatial sense in that it offers a decentralised narrative perspective focused on ordinarily marginalised voices. In this respect, regional dialect provides a voice for a voiceless constituency, providing a polemical challenge to the authorities and conventions (both literary and political) whose vested interests in British Unionism have been maintained by neglecting the voices of deindustrialised communities but also through persistent insular images of provincial locales. On the other hand, the association of regional dialect with otherness and the parochial undercuts the political potential of this decentralised narration. Cartwright's use of regional dialect to prioritise working-class voices is complicated by what Raymond Williams terms 'the orthography of the uneducated' (Williams, 2001, p. 245). In the novel, the narrative voice and Grace's speech are written entirely in Standard English, while only Dudley's residents' speech is represented in dialogue with an unconventional spelling. According to Williams, the 'error' is in 'supposing that the ordinary spelling indicates how proper people speak' (Williams, 2001, p. 245). Cartwright's use of 'you' for the narrator, and 'yer' (Cartwright, 2017, p. 63) for Dudley's residents reinstates the community's otherness due to their difference from a standardised national, linguistic form. This tension is reinforced by the novel's use of social realism, a style 'heavily associated with the depiction of (especially) northern life' and 'authentic' (Head, 2008, p. 5), gritty, working-class, cultural representation. Thus, regional dialect forms a stumbling block for the novel, signalling an impasse in its devolutionary politics; it is both politically enabling and a self-exoticising lens that reinforces uneven power relations between the North and South of England.

Similarly, *The Cut* critiques the way in which the media perpetuated stereotypes of a monolithic, working-class 'North'. Indeed, we can read Grace in a similar way to the Millingtons in *Missing Fay*: she stands as a symbol of metropolitan authority and class privilege, while Cairo serves as a metaphor for the working-class dispossession associated with the 'left behind'. Cairo and Grace's relationship is defined by this disconnection. During one of their first meetings, Cairo expresses his frustration at this tendency, explaining how: 'on the telly and that, papers, just been told we'm all stupid, held up for ridicule' (Cartwright, 2017, p. 43). Cairo's lament situates the representation of majority Leave-voting areas in the media within a larger history of prejudice against towns such as Dudley, possibly referring to the Dudley Ferris Wheel construction in 2016. The event led to media coverage humiliating the town and residents' despair that much-needed public funding had been spent on 'Britain's worst tourist attraction', offering views of factories, concrete buildings, and car parks.[15] Consequently, the area and its inhabitants were mocked by the press in an ideological manoeuvre that held up the town and its residents as embodiments of regional backwardness and a nostalgic opposition to modern urban development. This contextual reference evidences precisely the kind of discourse that featured during Brexit – it neglects the nuances of a social geography in which 'the subjective notions of class are bound up with place and location' (Savage, 2015, p. 295). As we have already seen in *Missing Fay*, there is a dominant narrative in the UK in which '"real people" need to be listened to and "respected", but in practice this tends to amount to the circulation of a one-dimensional portrait of "provincials"' (Kennedy, 2018, p. 11). The reference to the Ferris Wheel engages with these tensions, paralleling a Brexit discourse that was invariably simplifying and always came down to a fallacious binary opposition between an uneducated working-class North and a socially progressive, liberal Southern elite.

The Cut's deindustrial aesthetics are inseparable from a longer history of English regional uneven development. The novel mobilises deindustrialisation as a mechanism for exploring contemporary class divisions, mapping the socio-economic inequalities that shape the region's place in the wider national imagination. As Williams writes of the Welsh industrial novel, 'industrial work and its characteristic places and communities are not just a new background: a new "setting" for a story. In the true industrial novel they are seen as formative' (Williams, 2005, p. 221). Industrial ruins and dilapidated buildings feature prominently in Cartwright's depiction of Dudley. Descriptive passages of the landscape are punctuated by buildings and factories that once signified economic progress and modernity in the town, but are now 'totally disintegrated' (Cartwright, 2017, p. 22) and left as out-of-place anachronisms of a forgotten place and time. Industrial remnants serve as temporally displaced, residual class symbols and architectural embodiments of long-term uneven development. The industrial wasteland on which Cairo works symbolises the alienation of communities systematically dismantled since the Thatcher period, but it is also a material registration of regional uneven development and persistent social and economic inequality. Throughout the novel, the space is an emblem for deindustrialisation. It becomes a magnified symbol of what Katherine Cockin terms the 'Northern wasteland' (Cockin, 2012, p. 1), forming a microcosm for an entire regional consciousness centred on industrial labour.

In *The Cut*, Dudley's urban environment forms a historical palimpsest that triggers nostalgia for industrial labour and the 'structure of feeling' (Williams, 1977, p. 134) of a futureless present. The persistence of deindustrialisation (and its implications) still structures the present, reflecting the Derridean process of 'hauntology' in which the present is disrupted by the past's persistent 'haunting' (Derrida, 1994). In Mark Fisher's application of the concept, hauntology signals 'the slow cancellation of the future', but holds political potential in its refusal to be consigned to the past in categories of 'retro' or 'heritage' (Fisher, 2014, pp. 4, 15). For Fisher, hauntology metaphorically represents '*the agency of the virtual*: with the spectre understood not as anything supernatural but as that which acts without (physically) existing' (Fisher, 2014, p. 12, original emphasis). The spectral presence of industrial labour, understood as both 'ghosts of the past' and material fragments that provoke memories of that past, haunt the novel in the way Fisher describes. It registers a socio-economic disconnection between region and nation through collective historical experiences manifested as a kind of haunting. For example, the spectral presence of industry characteristic of Dudley's townscape renders acutely visible the way in which the spatial divisions of labour are constructed and reconstructed over time, solidifying the processes of uneven development in the contemporary:

> Cairo would bolt down the hill, racing the water that ran off and ended up in the Severn, down and over the Rowley Road and through Warren's Hall and past the ponds and the gravel where they used to sometimes torch the cars and down the black paths, past the ruin of the engine house where the engine had pumped water from the mine, and the coal had fired the engines and the furnaces, and forged the country as it became. And here were the ruins, and here were the ghosts of people among them.
>
> (Cartwright, 2017, p. 100)

These frequent references to the closure and subsequent privatisation of steelworks during the 1990s textually replicate the community's inability to escape deindustrialisation's spectral presence and its aftermath, despite their labour 'forg[ing] the country'. Yet, unlike the political potential Fisher ascribes to hauntology, the presence of the past in Dudley's deindustrialised landscape is closer to a restorative nostalgia in *The Cut*. The shift from localised spatial co-ordinates to nameless 'ruins' and 'ghosts' utilises the language of the spectre, and represents the local community as being stuck in the past and isolated by a prevailing image of stasis; the material environment and its populace are both haunted by and trapped within a regional iconography 'dominated by nostalgia and a spectral history of oppression' (Phillips, 2017, p. 151).

These architectural anachronisms also articulate the cultural inertia and political powerlessness felt within deindustrialised, working-class communities and help establish what Williams describes as a 'residual structure of feeling' (Williams, 1977, p. 134). Williams emphasises that this residual structure is formed in the past but remains very much alive in the present:

> [t]hus certain experiences, meanings, and values which cannot be expressed or substantially verified in terms of the dominant culture, are nevertheless lived and practiced on the basis of the residue – cultural as well as social – of some previous social and cultural institution or formation.
>
> (Williams, 1977, p. 122)

Williams goes on to suggest that this residual structure of feeling may have an alternative or even oppositional relationship to the dominant culture. Likewise, in *The Cut*, the affective experience of widespread political inefficacy stands in opposition to a national politics that neglects deindustrialised communities:

> 'We've had enough,' is what [Cairo] said [to Grace], with the sun on the footballer, and the church and the castle behind him and the soft shadow of the buildings and his face dusted with some unknown material, which he would no doubt breathe in and whatever it was would be there in his lungs, *burning through the years*.
>
> (Cartwright, 2017, p. 27, original emphasis)

This alignment of Cairo's body with the inevitability of the side-effects of industrial work and its health implications not only symbolises a regional democratic deficit in his lack of agency and voice, but corporeally registers years of industrial decline that continue to shape perceptions of the region and its inhabitants. The spectral image of Cairo standing in the town inhaling debris from disintegrating buildings aptly depicts the dangers of industrial work, but also how it was nonetheless central to the formation of the self.

In terms of individual agency, the novel's nostalgic narrative mode also articulates the loss of labour as a form of place-bound self-identification. In Dudley, as in many other industrial English towns, identity – particularly working-class masculinities – was at one time something forged through work.[16] Now, in the late capitalist era of globalisation and flexible accumulation, employment is scarce and, in *The Cut*, usually takes the form of insecure manual labour. Cairo embodies this shift in his casual role clearing an industrial wasteland, describing how his manager, Tony,

> pays them all in dog-eared notes in cash bags from the post office like they are men from some bygone era. Like they are men who would go walking up the lane here from this factory back when it was still standing, men with an early Friday finish, going to tend their allotments and stand up at bars and walk their dogs and go home to their families and fill in the football coupon and dream of a week at the seaside. As if there is any of that anymore.
>
> (Cartwright, 2017, p. 37)

This restorative nostalgia for a working-class culture is a comment on how class discourse in Britain has shifted from blue-collar respectability to that of an idle underclass that reduces class identity to a moral choice (see Tyler, 2013). Cairo is mourning the loss of his respectability, a specifically localised formation of culture and place-bound identity gone by.

The Cut's nostalgia does not primarily concern the financial implications of industrial decline, but the displacement of a specifically gendered, working-class culture and identity. During an interview with Grace, Cairo's father reflects that 'there used to be work for all the men. Man's work, not like now … There used to be a culture that went alongside the work' (Cartwright, 2017, p. 55). Cairo's father experiences the contemporary through loss, now that the material security of industrial labour has given way to precarity. Here, nostalgia pertains to a particular form of working-class subjectivity tied to productive industrial labour. This is an identity to which Cairo's father has a deep personal affiliation – his ancestors were 'nailers', 'puddlers', 'coal pickers', and 'navvies' (Cartwright, 2017, p. 46) – but which he cannot translate into the contemporary employment landscape centred on cognitive or alienated labour. As Sherry Lee Linkon writes, although the work itself was often unpleasant and dangerous, 'the mythology surrounding productive labour, with the associated benefits of the family wage, labour, solidarity, and physical prowess has long played a key role in defining working-class masculine identities' (Linkon, 2014, p. 148). In a similar vein, *The Cut* explores how the modern condition of flexible, post-Fordist production methods prevent the forging of shared communal histories, instead, creating a form of cultural alienation in which the spatial divisions of labour compound the relations of gender and class. We can therefore think of the disintegrated factory and ruins of industry as nostalgic symbols emblematic of disaffection with the flexible production methods of the global contemporary, and a subsequent desire to return to a more stable past.

Unlike the identity-bearing capacity of community-based labour, the 'gig-economy' of zero-hours contracts results in a contaminated historical presence of industrial labour; it is 'like a plague, eating away at them all' (Cartwright, 2017, p. 101), continually haunting the present. The loss of localised manual labour highlights the socio-economic and cultural resources for constructing masculinity that industrial work made available for most of the twentieth century throughout the UK. Yet, despite offering the class solidarity associated with manual labour, this version of nostalgia is at risk of being restorative in that it masks the hardships of industrial work. Cairo's father's longing for the stability of Fordism thus succumbs to a limitation of nostalgia insofar as it 'gloss[es] over contradictory or negative components that compromise the sense of possibility found in such spaces and in such sources' (Tannock, 1995, p. 457) and does little to imagine alternative democratic possibilities. The 'plague' that is 'eating away' at Cairo's father and others like him refers both to the literal contamination from exposure to asbestos in industrial work, and a figuratively corrosive, restorative nostalgia.

The capitalist reworking of public space also occurs alongside the elimination of identity-bearing productive labour in the novel. On the way to an interview with Grace, Cairo approaches the new Castlegate leisure complex, a development which appears at odds with the local environment: Cairo describes how 'the name of the complex was new, the whole development, cinema, gym, diner and so on, like it was bloody California' (Cartwright, 2017, p. 39). The example of California provides a comparison between globalised 'world cities' such as Los Angeles – the centre of the Hollywood entertainment industry and American 'mall culture' – and places where globalisation manifests itself in vast, uneven development and sectoral decline (Massey, 2007, p. 1). Marked by profound loss, Cairo's nostalgia responds to the removal of places that enable personal connection through productive labour and the rise of non-places offering only service work.[17] For example, the old County Ground that Cairo's great grandfather helped to construct is now the site of the business park. His relationship with the business park recalls Marc Augé's assertion that supermodernity and globalisation have produced identity-less places marked only by the exchange of capital; these identity-less 'non-places' (Augé, 1995, pp. 77–78) have replaced former places which are strongly settled in space and time, leading to the loss of an area's tradition and history. Spatial exclusion configures this erasure, with Cairo experiencing a kind of cultural disenfranchisement from local space due to urban regeneration initiatives. Recollections of his childhood are interspersed in his conversation with Grace, remembering how he snuck 'on to the site as a kid with his mates, after it had been abandoned' (Cartwright, 2017, p. 40). Despite his personal and ancestral links, the material processes of capital have erased his historical connection with the space:

the site 'used to be somewhere' (Cartwright, 2017, p. 44) but exists in the present only as an assemblage of empty signs that are devoid of all meaning.

Similarly, *The Cut* also mobilises nostalgia as a response to how the processes of neoliberal modernity exist in tension with the priorities of Dudley's local community. Cartwright associates the affective experience of simultaneous deindustrialisation and the creation of corporate non-spaces with a democratic system that ignores the implications of uneven development:

> [People] are tired. Tired of clammed-up factory gates, but not even them anymore, because look where they are working now, digging trenches to tat out the last of whatever metal was left. Tired of change, tired of the world passing by, tired of other people getting things that you and people like you had made for them, tired of being told you were no good, tired of being told to stop complaining, tired of being told what to eat, what to throw away, what to do and what not to do, what was right and wrong when you were always in the wrong. Tired of supermarket jobs and warehouse jobs and guarding shopping centres.
>
> (Cartwright, 2017, p. 101)

Illustrating the local community's political inertia, Cartwright's depiction of Dudley's community evokes a regional iconography characterised by stasis, nostalgia, and anachronism. This operates within a broader narrative of division that dominated media and political discourse during the referendum, as deindustrial, working-class identities are positioned as out-of-time, juxtaposed against the country's metropolitan areas and the rest of the world 'passing them by'. Despite the scene's sentimental characteristics, Cairo's nostalgia is not a restorative desire to return to the past but appears closer to a reflective nostalgia that is a product of the inadequacies of the British centralised state form. This reflexivity emerges in the passage's direction at Grace and the use of oppositional language. Here, Cartwright establishes an 'us' and 'them' dichotomy from a *local* perspective in a subversion of the hierarchies of media and political discourse that render communities such as Cairo's voiceless.

If there is a degree of devolutionary potential to be found in *The Cut*, it resides in the ways the novel makes visible how the Leave vote was invariably implicated within constitutional questions of democratic deficit and the need to resolve England's regional inequalities. Clearly embedded in both Cartwright's representation of regional-national relations and the Leave campaign's slogan of 'taking back control' was the desire to revolt against the injustices of centralised power in Britain and could be directed at both Brussels and a Westminster-located political elite. Ultimately, Cairo's contempt at being told 'what to do and what not to do' encapsulates how the continual marginalisation of several working-class groups has 'led to their democratic rejection of the UK's membership of the EU as another layer of government' (Virdee and McGeever, 2018, p. 268). The way *The Cut* mobilises reflective nostalgia as a vehicle for regional devolution indicates scepticism of the novel's ability to reconcile the 'two Britains' of Brexit and present a unified nation.

The Limits of Nostalgia

Thus far, I have argued that Cartwright utilises nostalgia to confront the ways regional uneven development, democratic deficit, and discourses of 'the North' played a decisive role in the outcome of the EU Referendum. In mobilising a locally particularised, working-class nostalgia for the industrial past, *The Cut* attempts to imagine a decentralised cultural politics. The persistent spectral presence of industrial decline sits uneasily alongside political discourses of a unified nation-state and the international orientation of capital central to the ideology of 'Global Britain'. In doing so, the novel's thematic concerns reflect an urgency for radical constitutional reform. In terms of its potential as a commissioned Brexit novel, as I have already argued, much of *The Cut*'s promise resides in the way it attempts to transcend media and political narratives that were primarily dominated by a homogenising and class-inflected version of the North that continues to exist in the cultural and national imagination. Furthermore, in focusing on an inherently placed politics at odds with unitary state-national politics, the novel offers a necessary account that seeks to 'break away from metropolitan stereotypes of small-town backwardness. To explore what happened with a sense of *where* it happened' (Barnett, 2017, p. 103 my emphasis). Thus, we might read *The Cut* as offering a cultural form of devolutionary politics which asks important questions about structural uneven development and political representation throughout England.

I want to draw my argument to a close by turning to one of the ways in which the deployment of nostalgia in *The Cut* ultimately prevents the realisation of alternatives to the present, suggesting that the novel's recommendation for routes out of a Westminster-dominated democratic system remain conflicted and ambivalent. The novel's aesthetic and thematic mobilisation of nostalgia equivocates between its potential as a devolutionary politics and as a barrier to imagining a radical alternative to the present. Nowhere is this ambiguity clearer than in Cairo's romantic, restorative nostalgia for his former boxing career, a pursuit that projects issues of political representation into the cultural sphere. Cairo's participation in boxing is self-actualising; it is associated with becoming democratically active in the public sphere and provides a route to reclaiming a cultural form of identity linked to a blue-collar, working-class masculinity located in the region's past. Cairo reflects that '[t]here is a whole history of men who got knocked senseless, in order to put food on the table, one of the many histories buried in the hill. He tells himself he is part of a proud Dudley tradition' (Cartwright, 2017, p. 12). Unlike his predecessors, Cairo's boxing does not serve as a source of financial income, but a cultural sphere in which to displace his desire for a political voice. In *The* Cut – like much of Cartwright's fiction – men construct an alternative 'imagined political community' (Anderson, 1983, p. 6) through sporting events in the absence of an adequate democratic system. This reclamation of boxing, a sport deeply embedded in Dudley's local history, functions as an attempt to retrieve a place-bound voice, conveying the desire for regional representation.

Cairo quickly becomes fixated on reclaiming his boxing career to gain control over his existence, equating boxing with a form of self-actualisation emerging from place-bound memory. Cartwright describes the running route Cairo takes in preparation for his boxing match in terms of its local specifics:

> Cairo turns left, along Watson's Green Road, into the gloom. He has the idea of running the opposite way up the hill, should meet the boy somewhere on Cawney bank, the other side of the watershed, where the water slips down the hill and on and on to the River Trent and then out to sea and then back again as rain on the hills.
>
> (Cartwright, 2017, p. 28)

Cairo's training is characterised by a desire to move through the town and recover its history. He becomes fixated on another runner – 'the boy from Lupin road' (Cartwright, 2017, p. 27) – and excavates individual agency through his physical capabilities.[18] In the face of political disempowerment, Cairo's spatial practices are aligned both with his individual identity, to 'prove to himself that he's still got it in him' (Cartwright, 2017, p. 27), and a reclamation of the region's history.

Despite Cairo's apparent mobility in this scene, his spatial pursuits eventually present themselves as failed attempts at agency that leave him stuck in the past. Realising that he is unable to keep up with the boy with whom he has become increasingly preoccupied, Cairo 'feels a sense of betrayal at this and he winds down the run as if he's slowing a clock' (Cartwright, 2017, p. 29). Here, the emphasis on temporality and the continual haunting of the past prevents Cairo's success in the present; despite his best efforts, he is unable to access the boxing community to the same degree as previously. Since Cairo's childhood, the industry has moved on and is now a kind of gentrified escapism from the demands of cognitive labour: there are 'white-collar bouts and unlicensed meetings on the first Friday of every month' (Cartwright, 2017, p. 10). Cairo's inability to reconstitute himself in the cultural sphere echoes the absence of self-government to liberate himself from the stasis that has come to characterise his present. Cairo's failed mid-life experimentation with his former boxing career signifies the novel's ambivalent deployment of nostalgia. While Cairo's nostalgia for his sporting youth becomes a source for 'value and meaning' (Tannock, 1995, p. 455), this romantic, restorative turn to the past fails to offer a resource for altering the present.

The limits of the cultural sphere to overcome the everyday realities of political and social abjection neatly capture the paradox of nostalgia. As Boym puts it, nostalgia 'works as a double-edged sword: it seems to be an emotional antidote to politics, and thus remains the best political tool' (Boym, 2001, p. 58). Cartwright places limits on nostalgia's capabilities and critiques – somewhat self-reflexively – how civic participation is often projected onto the cultural sphere in the absence of political representation in the public sphere. The novel is perpetually stuck at this impasse, between nostalgia as longing for a particular cultural-historical moment and its potential as a vehicle for constitutional change. *The Cut*, then, does not offer a straightforwardly restorative nostalgia, but multiple nostalgic forms that are competing and culturally cross-cutting.

This chapter has examined two Brexit novels which respond to the referendum as a symptom of the crisis of the centralised British state form and uneven development throughout England. The first half suggested that *Missing Fay* articulates the ways in which the idea of England as a 'local' counterpoint to 'Global Britain' was central to the desire for political representation emerging during the referendum, while the second half considered the idea of local England in a specifically 'Northern', deindustrialised frame. Here, I argued that *The Cut*'s dominant trope of deindustrialisation articulates the ways in which the North continues to occupy a discursive and political role as a provincial counterpart to the modernity associated with London. Taken together, *The Cut* and *Missing Fay* present Brexit as an emphatically non-metropolitan story bound up in the regional economic inequalities and the relationship between the political elites of Westminster and 'England-without-London'. In this sense, these fictions demonstrate that there was more at stake in the referendum than the future of the UK's relationship with the EU; at stake too was the viability of Britain as a multinational state and the political status of its largest component territory, which may be redefined, it seemed, from the peripheries.

However, to varying degrees, these novels simultaneously end up repeating the polarisation and dichotomies on which they are based. The multiple ways Thorpe and Cartwright represent their spatial settings and their communities augment a reifying image of Northern England. Neither text imagines their localities beyond the rigid class stereotypes that characterised much political discourse during the referendum campaign. *The Cut* is a regional polemic, but its reliance on restorative nostalgia and deindustrial aesthetics exists in tension with its decentralising potential. The central dichotomy between Grace and Cairo likewise relies on a contemporary manifestation of the North–South divide. *Missing Fay* also registers the profound difficulties of imagining Lincoln beyond the regional and class stereotypes that characterised political and media discourse during and after Brexit. The novel also deploys overdetermined, class-based archetypes of 'Little England' that reinforce the barriers to imagining a progressive English civic nationalism. Both novels grapple with the regional novel's formal and stylistic limitations and its association with working-class nostalgia, posing the question of a literary form that can adequately go beyond Brexit's political discourse. Both texts offer only ambivalent prognoses for the role of culture in altering Britain's political imaginary after the referendum. This ambivalence leaves the question of the Brexit novel's capacity to reconcile the regional and the national – and the local and the global – unanswered. It is to this question that we turn in the final chapter.

Notes

1 This rhetoric was likewise mobilised during May's general election speech in which she urged the public to 'remove the risk of uncertainty and instability' and give Britain 'the strong and stable leadership it demands'. Theresa May (2017), 'PM Statement: General Election 2017'. Delivered 9 June. Available at: https://www.gov.uk/government/speeches/pm-statement-general-election-201> [accessed 28 July 2020].

2 For a rare critique of this narrative in the media, see Zoe Williams (2016), 'Think the North and the Poor Caused Brexit? Think Again', *The Guardian*, 7 August. Available at: https://www.theguardian.com/commentisfree/2016/aug/07/north-poor-brexit-myths [accessed 17 September 2019].

3 See *BBC News* (2016b) 'Lincolnshire Records UK's Highest Brexit Vote', 24 June. Available at: https://www.bbc.com/news/uk-politics-eu-referendum-36616740 [accessed 22 September 2020].

4 See Anthony Cummins (2017), 'Missing Fay by Adam Thorpe Review – Gone Girl in Lincolnshire', *The Guardian*, 11 June. Available at: https://www.theguardian.com/books/2017/jun/11/missing-fay-adam-thorpe-review [accessed 20 December 2019].

5 McGregor's prequel, *The Reservoir Tapes* (2017), relies more forcefully on investigative tropes of the conventional crime novel.

6 See Phyllis Bentley (1941), *The English Regional Novel*. Crows Nest, New South Wales: G. Allen & Unwin.

7 See, for example, Gillian Evans' analysis of far-right populism and post-industrial communities in Evans (2017), 'Brexit Britain: Why We Are All Postindustrial Now', *American Ethnologist*, 44 (2), pp. 215–219; Ben Pitcher (2019), 'Racism and Brexit: Notes towards an Antiracist Populism', *Ethnic and Racial Studies*, 42 (14), pp. 2490–2509.

8 There is also a further irony here, in that the English nationalist sentiment Farage so readily harnessed heavily relied on the Anglo-British suppression of a civic, political Englishness in favour of an ethnonationalist English identity. The day after Brexit, Farage declared that 23 June would be remembered as Britain's 'Independence Day', a claim which redirected legitimate claims for representation away from the political elite to Brussels and immigration.

9 For a comprehensive examination of this development, see Ina Habermann (2020), 'Introduction: Understanding the Past, Facing the Future' in *The Road to Brexit: A Cultural Perspective on British Attitudes to Europe*. Manchester: Manchester University Press, pp. 1–18.

10 With a 15.4 per cent majority, Yorkshire and the Humber returned the fourth highest regional vote in favour of Leave. Former fishing town, Hull, for example, voted Leave by a decisive 67.6 per cent versus 32.4 per cent, in favour of Leaving the EU. 'Results and Turnout at the EU Referendum', *Electoral Commission*, 25 September. 2019. Available at: https://www.electoralcommission.org.uk/who-we-are-and-what-we-do/elections-and-referendums/past-elections-and-referendums/eu-referendum/results-and-turnout-eu-referendum [accessed 22 July 2020].

For a geographic analysis of uneven development and the referendum, see Gordon MacLeod and Martin Jones (2018), 'Explaining "Brexit Capital": Uneven Development and the Austerity State', *Space and Polity*, 22 (2), pp. 111–136.

11 See, for example, Channel Four's *Benefits Street* series. Lynsey Hanley's *Estates: An Intimate History* and Owen Jones' *Chavs: The Demonization of the Working Class* also critique of the ubiquity of the council estate in contemporary British culture.

12 While Thatcher's 'enemy within' referred to trade unions during the Miners' Strike, the term has since been deployed extensively in various disciplines to refer to social groups who were marginalised under Thatcherism. See Imogen Tyler (2013) *Revolting Subjects: Social Abjection and Resistance in Neoliberal Britain*. London: Zed Books, pp. 153–178.

13 There is a further irony here in that *Little Red Riding Hood* by Charles Perrault is of European origin.

14 This trope is later reinforced when Fay's skin is described as 'snow-white' (Thorpe, 2017, p. 135).

15 *The Telegraph* captured the public outrage caused by the wheel. See '"Britain's Worst Tourist Attraction": Ferris Wheel Gives Panoramic Views … of Dudley', The Telegraph, 15 March 2016. Available at: https://www.telegraph.co.uk/news/newstopics/howaboutthat/12194700/Britains-worst-tourist-attraction-Dudley-West-Midlands-ferris-wheel.html [accessed 20 November 2019].

16 For an excellent account of deindustrial labour and masculinity in a transnational context, see Sherry Lee Linkon (2018), *The Half-Life of Deindustrialization: Working-Class Writing about Economic Restructuring*. Ann Arbor: University of Michigan Press.

17 There is a further irony in that the Dudley Sports Centre was rendered unsafe by and eventually closed due to mining subsistence. See http://www.blackcountrysociety.co.uk/articles/holeinground.html [accessed 14 June 2019].

18 The idea of running as liberating or emancipatory may also be an intertextual reference to Alan Sillitoe's *The Loneliness of the Long Distance Runner* (1959), in which running offers a form of resistance to institutionalisation and class domination.

4 Global Britishness and the Neo-Primitive North

There is a scene in Sarah Moss' 2018 novel, *Ghost Wall*, in which seventeen-year-old Silvie attempts to reconcile the European travel of university students her age with her own rootedness in place: 'Rome and Paris. Now you can go to Prague and Budapest too ... Pete had already been to Berlin, after his exams, had seen some of the wall come down' (Moss, 2018, p. 16). During a period of accelerated European integration during the 1990s, the students reflect on their plans for inter-railing, while Silvie cannot comprehend how 'just moving around counted as a rational use of time and money' (Moss, 2018, p. 16). Unlike the carefree mobility of the students from an unnamed city in the South of England, Silvie's outlook from rural Northumberland is tentative and cautious, observing several social and geographical borders:

> How do you get to Berlin? Can you start at the bus stop, do you take an aeroplane or the train, several trains? I knew many of the British Isles, Holy Island and Anglesey, the Orkneys and several of the Hebrides, but I had never been overseas. We didn't have passports. Where was the money coming from, what did Dan and Pete and Molly's parents think of these plans?
>
> (Moss, 2018, p. 17)

Although the novel takes place during an unspecified period shortly after the crumbling of the Berlin Wall, Silvie cannot comprehend European citizenship or travel. The historical backdrop for the narrative is not only the unification of Berlin, but the interconnection of multiple national forms facilitated by globalisation. The fall of the Berlin Wall both resulted in closer European integration for the UK and the triumph of neoliberal globalisation as the only viable expression of Western liberal democracy (see Fukuyama, 1989).[1]

In *Ghost Wall*, the symbolic significance of the Berlin Wall resides in its capacity to historicise, forging connections between the 1990s and the contemporary moment. Padmaja Challakere describes the disintegration of the Wall as 'a model for a landscape without barriers' in Zadie Smith's *White Teeth* (2000) and Nicholas Royle's *Counterparts* (1996), suggesting a function

DOI: 10.4324/9781003388722-7

akin to that in *Ghost Wall*. For Moss, this reference point establishes a connection between the 1990s and Brexit as politically significant moments in European history which are marked by the renegotiation of national and supranational borders. Challakere concludes that contemporary fiction 'must refuse to narratively reproduce the cozily optimistic allegory of the fall of the Berlin Wall' and instead, 'reimagine "globality" as the experience of being "haunted by walls" if it is to become aesthetically and politically dynamic and cosmopolitan' (Challakere, 2007). *Ghost Wall*'s depiction of Britain shortly after the unification of Berlin is certainly 'haunted by walls', but what emerges is far from 'cozily optimistic' or cosmopolitan. The differing spatial optics of Silvie and the university students – one delimited by the archipelago's geographical boundaries, and the other European, unhindered by territorial borders – embody the ongoing division between the English local and a Europe-facing Britishness. As we saw in the previous chapter, this dualism was central to the government's politics of nation after the EU Referendum and was captured most acutely in Theresa May's rhetoric of 'Global Britain'.

By 2019, May's construction of Britain as a global power after Brexit had been condemned as 'intractable' (Daddow 2019, p. 5) and a dangerous 'Empire 2.0' (Olusoga, 2017), with the UK Parliament's Foreign Affairs Committee suggesting it risked being 'a superficial branding exercise' (Foreign Affairs Committee, 2018). In his polemic, *The Road to Somewhere*, David Goodhart borrows May's anti-cosmopolitanism rhetoric, seeking to explain Brexit through a caricature of two groups he describes as 'Anywheres' and 'Somewheres' (Goodhart, 2017, p. 3). Goodhart argues that 'the old distinctions of class and economic interest have not disappeared but are increasingly over-laid by a larger and looser one – between people who see the world from Anywhere and the people who see it from Somewhere' (Goodhart, 2017, p. 3). In Goodhart's hierarchy of mobility, the latter are more situated in place and identify with their local environment, encompassing groups such as 'the left behind', while the former have 'portable' identities, and comprise a university-educated, liberal metropolitan elite (Goodhart, 2017, p. 3). There is much to take issue with in Goodhart's analysis – not least its handling of social class – but what is most relevant here is the failure to account for how the very idea of 'Global Britain' was a unitary *nationalist* project. In the post-Brexit-vote context, 'Global Britain' was far closer to an evolution of Blair's multicultural Britishness than a cosmopolitan project.

By Goodhart's logic, Silvie appears to be a 'Somewhere': her identity is emphatically placed and, according to Moss, her name translates to 'Northumbrian goddess'. Conversely, the university students are 'Anywheres' who possess a transnational outlook and appear indifferent to place-bound attachments. Yet, unlike Goodhart's dualisms, Moss' narrative explores the complex, shifting dynamics of these two positions – crucially, *Ghost Wall* presents the local and the global less as disparate poles than a

Venn diagram, each perspective positioned side by side with points of overlap. Exploring the tensions between a past which is anchored in place and an increasingly borderless future, *Ghost Wall* tells Silvie's story as part of her father's re-enactment of British pre-history. Originally from an unspecified town in the North-West near Burnley, Silvie and her family travel to a remote rural location in Northumbria, are joined by Professor Slade and a group of university students, and take part in an experiential archaeology project. Living as Ancient Britons, they leave technology behind, dress in Iron Age tunics, eat an Iron Age diet of foraged or hunted foods, and observe Iron Age rituals. Silvie's father, Bill, obsessively idealises the Iron Age, driven by a xenophobic desire for an ethno-purist Britishness. For Bill, the trip is more than a simple pastime. It presents the opportunity to validate his belief that there is 'some original Britishness somewhere, that if he goes back far enough he'll find someone who wasn't a foreigner' (Moss, 2018, p. 20). Bill's conception of Britishness does not appear to include anywhere outside England, however. Told from Silvie's perspective, the narrative centres on Bill's search for 'his own ancestry, a claim on something, some tribe sprung from English soil like mushrooms in the night' (Moss, 2018, p. 45). In the isolation of a make-shift camp near Hadrian's Wall, Silvie's life is contingent on Bill's obsession with recreating Iron Age Britain; rather than travelling the globe and immersing herself in other cultures, she is living as Ancient Britons did, hunter-gathering and 'learning to walk the land the way they walked it two thousand years ago' (Moss, 2018, p. 34).

The global citizenship of Britain's 'Anywheres' was the target of May's now-infamous assertion that 'if you believe you are a citizen of the world, you are a citizen of nowhere' (May, 2016b). The former prime minister's attack on cosmopolitan identities appears to contradict her commitment to 'Global Britain' in the very same speech, indicating acceptance of 'the global' only insofar as it is part of a 'progressive' reframing of Britishness as a world power outside the EU. As the previous chapter demonstrated, tensions between England as an anachronistic and localised counterpoint to a 'global' Britishness are a recurrent preoccupation within literary responses to Brexit. However, while *The Cut* and *Missing Fay* grapple with the difficulties of transcending Brexit's polarising tendencies, *Ghost Wall* is perhaps more successful in attending to the nuances underlying the referendum. While at first glance Silvie appears to be a 'Somewhere', the perspective of *Ghost Wall*'s protagonist operates at the intersection of a placed isolationism and a more interconnected social outlook, gesturing towards a dialogue between these two opposing sides of Brexit's culture war.

Ghost Wall is not the only Brexit novel which is characterised by an emphasis on place. Fiona Mozley's *Elmet* (2017) also centres on a family's isolation from the outside world. Located in a remote, unnamed rural area of North Yorkshire, *Elmet* tells the story of Cathy and Daniel Price and their father, John. After the disappearance of Cathy and Daniel's mother, they move from the city to a house that John builds with his bare hands from the nearby wood, living self-sufficiently – but unlawfully – on unused land. According to John, the copse is 'theirs alone', with the family's self-contained lifestyle a deliberate attempt to keep the children away from what John perceives as the dangers of modern life; he wanted to 'keep us separate, in ourselves, apart from the world' (Mozley, 2017, p. 48). Cathy and Daniel are raised with little contact outside their family and a few trusted friends, living without technology, mostly eating the seasonal produce that they hunt and gather. Central to both novels is a concern with time, pre-capitalist social practices, and place-identity established through environmentalism. Yet, neither *Ghost Wall* nor *Elmet* were published as historical novels. In both texts, the past occurs alongside the present as a response to the spatial and temporal implications of an increasingly 'global' Britishness.

Following on from our discussion of *Missing Fay* and *The Cut*, the processes of what is another form of localised nostalgia will be the central focus of this final chapter. Chapter 3 argued that nostalgia had been mobilised in Brexit fiction as a rejection of the centralised British state form, demonstrating how the freighted relationship between the deindustrialised heartlands of England and its metropolitan core and questions of England's political status remain urgent constitutional concerns. This chapter explores the literary articulation of nostalgia as symptomatic of a desire emanating from formerly industrial Northern towns for the realignment of space, place, and labour. In both texts, the allure of neo-primitive lifeways resides in its efficacy as a place-based praxis. While *Elmet's* approach to primitivism centres on environmentalism as a basis for establishing localised democratic forms, *Ghost Wall's* primitivist emphasis on place is far more ambiguous – territorial affiliation is, at least partly, the outgrowth of what Paul Gilroy calls 'postimperial melancholia' (Gilroy, 2005). Despite these differences, the neo-primitive thrust of both Moss and Mozley's novels is born out of nostalgia for pre-modern, place-based democratic and social forms. In his theorisation of the radical potentialities of nostalgia, Alistair Bonnett explains that

> [i]n the time of modernity, solidarity and authenticity become idealised and identified with the past. Thus the hope of regaining community and the reintegration of life and labour constantly threatens to offer, or resort to, the pre-capitalist and organic past as a source of socialism's most basic hopes.
>
> (Bonnett, 2010, p. 29)

Ghost Wall and *Elmet's* primitive aesthetics echo Bonnett's view of nostalgia's radical properties, particularly via a 'reintegration of life and labour' and return to a territorialised experience of space and time. By examining this new formulation of the primitive mode as a politics of place, I argue that *Ghost Wall* and *Elmet* attempt to place or 'reterritorialise' England in response to the globalising impulses of the British state.

Neo-Primitivism as Reterritorialisation

The concept of globalisation is difficult to define singularly. Fredric Jameson captures the elusiveness of the term, describing it as a 'postmodern pro-verbial elephant' existing 'in the absence of a single persuasive and dominant theory' (Jameson, 1991, p. xi), while for Michael Hardt and Antonio Negri, globalisation 'is not one thing, and the multiple processes that we recognise as globalization are not unified or univocal' (Hardt and Negri, 2000, p. xv). Some of the earliest and most influential engagements with globalisation approached the phenomenon as both an economic and spatial process. From the 1970s onwards, globalisation became associated with neoliberalism, pri-marily 'the deregulated expansion of speculative capital; rapid technological development, especially in communicative technology; transnational produc-tion and the weakening of labour movements; the reforming of some inter-national trade agreements and an increasing multinationalisation of some corporations' (Connell and Marsh, 2011, p. xvii).

David Harvey connects globalisation's economic and spatial consequences, arguing that the economic processes of combined and uneven development are felt as, and intensified by, a particular spatio-temporal characteristic of global modernity. In his landmark study, *The Condition of Postmodernity*, Harvey coins 'time-space compression' (Harvey, 1989, p. 240) to describe a deterritor-ialising process whereby territorial borders are rendered insignificant by tech-nological developments. While 'deterritorialisation' has a philosophical understanding in the work of Gilles Deleuze and Felix Guattari (1972, 1980), my comprehension of the term evokes Harvey's spatial-anthropological appli-cation within globalisation studies. Indeed, for Ursula K. Heise, deterritor-ialisation describes 'the emergence of new forms of culture that are no longer anchored in place', registering 'the detachment of social and cultural practices from their ties to place that have been described in theories of modernisation and postmodernisation' (Heise, 2011, p. 158). Writing in a similar key, Anthony Giddens coins the term 'time-space distanciation' to account for technological developments which, in the spirit of globalisation's universalising impulses, have 'emptied out' localised space by uprooting identities from fixed spatial and temporal coordinates (Giddens, 1990, p. 20).

In this condition of universalising globality, primitivism's emphasis on place and the local can be understood as a process of *re*territorialisation. One of the earliest manifestations of primitivism from the 1750s onwards may be found in the imperialist construction of the 'noble savage', who was, in the European imagination, taken to represent a lost time of ecological simplicity and authen-ticity.[2] Michael Bell suggests that the term refers to 'the recreation of what many anthropologists have believed to be the most essential qualities of pre-civilised feeling and thought' (Bell, 1972, p. 8). However, Northern literary uses of pri-mitivism are distinct from former imperial uses which signify Eurocentric modernity defined against an apparently uncivilised 'other'.[3] In *Literary Primi-tivism* (2018), Ben Etherington proposes that contemporary manifestations of primitive social practices may be re-deployed in literature and culture as a negation of the capitalist world system, touching briefly on the significance of primitivism's localised or spatial characteristics:

> literary primitivism's futurity was decidedly local, pointing to the dis-aggregation of social realities rather than their unification. ... [W]e might call this 'world's literature': literature that projects divergent realities, creating a situation in which the universal will consist of the deepening and coexistence of all particulars.
>
> (Etherington, 2018, p. 172)

Taking Etherington's proposition that literary primitivism might initiate 'the deepening and coexistence of all particulars', this chapter focuses on a contemporary version of primitivism that I refer to as neo-primitivism. Victor Li offers an instructive explanation of the shift from primitivism to neo-primitivism, arguing that the latter 'follows the trajectory of Western thought from nineteenth-century evolutionism and the belief in universal histories of progress to twentieth-century cultural relativism and the so-called postmodern incredulity towards modern universalist narratives' (Li, 2006, p. 3). Neo-primitivism in this chapter thus describes a literary response to Brexit which attempts to represent England in localised, placed terms. To varying degrees, *Elmet* and *Ghost Wall* hint at a placed version of neo-primitivism located in both North Yorkshire and the North-East that pulls against a state-led narrative of globalism, contributing to a territorialised representation of the North in particular and England as a whole.

While these novels acknowledge the political potential of a placed neo-primitivism, they do not provide utopian engagements with the past. Their reworking of the primitive mode as a placed alternative to a deterritorialised global Britishness helps to articulate the roots of anti-globalisation sentiment, rather than being offered as a tangible political project. Both *Elmet* and *Ghost Wall*'s premodern lifeways are characterised by the persistence of historic social hierarchies including sexism, xenophobia, and, for adolescent narrators Daniel and Silvie, alienation from the longed-for outside world. While both *Ghost Wall* and *Elmet* imagine neo-primitive ethics centred on localised democratic relations, social collectivity, and ecological awareness, this devolutionary potential is undermined by gender-based violence, social isolationism, and, in *Ghost Wall*, attachment to an ethno-purist Britishness. Moss and Mozley's engagement with the neo-primitive thus remains cautious and ambivalent, unable to imagine democratic alternatives to a centralised and universalising Britishness.

Decelerated Times and the Environmental Ethics of Place: Fiona Mozley's *Elmet*

Elmet's neo-primitivism negates the processes of global modernity by initiating a reconceptualisation of the relationship between time, space, and place. The novel's title and epigraph, for example, not only reference a heavily decelerated 'glacial' temporality but also situate the text within Yorkshire's longer cultural and political history:

> Elmet was the last independent Celtic kingdom in England and origin-ally stretched out over the vale of York ... But even into the seventeenth century this narrow cleft and its side-gunnels, under the glaciated moors, were still a 'badlands', a sanctuary for refugees from the law.
>
> (Mozley, 2017, n.p.)

Both *Elmet*'s title and epigraph are taken from Ted Hughes' poetry collection, *Remains of Elmet* (Hughes and Goodwin, 1979), which is similarly embedded in the material geography of West Yorkshire. The collection presents Hughes' poetry alongside photographs of the Calder Valley where he grew up, a landscape which – as *Elmet* demonstrates – is saturated with history and the socio-economic implications of deindustrialisation. Pub-lished one month after Margaret Thatcher's election victory, the bleak tone of Goodwin's black-and-white photographs alongside Hughes' poetry aptly captures the disaffection felt throughout Northern England which, as we have already seen, is often articulated in the landscape.[4] This location of place within an intertextual historical lens works productively to reconnect space and time in the process of reterritorialisation, echoing neo-primitivism's prioritisation of local history as a kind of 'claim' to the land. The epigraph goes further in framing Elmet's territory in politics terms: the place is described as a 'badlands', a 'sanctuary for refugees from the law', an 'independent' area outside the jurisdiction of the centralised Brit-ish state and its laws. The area's status as the Celtic Kingdom also alludes to long-standing competing nationalisms within the Union, while devolu-tionary momentum remains high at a grassroots level in Yorkshire. These histories work productively to situate the novel within the context of Brexit and current debates surrounding democratic deficit in Northern England.[5] Indeed, frequent allusions to old stories and myths of the land root *Elmet* within North Yorkshire's literary and cultural history. *Elmet*'s neo-primitive rural wilderness evokes Yorkshire's previous literary func-tion as an anti-pastoral place of wildness and resistance. Emily Brontë's *Wuthering Heights* has been read as utilising the North Yorkshire Moors to resist the South-East of England's internal colonisation of the North, serving as a symbolic, uncivilised, primitive space (see Markwick, 2018).[6] Reviewers have also identified Mozley's mythologisation of the landscape, describing the novel as being at the forefront of 'Folk Realism', a new lit-erary subgenre David Barnett (2018) argues is particularly suited to York-shire's rural landscape. Similarly, *Elmet* has been described elsewhere as 'digging deep into the psychogeology of Yorkshire' (Taylor, 2017), reflect-ing the turn towards place in contemporary Northern English literary production that we have traced thus far.[7]

Elmet's multi-layered decelerated temporalities occur in opposition to a universal standardisation of time. Anthony Giddens identifies the invention of the mechanical clock as key in the separation of time from space and the onset of modernity, solidified by uniformity in the social organisation of time; this standardisation of time established the pre-conditions for the 'emptying out' of space, the detachment of space from a sense of place (Giddens, 1990, p. 18). In contrast to this process of 'time-space distancia-tion', oral stories serve as historicised modes of belonging, providing a means for Daniel to develop a relationship with the land. Local stories that inflect the lives of its inhabitants infuse *Elmet*'s geographical setting; Daniel describes how 'the soil was alive with ruptured stories that cascaded and rotted and then found form once more and pushed through the undergrowth and back into our lives' (Mozley, 2017, pp. 5–6). Later, he watches a hare running across the fields 'unlike any other' he has seen, describing it as an almost otherworldly creature, but also as a symbol of the mythological nature of Elmet's terrain: 'if the hare was made of myths then so too was the land at which she scratched' (Mozley, 2017, p. 5). Here, geography and history enmesh, with 'the ghosts of the ancient forest … marked where the wind blew' (Mozley, 2017, p. 5). Likewise, the stories John tells Daniel and Cathy are 'precious heirlooms' (Mozley, 2017, p. 16) as they too become part of the history of the place. John is most obviously represented as part of a local mythology based on masculinity and violence, with a reputation '[a]mong certain types in the Yorkshire ridings and in Lincolnshire' and 'in the counties around there were few who had not' (Mozley, 2017, p. 19) heard of him and his unparalleled physical strength.

Elmet's non-linear narrative also articulates a temporally fragmented present. The opening scenes focus on the aftermath of the narrative's tragic conclusion, with Daniel walking up the railway line searching for Cathy before rewinding to the events leading up to the conflict that separated them. These brief passages in which Daniel retells the past are printed in italics and are rich in symbolic description, differentiating them from the realism of the narrative proper. At the same time, however, these mytholo-gical descriptions occur against a recognisably modern backdrop of motor-ways, lorries transporting both goods and migrants, and roadside cafés. When the narrative switches to Daniel's present, he describes how the memory of '*that evening in our house in the copse does not loosen. The stills do not fall from their reel. Each face and each gesture confirms its shape. Nothing slackens*' (Mozley, 2017, p. 16, original emphasis), echoing the persistence of the past and anticipating the violent final scenes of the novel.

The persistence of history and a decelerated experience of time are bound up within *Elmet*'s neo-primitivism. The narrative encompasses contrasting temporalities between the past and present, including a motif of seasonal change; nearly all of the chapters open with a description of local ecosys-tems and the season in which it is set, and descriptions of everyday life are dictated by seasonal changes. The first thing Daniel recalls of moving to the copse is that they 'arrived in the summer when the landscape was in full bloom' (Mozley, 2017, p. 4), and begins to root himself and his home within this ecosystem:

> As soon as the external walls were up I planted seeds and bulbs .... It was the wrong time of the year to plant but some shoots came up and more came the following year. Waiting is what a true house is about. Making it ours, making it settle, pinning it to the seasons, to the months and to the years.
>
> (Mozley, 2017, p. 9)

Daniel's planting of seeds and bulbs is an environmentally conscious process of embedding, rooting himself and his house within a particular place and time. These gardening practices require patience and prolonged waiting periods, indicating a kind of permanence that allows an individual to dwell and form a place-bound sense of belonging. Such a desire to be 'in place' is reiterated in their home, which John builds using 'materials from the land and here about' (Mozley, 2017, p. 8). Daniel boasts that it 'will last many dozen seasons longer' (Mozley, 2017, p. 8) than houses in the nearest city, again returning to the idea of seasonal time as a controlling force of everyday life and prioritising a stake in the land established through situatedness in place.

The decelerated pace of seasonal time contrasts with the intervals of trains that run along the edge of the wood, indicating a simultaneously occurring modernity. Daniel, Cathy, and John live beside the East Coast mainline, where trains travel from London to Leeds and further up to Edinburgh; these trains 'had timetables and intervals of their own' contrasting 'the long, indigo Adelantes and Pendolinos that streaked from London to Edinburgh' while the 'carthorse-trains chugg[ed] up to the knacker, they moved too slowly for the younger tracks and slipped on the hot-rolled steel like men on ice' (Mozley, 2017, p. 7). These multiple velocities pull against the accelerated, dematerialised experience of everyday life under time-space compression. Daniel's recognition that '[i]n another world we might have grown up faster, but this was our strange, sylvan otherworld, so we did not' (Mozley, 2017, p. 48) reiterates this deceleration. The ability to dwell is a precondition for a kind of place-bound belonging which is contingent on living synchronously with the rural environment and its seasonal cyclicality.

Elmet's environmental consciousness establishes attachments that privilege the local. This ecocritical dimension relies on ethical and sustainable production methods, emphasising biocentrism and a non-hierarchical relationship with the non-human environment, and the ability to live from local produce that can be hunted or gathered without technology. While not strictly hunter-gatherers, Daniel, Cathy, and John's diet mostly consists of meat they have caught nearby. Using a bow and arrow, John hunts 'wood pigeon, rock dove, collared dove, pheasant and woodcock, if he caught them in the evenings coming to cover' and 'in the right season there was smaller game for breakfast' (Mozley, 2017, p. 12), indicating an approach to food consumption which is environmentally conscious and sustainable. Importantly, it is comprised mostly of local animals and dictated by seasonal availability. *Elmet*'s localised spatial setting echoes a new conceptualisation of the primitive marked by environmental consciousness, representing 'a world to which we should, apparently, wish to be returned, a world in which culture does not challenge nature' (Kuper, 2003, p. 395). *Elmet*'s association of the local with the environmental bears a resemblance to the social and political movement of 'bioregionalism', which, as Timothy Clarke writes, 'proposes that human societies, their modes of production and cultures should reform themselves from the bottom up, decentralising to become communities with close and sustainable relations to their local bioregions' (Clarke, 2013, p. 130). As Clarke puts it, the goal of bioregionalism is to reduce to a minimum the physical distance between consumers and producers while the region becomes 'a crucial agent in human identity and social organisation' (Clarke, 2013, p. 131). In this sense, like the re-wilding project in Hall's *The Wolf Border*, *Elmet*'s environmental neo-primitivism is imbricated with a regional impetus.

These 'devolutionary', neo-primitive ethics are part of what Ursula Heise calls an 'environmentalist discourse of place' (Heise, 2011, p. 157), which confronts ecological challenges through an emphasis on locality. These approaches emphasise 'the importance of a sense of place, the reinhabitation of the local through residence, intimate familiarity, affective ties and ethical commitment' (Heise, 2011, pp. 157–158). The ethical correlate to neo-primitive hunter-gathering is visible in the shift away from anthropocentrism towards a non-hierarchical relationship with the land and the animals that inhabit it. For instance, John's hens live close to the house to protect them from the winter cold, and there is a marked degree of care when he kills his prey: 'he would take it in his hands as quietly as he could then snap its fragile neck. The little creatures never even knew they were dead' (Mozley, 2017, p. 114). Here, neo-primitivism's environmental consciousness prioritises sustainable production practices in contradistinction to the ecologically harmful practices of global corporations – a modern presence echoed in the persistence of heavy goods vehicles that run alongside the setting of their home.

Aside from occasional cakes and biscuits in the homes of their small circle of friends, the family follow a Palaeolithic diet, supplemented by eggs laid by hens they keep in their garden beside their vegetable patch and berries picked from the sides of the road. In addition to the game caught by John and Cathy, the family source vegetables from the local market, or John occasionally exchanges goods with Andrew for meat, which is either bargained for or paid 'in kind' through John's labour. Lengthy descriptions of meal preparation throughout the novel prioritise a localised food economy.

For example, when Daniel fries eggs from his hens for the family breakfast, he describes the process as follows:

> The bacon was from the butcher, Andrew, who was also one of Daddy's few friends. It was well salted and he had cut it thickly but I made sure the rind was crisp before I lifted it from the skillet. The eggs fried quickly in the bacon fat and took on the salt from the meat so their bottoms formed caramel crusts while the yolks remained golden. I warmed the plates first in the oven, then finished them with a fresh slice of bread.
>
> (Mozley, 2017, p. 126)

This highly particularised description of Daniel's food preparation – from tending to the hens to consuming their eggs – indicates a grounded production and consumption method that requires local social exchange, time, and care, contrasting with the mass food production enabled by time-space compression. This global market hinges on the illusion of the seemingly endless productive capacity of land and food resources from around the globe, and a detachment between production and consumption due to dependence on food imports and, often exploitative, labour.

The opposition between this situated, environmental neo-primitivism and burgeoning capitalist domination forms the central antagonism of the novel, and one which is primarily explored through the politics of land ownership and the right to habitation. The freighted relationship between John and Mr Price arises from the tension between John's personal stake in the land and Price's legal ownership. The latter signifies a dematerialised capitalist hegemony, a form of deterritorialised power enabled by wealth and rentier capitalism. When Price's two sons go to John's house on the suspicion that he has killed one of their pet pigeons, this class-inflected dynamic is acutely visible. Tom and Charlie Price 'ascend the hill in their land rover' wearing 'green wellington boots and waxed jackets' (Mozley, 2017, pp. 111–112). In contrast, Cathy and Daniel are 'sitting among the trees of the copse, watching from afar; Daniel is whittling green ash' having 'stripped the tender bar from a piece the length of [his] handspan' while Cathy 'held the corpse of a small mallard between her knees and was pulling fistfuls of feathers from its dappled skin' (Mozley, 2017, p.112). In this early juxtaposition of the two families, *Elmet* contrasts a visceral, environmentally conscious attachment to the land with Price's disembodied, contractual ownership. John's approach involves harvesting the land's produce sustainably, while Price's claim to the land is conceived in terms of its financial value; it is underpinned by a distance between the individual and material territory in a way that is analogous to the way space is conceived under globalisation.

This moral distinction legitimises John's claim to the copse on which his family live, despite not possessing legal rights to it. When Price threatens to drive John and his family off the land, John bemoans that he

knew [he and his family] would care for this land in a way Mr Price
never could, and never would. Mr Price does nothing with these woods.
He doednt work them. He doednt coppice them. He doednt know the
trees. He doednt know the birds and animals that live here.

(Mozley, 2017, p. 121)

An environmental commitment underpins John's pre-capitalist form of
ownership here, but the land is also the place where Daniel and Cathy's
mother used to live. The repetition in John's dialogue points towards his
deep personal affiliation; the very idea that 'a person can write summat on a
bit of paper about a piece of land that lives and breathes … means nowt' to
him (Mozley, 2017, p. 202). Presenting multiple and competing claims to the
material terrain, the novel privileges a neo-primitive place-bound affiliation
based on environmental consciousness.

Mr Price's absentee landlordship and exploitation of his employees also
signifies his hegemonic capitalist authority. When John, Daniel, and Cathy
begin their plan to overthrow Price, they listen to local stories within the
community, learning that Price has mostly inherited the land he owns or
bought up former Right-to-Buy council homes. Reflecting on the experience
of privatisation, a member of the community describes how:

At least when I paid rent to council, I felt I could get things fixed. It
were a slow process, always, but someone would come eventually and
see to cooker, or whatever. I knew who to go to. I knew there were
some kind of, what's word, process, no matter how tricky. I gave my
money to council and I kept place nicely and in return I got a decent
place to live. Now it's a private landlord and he doendt give two stuffs.

(Mozley, 2017, p. 169)

This scene captures the effect of rentier capitalism in which Price represents
a land-owning class that no longer invests in productive industry to generate
profit, and increasingly relies on rents which have no productive value.
Contrastingly, despite its flaws, social housing during the post-war con-
sensus at least offered a tangible process in which tenants knew 'who to go
to' to address property inadequacies. In the novel's present, it appears that
unproductive profit mechanisms such as rents underpin capitalism's self-
sustaining tendencies. These disembodied, expansive economic conditions
neglect the material conditions of everyday life and augment a class system
signified by landownership.

Subtle references to deterritorialised economic systems in the novel also link
the abstract nature of capitalist control to powerful, but faceless, networks. For
example, in the local area,

most people … rent their homes from Mr Price … and if they don't rent
from Mr Price, their landlord is a friend of his. All the landlords round

here go drinking and shooting up at the manor. They all have dealings, as they say. They'll have some money invested together, bubbling in the same pot.

(Mozley, 2017, p. 130)

This scepticism towards the possibility of overthrowing Price and his class of fellow landlords highlights how deterritorialised forms of power intensify the effects of existing social hierarchies imbricated in the politics of land-ownership. Despite the fact Price and the tenant reside near one another, Price's faceless wealth and abstract business connections in *Elmet* are analogous to the ways in which businesses operate under globalisation, forming a social distance between the two. Daniel and Cathy's temporary work on Price's potato farm reiterates Price's association with an unequal and deterritorialised global financial system. The other farmhands are mostly individuals recently released from prison, who warn Daniel and Cathy that work on the farm is so exploitative that '[h]ardly anyone wants to do it – not even the Lithuanians – not worth it', explicitly locating Price within an economy of global processes whose systems of inequality inform and shape remote, non-metropolitan areas of England (Mozley, 2017, p. 159).

Elmet's engagement with the neo-primitive is not straightforwardly utopian. While these glimpses of unequal systems emphasise neo-primitivism's social and environmental benefits, the neo-primitive is complicated elsewhere, becoming much more critical and ambivalent. As the novel progresses, the idealised image of a close-knit family and their rural seclusion begins to falter. The family's neo-primitive isolationism must give way to enable a localised, collective revolt against Price. The narrative foregrounds the family's isolation as part of neo-primitive social practices, yet frequently alludes to its limits and resultant alienation. Even Daniel pines for a world outside his family and the copse, reflecting that 'though I loved watching birds and beetles, watching human beings was the thing I loved best' (Mozley, 2017, p. 146). While John hopes that isolationism will strengthen his children 'against the dark things in the world', as Daniel reminds us,

there was nothing of the world in our lives, only stories of it. We had been taken out of our school and our home town to live with Daddy in a small copse. We had no friends and hardly any neighbours.

(Mozley, 2017, p. 83)

It is through speaking to the local community, and conversations with old friends, that John can foment enough support to help overthrow Price. John's political project requires an abandonment of the primitive isolationism that has characterised the family's existence in the novel thus far in favour of a political community centred on meaningful relationships, social collectivism, and hospitality. John, Cathy and Daniel have 'been alone for too long' and when they host a dinner to assess the possibilities that lie in the community, Daniel describes how 'the prospect of so many faces coming up the hill to see us felt strange, like we were to be stripped naked and paraded' (Mozley, 2017, p. 165). Yet, he feels 'excitement as well as fear' (Mozley, 2017, p. 165), as his own character develops through hospitality and the opportunity to foster personal connections outside his immediate family. This transition is apparent in Daniel's preparations for the event:

> I busied myself with arrangements for the food we would serve. I calculated the amount we would need and saw that we got it in the day before. I picked spring vegetables from the patch and chopped them into chunks before setting them on skewers to char over the fire ... Daddy sorted most of the meat but I ground offcuts and entrails and made little patties with barley and spice.
>
> (Mozley, 2017, pp. 165–166)

The everyday act of preparing food for the community is a form of participatory politics as Daniel becomes part of a social network centred on openness and localism. Here the novel presents us with a pre-capitalist ethics centred on collectivity in opposition to the individualistic ideologies of Price. Social collectivism underpins Daniel's preparations and challenges a global conception of space and time defined by dematerialised capital. The simplicity and ordinariness of the tasks and use of local produce emphasise the importance of place, community, and belonging, while Daniel's use of every part of the animal including 'offcuts and entrails' indicates an environmental sensibility that is attuned to issues of waste. The lengthy descriptive detail and the collective sentiments underpinning the act indicate that placed manifestations of community are more conducive to ethical values and meaningful democratic forms, but it also suggests the limits of isolationism.

Elmet's historical backdrop of deindustrialisation also works productively as a reterritorialisation of space and time. Chapter 3 identified how deindustrialisation has been represented in post-Brexit-vote fiction as a process of place, often manifesting in the present through nostalgia or in the material environment as a reminder of localised and identity-bearing manual labour. *Elmet* draws on the social qualities of industrial work in the revolt against Price as a form of collective action that prioritises a placed social network. For instance, the preparations and relationships forged by group meetings are inflected with a kind of reflective nostalgia for the camaraderie and economic stability of industrial labour and trade unions:

> The jobs had gone twenty years ago or more. There was just a couple of warehouses where you could get work shifting boxes into vans. At Christmas-time there were more boxes and more vans but still not enough. There were jobs here and there for women: hair-dressing jobs, nannying jobs, shop-assistant jobs, cleaning jobs, teaching-assistant jobs

if you had an education. But if you were a man and you wanted odd jobs or seasonal farm work [the carpark behind the Working Men's Club] was where you met.

(Mozley, 2017, p. 151)

This is what Sherry Lee Linkon calls the 'half-life' (Linkon, 2018, p. 1) of deindustrialisation, a temporal process in which the effects of deindustrialisation continue to manifest socially and culturally even if the community itself has developed a new economy. *Elmet* presents a contemporary neoliberal employment landscape shrouded in immobility and stasis, centred on low-skilled service work. The scene testifies to the ways globalisation brings about 'the uneven insertion of different territories and social formations into the capitalist world market' (Harvey, 1988, p. 49). Unable to recover from deindustrialisation and successive waves of governmental neglect, the area's employment opportunities are far from the promises of 'Global Britain'. Instead, individuals engage in a technologised, mass-produced globalised market from below. Rather than experiencing globalisation in the form of planetary connectivity and mobility, globalisation manifests itself in warehouse work and precarious forms of labour that do not offer a secure income but unstable work lifting boxes into vans before being transported across the globe.

While the deindustrial past appears to signify place-bound social relations and meaningful forms of embodied manual labour, *Elmet* presents a tentative and cautious view of the romanticisation of the past. Ewart, a former labourer and friend of John's, 'spoke of the way things had been when people who lived together in the same communities also worked together, drank together, voted together and went on strike together' (Mozley, 2017, p. 141). The self-actualising potential of manual labour enables a historicised and 'placed' mode of belonging, representing the 'spirit' and 'pride' (Mozley, 2017, pp. 171, 19) of both the work and the camaraderie that came with it. Yet, even this community spirit proves to be less aspirational than it at first appears. *Elmet* distinguishes between Boym's politically enabling reflective nostalgia and reactionary restorative nostalgia, with the novel cautioning against idealisation of the past. After one of their meetings, Vivien confronts Ewan's outright celebration of the industrial years, pointing out that '[t]hose men who would come together so naturally to support one another would go home drunk and beat their wives' (Mozley, 2017, p. 172). Vivien punctures Ewan's restorative nostalgia, stating that '[t]here are dreams, Ewart, and there are memories. And there are memories of dreams' (Mozley, 2017, p. 172). So, while the novel highlights the inequalities of the contemporary globalised world, *Elmet* does not offer a straightforward advocation of returning to the past as it emerges in both primitive isolation or the localised communities formerly associated with industrial work. Instead, Elmet's neo-primitive vision is shot through with social hierarchies, oppression, and marginalisation.

The novel's treatment of gender elsewhere also complicates neo-primitivism's political potential. While Mozley's neo-primitivism initially appears to facilitate anti-capitalist social and environmental practices and a meaningful place-bound affiliation, it is also characterised by a kind of 'primal' masculinity which is contingent upon acts of violence. John's livelihood has primarily been sustained by working for Price as a bare-knuckle fighter. Daniel tells us early on, that John has fought and killed men 'in the peat fields of Ireland' or 'in that black mud of Lincolnshire' (Mozley, 2017, p. 13), but never in gymnasiums or auditoriums. John is frequently likened to an animal throughout the novel, blurring the boundary between the 'human' and 'animal' to present the violence of bare-knuckle fighting as an innate characteristic of primitive masculinity. During a fight, John stands '[a]s still as a wolf. His eyes ... fixed on his prey' (Mozley, 2017, p. 218), with this physical prowess an essential part of John's identity, instilling primal animalism from which he draws physical and mental strength. Likewise, Vivian compares John's fights to the breach of great whales, suggesting that, for John, fighting serves a similar, almost meditative purpose: 'But bloodier, much bloodier. And it isn't a lone act. It's not just an animal and the elements. But it's the same. It quenches him' (Mozley, 2017, p. 95).

As the tension between John and Price reaches its apotheosis, John is eventually convinced to 'return to the fold' by Mr Price in the hope of winning the legal rights to the land. Here, the physicality of bare-knuckle fighting represents a neo-primitivist rejection of disembodied capitalist modes of production, offering a corporeal form of productive labour. As John explains:

> I win fights because I am suited to the rules of those fights, Cathy. They're a test of strength and speed and endurance and I am the strongest, fastest and toughest man in Britain and Ireland. But take away those rules and it's anyone's guess who'd win. If someone pulled a knife on me, or a gun ...
>
> (Mozley, 2017, p. 123)

John's admission creates a juxtaposition between capitalist and embodied labour. Bare-knuckle fighting's emphasis on the capabilities of the male body resists the ways in which global economies appear to prioritise technology – represented here by the knife or the gun – and an inherently disembodied labour form. Resembling the physical prowess of industrial work, Bill's world is 'about muscle' (Mozley, 2017, p. 21), pulling against the dominance of cognitive work under contemporary capitalism. The fact that John's body is 'all [he] owns', illustrates how, in *Elmet*'s gendered labour economy, the dematerialised currency of modernity has been replaced by the body as a form of corporeal economy (Mozley, 2017, p. 112).

At the same time, Mozley is careful to emphasise how John's primitive masculinity ultimately restrains him and limits his freedom in the present. John's physical capabilities keep him tethered to Mr Price and operate within a capitalist logic centred on the male body's exchange value. Keen to accumulate John's physical labour for his own ends, Mr Price monopolises John's reputation as 'the strongest, fastest and toughest man in Britain and Ireland' (Mozley, 2017, p. 123) as leverage in their long-standing feud. This commodification of the masculine body is clear in Price's warning to Daniel that, if John loses the fight, 'he must return to the fold' (Mozley, 2017, p. 200). Price boasts of earlier times when John would work for him, earning him money when individuals would bet on John's opponents during a fight. Price 'used to own' John's muscles and 'his mind …, his fists, and his feet, his eyes and his ears and his teeth' (Mozley, 2017, p. 200), echoing capitalism's hegemony and an economic system that reduces John's body to the parts that produce capital. Significantly, John's opponent, 'The Bear', has travelled to England from Eastern Europe. In this battle, the right to habitation rests on the defeat of a European 'other' figure. The fact that the the brown bear – the largest predator native to Britain – was last seen in England in Yorkshire between 425 and 594 (Briggs, 2018) indicates a bridging of medieval history and the present, and allegorises the tension between the English local and European integration as a process of globalisation. In *Elmet*, 'The Bear' is predatory once again, and comes to represent both the direct competition for labour power constituted by economic migrants from Eastern Europe and a burgeoning borderless world. As such, while *Elmet* utilises a neo-primitive mode insofar as it represents an environmentally conscious politics of place, the novel offers only a tentative prognosis for its potential as a democratic alternative to the unequal global present.

Simulated Neo-Primitivism and Archaeologies of Britishness: Sarah Moss' *Ghost Wall*

While *Elmet* presents us with a cautious engagement with neo-primitivism as a politics of place, *Ghost Wall*'s mobilisation of pre-modern lifeways is even more sceptical. In Moss' novel, the democratic and environmental affordances of neo-primitivism are tainted by a reactionary nostalgia for nation. This is a nostalgia which is rooted in xenophobia and sexism, emerging primarily as a means to simulate an 'authentic' British past. Bill's propensity for an ancestral British pre-history is a comment on a geographically and class-inflected stereotype played out during the run up to the EU Referendum and after, offering a satirical critique of the attachment to a mythological national past which, as we saw in the previous chapter, was associated with an equally mythological Leave-voting 'left behind' in the North. While the novel is clear in its condemnation of reactionary – and often xenophobic – attachments to a British national past, Moss attempts to go beyond polarising stereotypes to make visible the complexities underlying such views. More specifically, the narrative locates how successive waves of regional uneven development culminating in deindustrialisation, democratic deficit, and a profound lack of agency are bound up in ethno-purist attachments to nation.

Ghost Wall's title foregrounds Moss' concern with territory and the symbolic significance of borders. 'Ghost Wall' refers to a battlement made by Ancient Britons, on which hang the skulls of their ancestors. Intended to close off outsiders and reassert a blood claim to the land, Ghost Walls were 'more of a symbol, rather than a military necessity' (Moss, 2018, p. 45). Moss evokes one of the last attempts by the Ancient tribes to resist the Roman Empire, but also Hadrian's Wall. While Bill views Hadrian's Wall as proof that the 'Britons' threatened the Roman Empire, Professor Slade reveals that it is simply 'a marker' of 'the edge of empire, it's not to keep the barbarians out so much as to show where they are' (Moss, 2018, p. 25).[8] An archaeological symbol of Britain's own ongoing internal fragmentation, the wall indicates that Bill's search for 'Ancient Britain' is more about locating a pre-Roman *England* than a unified Britishness. In Bill's view, the repercussions of the Roman Conquest are tangible today, and he dedicates his life to reclaiming a pre-Roman 'pure' and 'authentic' Britishness through reproducing their lifeways and rituals. When Bill looks at the remains of the Roman Wall, Silvie notes how it 'was only a ditch, that first day, but at least it was a Roman ditch, a physical manifestation of Ancient British resistance marked on the land', with Bill 'drawing strength from it' (Moss, 2018, p. 26).[9] A slippage between England and Britain underpins the entire archaeological project; it is a product of the desire to find 'some tribe sprung from English soil like worms in the night' (Moss, 2018, p. 45). Bill's attraction to pre-history is emphatically Anglo-British, relying on a vision of England which is interchangeable with Britishness. While the novel remains sceptical of the destructive potential of nationalism, repeatedly drawing attention to the constructedness of 'nation', this slippage between England and Britain, along with references to the Roman invasion, Hadrian's Wall, and a concern with a close relationship with the land, all exist in tension with the way Britishness is experienced as a deterritorialised statehood, rather than a place-bound civic nationalism.

Ghost Wall's neo-primitivism centres on the mythic and spiritual qualities of the bog people, and their association with an ancestral blood-claim to the land. Living in a remote rural settlement as pre-modern hunter-gatherers, the lifeways Bill instils in his family and the university students are modelled on the lives of the Ancient British tribes, who sacrificed bodies to be preserved in bogs as part of a ritualistic practice. As both literal and symbolic bodies of the land, the bog people function in Bill's view as an archaeology of Britishness that is connected to geographical territory and historical lineage. *Ghost Wall* shifts temporally between Ancient Britain – indicated through the representation of sacrificial practices – and the 1990s. The novel's opening scene anticipates *Ghost Wall*'s ending, describing a female victim hanging over the bog as she occupies the liminal space between her present life and her future as a historical artefact. An omniscient narrative voice tells us that there is an art to holding her in the place she is entering now, on the edge of the water-earth, in the time and space between life and death, too late to return to the living and not time yet, not yet, not for a while, to be quite dead.

(Moss, 2018, p. 3)

Throughout the novel, the pre-modern rituals of putting bodies into the ground to be preserved allegorises Bill's desire for a place-bound identity and ancestral lineage. For him, the bog people represent an ancestral Britishness established through place, history, and violence.

What makes bogs an appropriate symbol of reterritorialisation is both their association with place and dwelling. The names of bog bodies are with very few exceptions place names – such as Tollund Man; Grauballe Man; Lindow Man; Yde Girl; Windeby Girl; Weerding Couple – gesturing towards a territorialised, place-bound affiliation. Bogs are also, notably, a liminal landmass – occupying the boundary between land and water – and the bog bodies themselves have a unique biological composition. Karin Sanders' explanation of the usages and particular biological properties of bogs is worth citing here:

The anaerobic condition of the bogs provides an environment that slows decomposition significantly. The bog water and the peat in some instances contain chemicals that naturally convert bodies into leather-like envelopes of preserved skin and hair. As a result, bodies in bogs have been able to survive for centuries with perfectly preserved features, fingerprints, nails, hair, and other distinct individual traits.

(Sanders, 2009, p. 2)

As Sanders notes, bogs have particular environmental associations, with the preservation of the bodies reliant entirely on climate conditions; the bogs must remain within a specific temperature range and not dry out, preventing the bodies from being exposed to the air. Yet, it is not the archaeological prospects of bogs or the biological features of preserved bodies that fascinate Bill; as Silvie tells us, her dad loved the fact that the bog people 'could now only exist as victim, as the objects of violence' (Moss, 2018, p. 69). Akin to *Elmet*, there is a clear environmental sub-text to *Ghost Wall*'s exploration of contemporary Britain and its socio-political fractures.[10] Frequent references to the wastage of food, energy, and natural resources indicate the novel's environmental consciousness, but for Bill, this awareness serves only as a legitimating pretext for his imperial desires. His neo-primitivism appears to be closer to a violent re-incarnation of *Elmet*'s environmentally oriented primitive aesthetics. Reading a book on a teenage girl recently recovered from a bog, Bill focuses only on the violence that might have caused her death, indicating an engagement with pre-history which is less about archaeological or ecological research, and more about the cruelty and recreation of social order through human sacrifice.

The ancestral qualities Bill attributes to the bog people and their rituals indicate that his fascination with this group is part of his imagination of Britishness predicated on bloodline. When Bill takes Silvie to a museum to see the Lindow Man, a bog body from Cheshire, he tells her 'that's where you come from, those folk, that's how it used to be' (Moss, 2018, p. 39), displacing the European origins of the bog people to present the body as a form of British heritage. The desire for the existence of a British pre-history is also evident in Silvie's description of her father's obsession:

> Dad would like to find a body up there, I thought, most of all he would like to be the one out gathering peat to see us through the winter, the one who, aching after hours of honest labour, leans on the spade once again, levers the clod that's lain for centuries over the compacted pre-historic trees of the peat bog and sees among the roots and frantic worms a human face, a face last seen two thousand years ago by the neighbours who led their friend naked across the moor, who bound him hand and foot.
>
> (Moss, 2018, p. 91)

Silvie's description of her father's desire for a version of Britishness he can excavate from the soil echoes a wider cultural functioning of the bog people, who have 'come to connote the sort of depth we associate with "roots" in the meaning of ancestry, pedigree, family tree, and national identity' (Sanders, 2009, p. 12). Bill's attachment to bog bodies alludes to an ethnonationalism centred on ancestry and deep historical lineage that is both articulated corporeally and heavily affiliated with place.

This place-bound sensibility is reiterated in Silvie's role as a pet project for Bill's obsession with Iron Age Britain. Her name speaks to the artifice underpinning Bill's mythologisation of Britishness and, according to the novel, originates from an Ancient British goddess. While Silvie believes her father's desire for her to 'have a proper native British name' (Moss, 2018, p. 18) is a product of his archaeological hobbies, the university students possess a degree of cultural capital attuned to the xenophobia underpinning Bill's primitive impulses. Pete diagnoses that

> he likes the idea that there's some original Britishness somewhere, that if he goes back far enough he'll find someone who wasn't a foreigner. You know it's not really British, right? I mean, Sulvia, its obviously just a version of Sylvia which means – *of the woods* in Latin, I said, yes, I do know, a Roman corruption of a lost British word.
>
> (Moss, 2018, p. 20)

The weight that Bill ascribes to ancestral lineage and a tangible, 'original' Britishness occurs in opposition to the perspective of the students, who understand the very idea of an innate Britishness to be a falsity. Bill wanted 'his own ancestry, … lineage, a claim on something. Not people from Ireland or Rome or Germania or Syria', echoing a regressive post-imperial nostalgia for a contracted and territorialised sense of national belonging (Moss, 2018, p. 45). It is also worth noting both the regional and Roman correlates of Silvie's name. According to Professor Slade, Sylvia is 'a local deity', a 'Northumbrian goddess of springs and pools, co-opted by the Romans' (Moss, 2018, p. 10). A product of the Celts and the Britons, the irony of Silvie's name forms another critique of the idea of Britishness as a 'native' identity to which one can return.

The intertextual significance of bogs in the wider context of the UK further complicates Bill's appropriation of the bog people as evidence of an 'original Britishness'. Seamus Heaney's well-studied 'bog poems' deploy the bog as a symbol for Irish national identity and its internal colonisation within the British Empire, with the poems becoming associated with The Troubles in Ireland.[11] Taken together, the literary significance of bogs in Heaney's poetry, *Ghost Wall*'s unspecified historical setting of the 1990s – a decade in which the Good Friday Agreement officially ended The Troubles – and Bill's outward hostility towards the Irish, all gesture towards a wider political backdrop of constitutional instability in the Union. While Heaney focused predominantly on the Danish bog (see 'The Tollund Man' and 'Punishment') to capture the violence of 1970s Ireland, in *Ghost Wall*, the sacrificial bog articulates mythologically a cycle of scapegoating and violence. Silvie tells us that her father 'didn't like the Irish, tended to see Catholicism in much as the earlier form of Roman imperialism', viewing them as 'foreigners' (Moss, 2018, p. 45). The Irish literary connection to bog people points to flaws in Bill's logic, an irony further intensified by the fact that bog bodies are found in several different countries and cultures, with many located in parts of Northern Europe (Sanders, 2009, p. 2).

Divisions of class and geography are also central to Moss' exploration of Brexit. The opposition between the regional stasis of 'Somewheres' and the infinitely mobile 'Anywheres' is played out in the dynamic between Bill and his family and Professor Slade and his students, who symbolise the local and the global, respectively. Professor Slade and his students are middle-class, educated, and well-travelled cosmopolites from a university in an unnamed part of the South of England. They appear to represent a stereotype of what Lisa Mckenzie describes as 'cosmopolitan Remainers' (Mckenzie, 2017, p. 271) who are typically middle-class, urban, white-collar professionals with significant levels of economic, social, and cultural capital. By contrast, Silvie's family are decidedly working-class; Silvie's mother is a supermarket cashier and her father, Bill, is currently a bus driver by trade, but not by choice, as his frequent nostalgic visits to Newcastle's industrial ruins and docklands suggest. These socio-cultural divisions map on to *Ghost Wall*'s exploration of globalisation, emphasising the complexities of discourses that dichotomise between an outward-facing cosmopolitan globalism and parochial localism. This is a duality which, as we saw in the previous chapter, dominated political and media discourses during Brexit. In *Ghost Wall*, primitivism's reconfiguration of contemporary social hierarchies complicate Brexit's narrative of division:

> The Professor appeared after breakfast and started organising people in a way that made me wonder if he thought they were Iron Age professors, or maybe as if he couldn't imagine that there were circumstances in which qualities other than being posh and having read a lot might put a person in charge of everyone else. My dad, I thought, knew as much as anyone about living wild off the land, foraging and fishing and finding your way.
>
> (Moss, 2018, p. 17)

In contrast to the university students and Professor Slade, Silvie and her father possess an intimate, 'ancient knowledge' of the environment that has been rendered meaningless in the global contemporary. In a similar way to John's environmental expertise in *Elmet*, *Ghost Wall* juxtaposes Bill's innate knowledge of the land against the metropolitan intellectualism held by Professor Slade, challenging the hierarchies of labour under neoliberal globalisation, which prioritise creative or cognitive work (see Florida, 2002). Bill's lifelong interest in the world of early Britons stems not from an elite education, but, rather, from nationalism.

After the socio-economic restructuring onset by deindustrialisation, Bill devotes himself to studying Roman Britain and establishes a relationship with several archaeologists; these are men 'who'd passed the eleven-plus and made summat of themselves, had begun to exchange his self-taught expertise in outdoor survival, foraging and mountain craft for their answer to his questions and offprints of their research' (Moss, 2018, p. 93). Here, *Ghost Wall* establishes a distinction between primitive 'self-taught expertise' and formally recognised knowledge, but more specifically, to the elitist education system of grammar schools associated with the Conservative Party. Moss references the inauguration of Britain's meritocratic education system whose hallmark feature was grammar schools and the eleven plus, communicating the way in which inequalities in Britain's post-war education system continue to structure twenty-first-century class struggle. For example, Bill's scepticism towards the intellectual elitism embodied by Slade recalls Michael Gove's now-infamous declaration that 'people in this country have had enough of experts' (Mance, 2016). This rhetorical stance was aimed to stir up, and quickly became attributed to, working-class groups residing in small towns or rural areas – typically with low levels of progression to university – perceived as being 'left behind'.

In contrast to the curricular knowledge prioritised by formal education, Silvie is preoccupied with environmental learnings:

> I indulged myself with the idea that ancient knowledge runs somehow in our blood, that in time I could forget who fought in the War of the Spanish Succession and how to solve quadratic equations, and

remember how to spin yarn and grind grain, to read the flight of birds and the growth of plants to tell me what was happening beyond my sight. My father's skills: redundant except for archaeological purposes.

(Moss, 2018, p. 106)

Silvie locates the complexities and double-edged nature of primitivism, emphasising how it prioritises a now-redundant environmental conscious-ness rooted in an ecological sustainability. Upon leaving the urban area in which she lives and moving to the experiment's isolated rural environment, Silvie describes a reorientation towards the land. This is especially the case, Silvie reflects, when wearing Iron Age clothing:

you move differently in moccasins, you have a different experience of the relationship between feet and land. You go around and not over rocks, feel the texture, the warmth of different kinds of reed and grass in your muscles and skin.

(Moss, 2018, p. 27)

Silvie's visceral, grounded spatiality opposes the time-space compression's deterritorialising tendencies and points towards the need for alternative, and placed, environmental practices in the present. Like *Elmet*'s environmental ethics of place, *Ghost Wall* draws connections between primitive isolation and environmental sustainability to critique the technologised, mass-production methods of the present. The archaeological experiment relies on an emphatically pre-industrial form of labour and production; the spinning of yarn and grinding of grain evokes a corporeal, embodied labour which, in Bill's case, suggests a displaced desire for industrial work.

The association of Professor Slade and his students with a cosmopolitan outlook and citizenship further emphasises *Ghost Wall*'s narrative of division. The students' ability to perceive the world as unhindered by borders contrasts with Silvie's limited spatial optic. She cannot comprehend the other students' spatial freedom in contrast to her own relative immobility, with Silvie's limited concept of the world extending only as far as the nearest town. The ordinary places she visits with her father comprise Silvie's world:

We held hands and I trotted, as always, to keep up with him, past the butcher where the pork and lamb and beef in the window were divided from each other like the animals on the toy farm at school by plastic grass, past the Post Office where I went with Mum every Thursday straight after school to pick up the Child Benefit and we queued on the dusty lino floor around the metal barriers, because Thursday was also the day you collected your pension so there were old ladies with sweets in their handbags for little girls who knew how to be winsome, which I didn't, mostly.

(Moss, 2018, p. 37)

There is a sense of ordinariness in this routine: the local shop, school, and post office are everyday places in the town, but they nevertheless form the boundaries of Silvie's world. The certainty with which Silvie explains that Thursday was the day you collected your child benefit, but also the day you received your pension, articulates an existence marked by cyclicality and sameness. Even Silvie eventually begins to recognise that her childhood has been far removed from the external world, describing university as an opportunity to 'leave childhood and dependence behind, to enter the world' (Moss, 2018, p. 29).

While *Ghost Wall* predominantly offers a critique of the reactionary qualities of the primitive, the novel also foregrounds the socio-economic structures that have contributed to Bill's character. Indeed, what is notable about *Ghost Wall's* socio-economic and geographic tensions – between a metropolitan cosmopolitanism and regional stasis – is their historicisation within a distinctly deindustrial frame that makes visible Northern England's long-term marginalisation. One example of this is when Silvie recalls her life prior to the re-enactment. She describes childhood memories in which Bill would take her to see the ruins of the docks in Newcastle:

> I followed him across the concrete waste. Cranes reared above us *like ceremonial pillars of a lost civilisation*, intricate with rust and disintegration. The windflowers and morning glory that are either holding together or pulling apart England's abandoned buildings and roads and railways flattened under the weather. Look at this, he said, look at it. Used to send ships all over the world from, here. Look at it now.
>
> (Moss, 2018, p. 23, my emphasis)

Here, once again, is a deindustrial landscape, similar to that which we have encountered in the work of Sahota, Thorpe, and Cartwright. The detailed description of the relics of industrialisation as 'pillars of a lost civilization' registers Bill's disaffection with globalisation's shift away from the production methods of local industries to deterritorialised global networks of finance capital. This passage complicates Bill's primitive nostalgia. His mourning for an industrial past suggests that his obsession with Ancient Britain itself is a reaction to the loss of a placed, manual trade heavily associated with masculinity, and the unequal present in which globalisation is experienced through disintegration, abandonment, and loss. Bill's preoccupation with Newcastle's industrial past registers a history of uneven development that has been exacerbated by globalisation, presenting neo-primitivism as a reaction to the inequalities of global capitalism and the spatial biases of British urban modernity.

This stasis and isolation from 'the world' are attributed to the family's status as 'Northerners'. Silvie does not realise until she meets the students that she and her family live 'up north' – 'up from where?' (Moss, 2018, p. 94), she wonders, when the university students talk about their experiences of Northern England as though it is an exotic country. Indeed, *Ghost Wall* points to a persistent, socio-spatial discourse whereby the North is presented as England's 'other' space, or, as Rob Shields writes 'as the complete antithesis to the civilization of the southern metropolises' (Shields, 1991, p. 5). In the novel, this 'otherness' is not only a result of material socio-economic inequality, but also geographic distance from London. The metropolitan lens of the students and Professor Slade is acutely visible when they mock Silvie's mother's accent, to which Silvie retorts: 'It's not another country, the North of England, it's not that far from you' (Moss, 2018, p. 95). Silvie and her family's Northernness reinforces their alienation and positions them at odds with the global urban modernity associated with the university students, highlighting how globalisation is inherently a metropolitan project, perceived as operating far away from the hinterlands of rural or post-industrial areas of Northern England. The trope of the North as 'other' is reiterated in the students' and the Professor's approach to the experiment as a whole. They are seeking only a 'flavour' (Moss, 2018, p. 7) of Iron Age life, while the re-enactment becomes part of Silvie and her family's lived reality. These differing approaches to the project enact a fundamental social cleavage during Brexit between an educated metropolitan elite and non-metropolitan – often deindustrial – working-class communities, in which the legitimate socio-economic concerns in Leave-voting towns were diagnosed as ailments of regional backwardness, cultural hostility, and parochial trivialities.

Elmet and *Ghost Wall* thus utilise the political efficacy of primitivism as a territorialising force. At the same time, though, these novels foreground the limits of neo-primitivism as a social practice reliant on social isolation and one which is at risk of reproducing oppressive social structures. Indeed, what is notable about *Ghost Wall*'s use of neo-primitivism is its self-conscious reflexivity. Unlike Mozley's naturalisation of environmental neo-primitive practices, Moss continually foregrounds constructed nature as a simulation. The novel hinges on a temporal tension between Ancient Britain and the modernity of the present, frequently foregrounding the contradictions inherent in Bill's psyche and the artifice of the re-enactment. Indeed, a key social division in the novel is the fact that Professor Slade and his students only ever play around with the idea of Ancient British life. As Silvie points out, 'the Professor's dodging of bloodshed pretty thoroughly messed up the idea that our experiences that summer were to rediscover the lifeways of pre-modern hunter-gatherers' (Moss, 2018, p. 10). Unlike *Elmet, Ghost Wall*'s neo-primitivism is overtly represented as an 'experiment' (Moss, 2018, p. 30). Silvie's quick-witted – often humorous – first-person narration primarily communicates this artifice. While largely sympathetic towards her father's desires, Silvie's internal monologue indexes the hypocrisy of her father's beliefs, and how he too is experiencing only a select version of Iron Age life. For example, Silvie critiques her father's idealisation of patriarchal social hierarchies, and reveals how Bill's rules are upheld only insofar as they reinforce his dominance over the group or suit his particular whims.

Silvie recalls how tampons were eventually won as a concessionary item, after Bill asserts that 'in the old days women weren't going round forever bleeding all over the place' (Moss, 2018, p. 13). Similarly, Silvie recognises the injustice of Bill's anger because she and her mother had overslept, 'when he'd made us leave our watches at home and kept talking about a world without clocks' (Moss, 2018, p. 15). Although Bill asserts that Iron Age British '[f]olk lived by their bellies and the sun' (Moss, 2018, p. 15), his desire for a return to solar time is compromised by a concurrent reliance on the social organisation of time.

Even the supposed 'wildness' of the re-enactment's location in rural Northumberland contradicts Bill's pre-modern sensibilities. Inflected with traces of tourism and modern agriculture, Moss situates the re-enactment within a rural environment which is clearly marked by human influence. The ecology of the landscape is not suited to hunter-gathering; when Silvie and the students are sent to nearby moorlands to forage for their evening meal, they can source only bilberries from this human-made landscape which, as Dan points out, has been specially cultivated for sheep farming. The narrative continually foregrounds how Northumberland's landscape has historically been shaped by human interests. Silvie notes how a 'green sign-posted footpath' stands out on their route, also commenting on how Hadrian's Wall looks like 'someone had drawn it with a ruler on a photo' (Moss, 2018, p. 23). The experiment's location in a rural landscape cultivated in the interest of both farming and tourism – and its proximity to another human-made border – reflects the impossibility of achieving an 'authentic' version of primitivism and, in turn, an authentic or 'original' Britishness.

The inability of *Ghost Wall*'s neo-primitivism to exist at a remove from mainstream society indicates a kind of critical self-reflexivity, embodying what Victor Li describes as a 'contaminated' neo-primitive 'alterity' (Li, 2006, p. 32). Drawing on the work of Jean Baudrillard, Li proposes a sub-genre of neo-primitive 'alterity' that encompasses '[p]articular, local forms of otherness [which] have been mobilized in the struggle against the universalizing metanarratives of a Eurocentric modernity' (Li, 2006, p. 122). Crucially, the 'radical otherness' and authenticity of this version of neo-primitivism is undermined by its inability to exist outside of capitalist structures. As he explains, 'though the primitive has not vanished completely, in its present hybridized or contaminated form, it can no longer be posed as a radical alterity or alternative to Western modernity' (Li, 2006, p. 32). A similarly 'hybridized' or 'contaminated' neo-primitivism characterises *Ghost Wall*'s experiential archaeology. The novel increasingly grapples with a temporal tension between pre-history and the present, with remnants of contemporary capitalism tainting the apparent 'authenticity' of the re-enactment. For example, when Molly convinces Silvie to take a break from foraging to visit the local Spar, Silvie notes her fascination at the presence of ice creams, Hula Hoops, and Mars bars and how she 'had almost forgotten to behave in the presence of electric lights and painted walls' (Moss, 2018, p.

82). Molly gradually becomes disillusioned with the project, noticing Bill's inability to separate the re-enactment from reality and how he and Professor Slade are focused more on fighting rather than hunter-gathering. This realisation leads to a tension between her and Silvie, who retorts:

> Of course I know it's not real, I said, but none of this is real, is it, this whole summer, the blankets came from a shop and you lot made the moccasins on a study day and the Prof had the grains delivered from the health food shop in Morbury, that's not the point. So what is the – she said.
>
> (Moss, 2018, pp. 121–122)

The objects' inauthenticity demonstrates how Bill's primitivist project is only an idealised simulation of the past, echoing Li's definition of neo-primitivism 'as a simulacrum, a model constructed by the human sciences precisely to replace the vanished or vanishing original' (Li, 2006, p. 53). The visibly constructed re-enactment alludes to the ways in which an 'anti-capitalist' or primitive way of life has been commodified to 'oppose Western modernity through its valorisation of primitive alterity, only to reveal its complicity with modernity's nostalgic fantasy of recovering premodern losses' (Li, 2006, p. 40). Allusions to the pre-modern or 'tribal' authenticity are ubiquitous in contemporary culture. In the health and fitness industry specifically, there has been a recent resurgence of faux tribalism, demonstrated in the popularity of 'Xtreme' sports alongside the commodification of thrift and vintage clothing, the Paleo diet, and digital minimalism (cf. Pitcher, 2022). Thus, while it might be tempting to read *Ghost Wall*'s neo-primitivism as a straightforward antithesis of modernity, it is only a simulation of pre-modern ethics. *Ghost Wall*'s neo-primitive mode might thus be read as a *product* of the broader globalising forces of capitalism, a symptom of post-modern nostalgia for a pre-modern past.

The novel's exploration of gender hierarchies, culminating in the denouement, renders the blurred boundary between reality and simulacra starkly visible, functioning as an allegorical warning against mythologising the pre-modern past. Like *Elmet*, *Ghost Wall* critiques neo-primitivism's ability to legitimate systems of oppression, with violence against women entrenched in both Mozley's environmental primitivism and Moss' neo-primitive re-enactment of Ancient British life. The numerous contradictions of Bill's belief system are bound in misogyny, an essentialist attitude towards gender roles, and the desire to govern women's bodies. Bill possesses a 'stretchy' version of Ancient British life that is contingent upon female oppression. Like Cathy, Silvie's gender dictates her participation in social activities; during the novel's first pages, she observes the male university students 'creeping off somewhere to do some boys' thing at which [she] would probably be more skilled' (Moss, 2018, p. 4). Again, mirroring Cathy's narrative in *Elmet*, Silvie's oppression manifests itself in a primal masculinity contingent upon successfully performing acts of physical violence. Bill exemplifies this kind of masculinity, legitimised through the guise of Iron Age rituals. Bill beats Silvie and her mother at times for no other reason than he just 'needed to' (Moss, 2018, p. 65) however, when Bill catches Silvie swimming naked in the lake, the threat of the female body results in a particularly severe beating. In a similar way to John's reaction to the physicality of bare-knuckle fighting, Bill appears to draw strength from the attack: 'it went on for longer than usual, as if the open air invigorated him, as if he liked the setting' (Moss, 2018, p. 62). Bill's physical violence against Silvie is almost a convalescence; the combination of the rural environment, the Iron Age belt, and a female victim enmesh in this scene to create the kind of power Bill associates with Ancient British life: that of misogyny and violence.

This blurring is intensified at the end of the novel, with Silvie's conscription into her father's ritualistic desires. This turn in the novel's neo-primitivist project is anticipated in an earlier scene, when the leader of the group's basket-weaving workshop explains to Silvie that replicas are made so that 'you can test them to destruction if you need to' (Moss, 2018, p. 33). *Ghost Wall*'s denouement sees the re-enactment 'tested to destruction' when Bill sacrifices Silvie to the bog:

> [T]hey wanted to kill me at sunset. To march me up onto the moor to the beat of the drums and the bass chanting, to tie my hands and my feet, to put a rope around my neck that could be tightened and loosened for as long as blades and rocks could hold me wavering between life and death.
>
> (Moss, 2018, p. 136)

The novel's denouement is a final reminder of the dangers of romanticising a mythological past. Silvie is stripped and taken to the edge of the bog, mirroring the female sacrifice on which the novel opens – here, reality and simulacra are rendered indistinguishable from one another. Bookended with scenes of female sacrifice, *Ghost Wall*'s cyclical narrative imagines neo-primitivism as more suited to reinforcing social systems of oppression than alternative egalitarian futures. If *Elmet* presents us with a self-consciously tentative mobilisation of primitivism, this criticality is reflected and, in many ways intensified, in *Ghost Wall*'s emphasis on the human cost of nostalgia and its inability to operate outside the structures of global capitalism.

Between Anywhere and Somewhere

Elmet and *Ghost Wall* thus offer guarded prognoses of neo-primitivism as a placed social and environmental alternative to 'Global Britain'. In terms of the efficacy of these novels as Brexit ecocriticism, while *Elmet*'s environmental primitivism appears to get closer to imagining an alternative egalitarian democracy based on ecological sustainability, the re-emergence of oppressive violence and social isolation undermines the local networks and social collectivity forged through neo-primitive lifeways. In *Ghost Wall*, neo-primitivism primarily emerges as the product of a reactionary nostalgia for an ethnopurist Britishness and cannot be imagined outside the structures of capitalist modernity. Taken together, these novels provide only a 'contaminated' neo-primitive mode as an aesthetics of place, registering the difficulty of imagining a post-British, progressive future for Northern England.

Despite this critical complexity, neo-primitivism indicates an ongoing need for the reconceptualisation of place-bound modes of belonging that goes beyond Brexit's polarising logic, and in which Northern England is not seen as necessarily regressive, anachronistic, or insular. This chapter has sought to show how *Elmet* and *Ghost Wall* provide placed Northern literary responses to 'Global Britain' in the post-Brexit-vote period. The inherently localised manifestations of neo-primitivism in *Elmet* and *Ghost Wall* attempt to reterritorialise England as a heterogeneous and politically active place, opposing the British state's appropriation of globalisation as a politics of nation. Contrary to the idea that globalisation will see the world 'shrink' and become 'one place' (Robertson, 1992, p. 8), the two texts I have considered here attempt to forge placed social and democratic practices in North Yorkshire and Northumberland. What these two novels suggest, then, is the need for a reconceptualisation of the relationship between the local and the global that goes beyond a simplistic dualism between a London-centred global Britain on the one hand and English regional or local isolationism on the other.

In this context, it is notable that both novels position their young-adult narrators as remedial counterpoints to the regressive correlates of primitivism exhibited in both texts. Occupying the space between childhood and adulthood, Daniel and Silvie also operate at the intersection of primitivism and modernity and can navigate these two opposing ideologies. Silvie dreams of freedom and entering the world of the university students but is simultaneously able to rationalise her father's obsessions, possessing an ecological understanding of the outdoors that they do not. As she tells us, '[i]t was not that I didn't understand why my father loved these places, this outdoor life. It was not that I thought houses were better' (Moss, 2018, p. 6). So, while Bill's neo-primitivism manifests in a reactionary attachment to a mythological British history that never existed in the way he imagines, Silvie's neo-primitivism is markedly more forward-looking and attuned to the social and environmental issues of the present. Rather than evoking the past, Silvie's neo-primitivism represents an ethical underpinning for a more environmentally conscious future. Likewise, despite Daniel's affection for the ecosystems of his local environment, his lessons with Vivien result in him becoming fascinated by 'history and poetry and her travels around France and Italy and about art' and he begins to see a 'world that suited me in a different way' (Mozley, 2017, p. 88). Noting a growing difference in disposition between himself and Cathy, Daniel tells us how he 'came to prefer the inside to the outside .... And while I sat and read and drank tea,

Cathy walked or ran through the fields and woods and, in her own way, she read the world too' (Mozley, 2017, p. 88). It is in this non-hierarchical co-existence of two separate worlds that these novels imagine an alternative future for their respective geographies within Yorkshire and the North East most successfully, offering visions of social relations centred on hospitality, empathy, and environmental ethics.

These momentary, optimistic glimpses of social relations occurring *within* a modern frame emerge for a final time at the end of both novels. *Ghost Wall* ends with Silvie being rescued from Bill and Professor Slade's ritual by Molly and the police before she is taken to stay in the safety of an acquaintance in the nearest city. Similarly, in *Elmet's* closing scene, Daniel waits in Edinburgh train station on the off chance he might find Cathy at the most Northern point of the railway line, watching 'the web of tracks that bring people to this city from every point of the compass' (Mozley, 2017, p. 309). What Daniel and Silvie come to represent, then, is the possibility of a placed England which is capable of navigating global modernity and its consequences, posing a challenge to the Unionist narrative of 'Global Britain'. This is a project which is commensurate with a new literary vision of Northern England that goes beyond regional stereotype, insularity, and otherness. In this context, a progressive and placed literary North has never been more politically urgent or timely.

Notes

1 Throughout this chapter, I deploy the term 'neoliberal globalisation' to acknowledge that neoliberalism and globalisation are not mutually exclusive processes and effectively coincided to create a singular and dominant capitalist economic model throughout the UK in the 1970s and 1980s.

2 See Parita Mukta and David Hardiman's study of the ecological sensibilities epitomised in the noble savage as a form of nostalgia: Mutka, P. and Hardiman, D. (2000), 'The Political Ecology of Nostalgia', *Capitalism, Nature, Socialism*, 11 (1), pp. 113–133.

3 See Victor Li's account of primitivism's colonial uses in Li, V. (2006), *The Neo-Primitivist Turn: Critical Reflections on Alterity, Culture, and Modernity*. Toronto: University of Toronto Press.

4 It is also worth noting that Hughes has been identified as contributing to the decentralising momentum in regional poetry in the post-Thatcher period. James Underwood argues, with reference to Hughes' work, that 'behind "diversity" and "regional inequality" there usually lies a history of political, economic and social trauma – the very factors that make divergence necessary' (Underwood, 2019, p.164). See Underwood, J. (2019), 'Pit Closure as Art', in Eileen Pollard and Berthold Schoene (eds) *British Literature in Transition: Accelerated Times, 1980–2000*, Cambridge: Cambridge University Press, pp. 162–177).

5 See the 'One Yorkshire' devolution agreement which is still being pursued by eighteen local authorities across the region: https://www.york.gov.uk/council/one-yorkshire-devolution/1 [accessed 14 December 2020].

6 The intertextual link to Wuthering Heights is also signified in the name of 'Cathy' for *Elmet's* female protagonist.

7 Other examples of this trend might include the novels of Ben Myers, Jenn Ashworth's *Fell* (2016), and Daisy Johnson's *Everything Under* (2017).

8 It is worth pointing out that Moss acknowledges that those involved in the fight against the Romans would not have identified as British. In response to Bill's valorisation of Britishness, Professor Slade replies: 'Celts, we tend to call them these days though they wouldn't have recognised the idea, they seem to have come from Brittany and Ireland, from the West' (Moss, 2018, p. 45).

9 Given the novel's concern with reactionary nationalism, further parallels may be drawn here to 'the wall', Donald Trump's proposed extension of the Mexico–US barrier.

10 The environmental thrust of *Ghost Wall* emerges more forcefully in Moss' most recent novel, *Summerwater* (2020). Set in a rural holiday park in Scotland in the aftermath of the EU Referendum, the novel explores Brexit within a wider frame of climate crisis, making several references to Britain's reliance on EU support for ecological conservation.

11 Rob Giblett notes Heaney's popular cultural association with the bog as a symbol of Irish national identity. See Giblett, R. (1996) *Postmodern Wetlands: Culture, History, Ecology*. Edinburgh: Edinburgh University Press, p. 245.

Conclusion: Regional Development and the 'Cultural Turn'

The regional English question at the core of *Rewriting the North* shows no sign of waning. Whether under the banner of the 'Northern Powerhouse', 'Midlands Engine', 'Levelling Up', or 'Build Back Better', geographic inequality remains hot on Britain's cultural and political agenda. In the run-up to the 2019 General Election, Boris Johnson homed in on England's so-called 'Red Wall' in a series of pledges to invest in neglected areas of England. However, like George Osborne's Northern Powerhouse rhetoric and Theresa May's promise to serve Britain's 'ordinary working-class families' (May, 2016b), Johnson's claim to solve England's persistent socio-economic and geographic imbalances materialised as an empty mantra, the distinct objectives of which were difficult to parse from previous regional policies (Tomaney and Pike, 2020, p. 43). Rather than being a year of 'Levelling Up', 2020 witnessed the limitations of regional devolution as divisions between several metro mayors in the North and Westminster hardened with renewed significance during the Covid-19 pandemic. Westminster's decision to force Greater Manchester into Tier 3 before reaching a deal regarding financial support communicated publicly the power disparities between local and regional governments and Westminster. Despite the political fallout generated by the stand-off between the Johnson Government and Andy Burnham (Greater Manchester) and Steve Rotherham (Liverpool), the structural weakness of the metro mayors' position meant that there was little subsequent political follow-up and no institutional change. This episode triggered a renewed focus on the nature of devolution in the English context and the highly asymmetrical character of the power relationship between centre and periphery (see Giovannini, 2020; Harris, 2020; Kenny and Sheldon, 2020; Morphet, 2021).

The geographic inequalities thrown into relief by Covid-19 also generated an explosion of government-led interventions which harnessed Britain's cultural industries as instruments of regional development. As part of a national response to counter the impact of the pandemic, the government launched its Cultural Recovery Fund while Arts Council England and the National Lottery established their 'Priority Places and Levelling Up for Culture Places' fund. The latter earmarked 108 places for targeted

DOI: 10.4324/9781003388722-8

investment between 2021–2024, with forty-two in the North, twenty-nine in the Midlands, twenty-two in the South-East, and fifteen in the South-West. These developments provide evidence of a 'cultural turn' in governmental approaches to addressing regional imbalance. In 2016, the UK's first Culture White Paper in fifty years pledged a focus on the cultural sector as part of a localised approach to economic development, with Arts Council England and the Heritage Lottery Fund later announcing a £20-million investment to place-making projects under the 'Great Places Scheme'. Aiming to highlight the ability of culture to generate income, creative place-making projects utilise arts activities as drivers of economic recovery and changing perceptions of declining urban areas. To date, cultural interventions associated with the funds have targeted formerly industrial towns and cities across the UK (mostly in the North of England), including Liverpool, Manchester, Kingston Upon Hull, Bradford and Glasgow. While the preceding chapters of this book have focused on formal, aesthetic, and thematic literary engagement with devolutionary questions, this concluding chapter aims to initiate a critical discussion of 'place-based' cultural policy in Britain. That is, the way that regional development initiatives augment the state's devolutionary agenda by addressing spatial inequality through 'cultural transformation' or the commercialisation of local 'cultural heritage', deflecting attention from larger structural problems. I want to end, then, by proposing that the regional-constitutional tensions explored throughout this book have been complemented by an emphatically centralised governmental cultural policy in Britain, and that future literary-critical assessments of the North must account for these wider ideological conditions of production and reception.

The UK 'City of Culture' scheme – inspired by the larger European Capital of Culture – is a highly developed expression of a government-led creative-industries framework designed to instrumentalise culture as a tool to bolster the economy. Often awarding bids from deprived areas, City of Culture aims to 'attract media attention, encourage national tourism and change perceptions' (DCMS, 2014, p. 4) through cultural transformation. In 2013 the Department for Culture, Media and Sport announced that Hull would be UK City of Culture in 2017. The award promised a renaissance for Hull, once celebrated as a great port city shortly behind London and Liverpool, leading to a programme of cultural activities and art pieces across the city. The installation of a 75-metre wind turbine sculpture, 'Blade', in Queen Victoria Square kicked off the festivities. The sculpture was a nod to the decision by Siemens, a German technology giant, to locate its turbine blade factory in Hull, bringing a £310-million investment which would rewrite the city's identity from a former fishing port to a global player in renewable energy. As far as cultural regeneration goes, 'Blade' is unique in referring to private economic investment – rather than arts activities - as a driver of regional recovery. However, the fact that the City of Culture positioned the sculpture at the fore of their cultural programme indicates a governmental approach to addressing regional inequality founded on utilising the creative industries as instruments of economic renewal. Indeed, a new identity for the city as a success story of governmental intervention was at the core of plans for Hull's development. This re-imagining primarily played out in the city centre, which was transformed into a cultural-creative hub. City of Culture left the trading history of the Humber Dock area in the Old Town unrecognisable: once the 'stock exchange' of Hull, the warehouses of the Fruit Market became bars, restaurants, galleries, and arts venues. With 'Change is happening' daubed across the brick walls, these buildings embodied architecturally Hull's commercial framing as an evolving urban enterprise, perfectly poised to look to the future.

Beyond Hull's now-gentrified Old Town, however, the city tells a different story. Promotional materials flaunt the language of change across the windows of retail spaces, but in places like Whitefriargate, they serve only to conceal long-term vacancy. Demonstrating that more is needed to secure Hull's long-term economic recovery, these empty buildings painted with the rhetoric of renewal eerily embody the fate of places selected for City of Culture after the programme ends. Indeed, the scheme has often been critiqued as a market-focused 'rebranding' exercise with the competition for visitors and investment offering limited long-term benefit for local cultural workers (Mooney, 2004; Wharton, Fenwick, and Fawcett, 2010) or the area's demographic more widely. The marketisation of 'local heritage' is perhaps a consequence of the way that policymakers involved in Hull's City of Culture programme aimed to replicate the successes of earlier models in Liverpool (European Capital of Culture) and Glasgow (City of Culture), whose 'aggressive branding strategies exploit[ed] local identity as a marketing device' (Howcroft, 2021, p. 47).

Moreover, a second narrative of transformation – from regional backwater to cosmopolitan world player – was vital in Hull's rebranding as the city's economic decline had been vital in its designation as City of Culture. The bid document evoked the city's past economic hardships, proposing that Hull was now 'finding its place in the UK, a city coming out of the shadows and re-establishing its reputation as a gateway that welcomes the world' (Hull2017, 2013). It could hardly have been predicted at the time of the announcement in 2013, but four years later, Hull's cosmopolitan, City of Culture status was perceived by some as contradictory (see Araujo, 2017). For policymakers, City of Culture signified the openness and cosmopolitanism of the host city (Howcroft, 2021), whereas post-Brexit media attention remained fixed on Hull returning one of the highest Leave-voting majorities in the country. According to the English Indices of Deprivation, Hull remains within the top ten poorest local authorities in the UK, a position the district has held on to for decades (Noble, 2019). The economic boost brought by City of Culture award was fleeting, offering little to alleviate the impact of long-term austerity.

The disconnection between the commercial narrative of Hull's 'cultural transformation' and the area's ongoing economic hardship is not specific to the city's circumstances or the City of Culture programme. Rather, it is a symptom of Britain's interconnected cultural and political economy, which takes as its expressive form centralised approaches to localised cultural policy. This interconnection is detectable in the ideological paradox of interventions like City of Culture, which purport to be 'place-making' policy interventions focused on the priorities of local communities (see Umney and Symon, 2020) but are administered from the top down. An illustrative example of this paradox is that funding for these schemes tends to be distributed through a centralised national body like Arts Council England, after which projects are delivered on the ground by smaller organisations.[1] There is much to take issue with here, not least the problem of a narrow, instrumentalist approach to 'culture' as a tool to reach 'managerial goals' (see Wharton, Fenwick, and Fawcett , 2010). Nevertheless, the paradox of a 'top-down' approach to 'place-based' cultural intervention is that it replicates the stabilising logic of political devolution: a larger, power-holding body grants temporary autonomy to a subordinate region. Likewise, it is notable that these interventions and their associated pots of funding tend to frame regional development as a part of a larger *national* project. Arts Council England, for example, describes its 2021–2024 Delivery Plan as 'strengthening our place-based approach and supporting levelling up' (Arts Council England, 2021), harnessing a governmental discourse of regional development that operates for the sole purpose of strengthening the entire nation. What this demonstrates is that the 'discomforting link' (Fowler, 2008, p. 6) between Britain's cultural and political economies has found expression in a centralising narrative of regional regeneration.

Manchester's unique development evidences this cultural and political recentralisation in a different way. The city has served as the primary location for commercial and governmental attempts to rebalance England's economy to the extent that, as Alex Beaumont argues, it 'occupies a contradictory status as a unique space' of neoliberal investment and as 'metonymic stand-in for Northern England' (Beaumont, 2015). An illustrative example of this contradictory status is the Northern Powerhouse, which since 2014 has focused on big-ticket infrastructural projects which would, according to George Osborne, put the North of England on an equal footing with London. In the Northern Powerhouse's early years, Osborne promised to make 'the cities of the north a powerhouse for the economy again' (Osborne, 2014), but delivered such a promise simply by making London more accessible to the Northern regions. Thus far, Northern Powerhouse policies have concentrated on establishing greater transport links to London for big cities like Manchester, Liverpool, and Birmingham, which would effectively facilitate the flow of labour to the capital city. The proposal of a high-speed rail link (HS2) to connect cities across the North to London is complementary to regional devolution's aim to deliver centralised policy more effectively to the regions. Less than three years after nine out of ten referendums in English cities rejected directly elected mayors, Osborne introduced a 'one-size-fits-all' executive mayor model for English governance. Like HS2, this model appeared to forget anywhere beyond Northern England's big cities. Northern Powerhouse's urban-metropolitan bias promised little beyond re-centralising finance and political power in cities across England, neglecting the region's towns, villages, rural areas, and coastal edge lands that comprise some of the most deprived areas of the country. Despite the project's promise to address a range of economic, cultural, and infrastructural regional disparities, the idea of a 'Northern Powerhouse' materialised as more of 'a label which can be applied to often pre-existing policies to give them coherence, focus and portray the government as acting for the North' (Lee, 2017, p. 480). Ultimately, the policies of the Northern Powerhouse reflect a centralising logic of administrative delegation, posing little threat to Britain's political status quo.

This governmental and infrastructural recentralisation has been matched in the cultural sphere by the establishment of Northern outposts of the BBC in Salford's MediaCityUK and HarperNorth in Manchester. MediaCityUK's Salford office is a consequence of a BBC initiative that aimed to position the corporation as less London-centric in the run-up to the renewal of its Royal Charter in 2007, with the objective of being more representative of their license fee payers. In economic terms, although the proposal was partly approved on the basis that it would 'be of considerable benefit to not only [the Salford Quays], the city as a whole, and the region in general', many of the additional jobs created were taken up by workers relocating from outside Greater Manchester (Salford City Council, 2006, p. 71; Bäing and Wong, 2018, p. 532). As an inherently corporate incursion, Salford's BBC office effectively made large parts of Manchester more attractive to a metropolitan – and often commuter – demographic, going hand in hand with the gentrification of the city's former industrial quarters as 'a nostalgic part of the heritage industry' (O'Neill, 2017, p. 288). In any case, despite the BBC's attempt to rebalance the disparity between its London base and its viewers, the corporation's vision remains staunchly centred on England's capital city, merely creating a dialogue between the continuing powerbase in London and the 'Northern' outpost in Salford (see Christophers, 2008, p. 2314).

Manchester's successful application for UNESCO City of Literature status in 2017 solidified its commercial rebranding as a part of the heritage industry. The city's libraries and cultural hotspots were readily marketed as powerhouses of Northern writing in an events programme that celebrated the decentralisation of Britain's cultural economy, with Manchester a success story of the nation's apparent 'levelling up'. However, as Sarah Brouillette points out, UNESCO's institutional resources 'tend to support and sustain existing metropolitan markets for culture, where relatively wealthy and leisured consumers are assumed to power the dynamism of the creative economy' (Brouillette, 2014, p. 101). UNESCO's tendency to accelerate the economic development of existing, largely middle-class, cultural centres replicates the urban and Manchester-centric bias of the Northern Powerhouse. In framing the city's civic spaces as proof of Northern

England's cultural value, Manchester's City of Literature status has offered a success story of the region's 'levelling up' in the absence of adequate structural change.

The concentration of 'devolved' Northern cultural organisations in Manchester is a prime example of how such initiatives are implicated in a government-led creative-economy framework founded on the 'yoking together of cultural, social, and economic goals' (Brouillette, 2014, p. 1). Just as 'place-making' cultural interventions like the City of Culture subscribe to a 'top-down' ideology of regional development, Manchester's status as a figurehead for 'Northern' culture is based on the logic of recentralisation, relying heavily on power relations between a metropolitan urban core and its periphery. While these interventions are very different in scope and objective, they nevertheless operate in a way that is analogous to regional devolution's pacifying character: that is, they perform regional liberation insofar as it supports a centralised and unitary Britishness. What political and cultural approaches to devolution have in common, is that they augment an asymmetrical power relation in which Britain's political, economic, and cultural capital remains concentrated in London.

Governmental policy has maintained the imbalances of power explored throughout this book. As we have seen, Northern England was at the fore of literary engagement with the British break-up in the first two decades of the twenty-first century. The ongoing devolutionary period has been characterised by literary reflection on the political status of Northern England, emerging from Britain's wider constitutional instability. From the urban geographies of Sheffield's inner-city streets, coastal towns, and mythological industrial wastelands to the rural 'wild places' of North Yorkshire, Cumbria, and Northumberland, Northern England's heterogeneous landscapes have been crucial to the literary exploration of democratic alternatives to the centralised state form. In this context, *Rewriting the North* has proposed 'the cultural politics of devolution' as a new way of reading literary engagement with Britain's territorial disintegration which brings together a decentralised literary-critical practice with attention to devolution's constitutional contours. Sunjeev Sahota, Sarah Hall, Anthony Cartwright, Adam Thorpe, Sarah Moss, and Fiona Mozley all engage with devolution as a political-constitutional process. Their attempts to imagine alternative political futures for the North and the English nation are related to democratic deficit, uneven development, political representation, and agency. Perhaps the most productive way that these writers engage with devolution, however, resides in the very literary structures of the texts. Whether through an ideological retreat to multicultural assimilation or rural pastoralism, or by reinscribing regional class stereotypes and the limits of nostalgia, literary attempts to subvert the North's regional iconography and imagine alternative democratic possibilities are either undermined by the formal, stylistic, or ideological contradictions of the texts or abandoned altogether. So, while these novels acknowledge the inadequacies of the centralised British state form, their regional projects are limited by the same stabilising structures as political devolution. The texts considered here engage with devolution – either through direct representation or political allegory – as a form of 'virtual liberation' (Nairn, 1998), which necessitates minor administrative adjustments rather than a constitutional rethink. This literary ambivalence reflects less the desire for an English regional governance than a post-British alternative – they index a contemporaneous Nairnite sensibility in which inequalities between England's North and South cannot be resolved by devolution 'as a form of Westminster-inspired "modernisation"' (Nairn, 2011, p. 267). This book has proposed a literary-critical approach which destabilises the dominance of London as Britain's cultural centre but is equally concerned with the methods by which literary texts register political devolution's limited constitutional charge. Looking ahead, the task of the discipline will be to address how governmental attempts at rebalancing England's cultural economy alter the conditions of literary production and reception.

Further literary discussion of regional English questions must also account for the national correlates of this debate. In the aftermath of the 1997 Devolved Parliaments Act, Nairn anticipated the difficulty of extracting England from Britain, suggesting that there is much deeper uncertainty attached to post-British England than to any dilemmas currently experienced in Scotland, Wales, or Ireland (Nairn, 2000). Nairn's predictions remain incisive and prescient two decades into the twenty-first century. Among the political uncertainties characterising post-Brexit Britain, there have been calls to abandon the 'English Question' altogether. In 2019, Alex Niven argued that '[t]he Break-Up of Britain must also be the Break-Up of England' (Niven, 2019, p. 128), writing in *The Guardian* the following year that 'we need to stop talking about the chimera that is English identity, and focus on more urgent, more tangible political projects' (Niven, 2020). Niven's qualms about Englishness are not without basis. From England's so-called 'island imaginary' during Brexit to the quick mobilisation of racist discourse following England's loss in Euro 2020, the prospect of a post-imperial Englishness appears far from view. Regarding the latter, England's football team had attracted controversy long before the final. The team had committed to 'taking the knee' before every fixture in solidarity with the 'Black Lives Matter' movement, attracting criticism from former Home Secretary, Priti Patel, who condemned the team for engaging in what she called 'gesture politics' (Patel cited in Stone, 2021). When Marcus Rashford, Bukayo Saka, and Jadon Sancho missed their penalties in the final game, the football pitch became a site of political contestation once again. This time, the English credentials of Gareth Southgate's Black players were the target of racist abuse on social media, leading to the defacement of the players' murals in Darlington and Manchester. Critical responses to the events have similarly noted how the game was shadowed by an Anglo-British imperial past. Les Back and Kelly Mills propose a parallel with the 1970s and 1980s, when 'England fans would routinely sing "there ain't no Black in the Union Jack"' (Back and Mills, 2021, p. 110) while Ben Carrington describes the penalty shootout as an evolution of Tebbitt's cricket test (Carrington, 2021). Sporting culture has long served as an unofficial form of mass democratic participation in England, but it also provides evidence of the nation's ongoing struggle to disentangle itself from ethno-purist ideology.

Despite the persistence of England's imperial shadow, the fictions examined in *Rewriting the North* suggest that this overdeterminism is no reason to jettison a progressive English civic nationalism. The fact that literary engagements with Northern England have so much difficulty imagining egalitarian democratic possibilities within the parameters of the British state indicates that a post-imperial, civic Englishness is even more urgent. A key task of *Rewriting the North* has, therefore, been to demonstrate the interconnections between the regional and national English Questions and suggest that literary constructions of the North are vital in resolving them via a place-based politics that Michael Gardiner calls 're-provincialisation' (Gardiner, 2012, p. 167). The methodological literary 'placing' of Northern England as a range of evolving and differentiated localities has constitutional implications for the region and the English nation. It pulls against a critical practice which naturalises Britishness in opposition to an exclusionary Englishness, and initiates a literary registration of England beyond the North–South divide.

A related question that this book has begun to answer is why literary representations of the North are central to England's national return. After all, the democratic possibilities offered up by dismantling the structures of the British centralised state form are not specific to the regions of Northern England. The answer concerns the relationship between England's political future and the 'growing abyss' (Nairn, 2011, p. 244) between its constructed poles of 'North' and 'South'. In the spirit of Nairn, I opened by proposing that a fundamental barrier to England's political realisation has been the construction of 'the North' as a placeless, class-inflected metaphor which originated in – and was later solidified by – literary culture. The codification of a monolithic 'North' as the nation's 'floundering periphery' (Nairn, 2011, p. 244) has persisted: from the social problem novels of the industrial revolution, kitchen sink realism, and the 'post-Thatcher novel', through to twenty-first-century literary culture. As we have seen, this geographically stretchy, cultural 'North' has been vital to a discourse of Englishness in which the nation cannot reconcile its competing internal poles.

Rewriting the North has opened up several areas for future enquiry. A key priority for literary-critical engagement with the region will be to dismantle its racial stereotype and examine how Black and Asian writers have utilised various locations across the North in the construction of England's postcolonial identity. Twenty years later, Procter's maxim that 'London persists as the cultural capital of black Britain' holds true (Procter, 2003, p. 164). Chapter 1 responded to the metropolitan character of race in the British 'multicultural' novel via a discussion of Sahota's *Ours are the Streets* and *The Year of the Runaways*, specifically how Sahota maps the contours of state-racism in Britain. But Zahid Hussain's *The Curry Mile* (2000), Nadeem Aslam's *Maps for Lost Lovers* (2004), and Caryl Phillips' *A Distant Shore* (2003), *In the Falling Snow* (2009), and *The Lost Child* (2015) have also situated diverse geographies across the North as loci of Black and Asian literary production after Empire, and a remaining area for future critical engagement is how writers negotiate experiences of Blackness in the North of England beyond the city. Even when London is discounted, urban space remains the default terrain for critical engagement with representations of Black life in Britain. One example is Anita Sethi's nature writing, *I Belong Here* (2019), which, in its response to Sethi's experience of racist hate crime on a TransPennine train, documents her long-distance walk across the Pennine Way as a journey of reclamation. An author focused study might also consider the work of Ben Myers, whose novels, *Beastings* (2014), *Turning Blue* (2016), and *The Gallows Pole* (2017) have constructed a dissident narrative of rural Yorkshire rooted in the region's political history. Class struggle has also been a recurring conceptual thread running through each of the chapters in this book. But class is never static, and more work is needed to adequately explore how neoliberalism has altered working-class experience across Northern England's own uneven geographies. Jessica Andrews' *Saltwater* (2019) and *Milk Teeth* (2022), for example, offer new, under-explored accounts of generational class difference, charting an emerging 'millennial' figure in the North-East marked both by economic precarity and social mobility (see Ashbridge, 2022).

Critical discussions of the North–South divide also risk occluding other socio-economically or politically marginalised areas of England. London remains heavily polarised and unequal. Zadie Smith's pessimistic portrayal of London in *N.W.* (2012) – set during the Conservative-Liberal Democrat Coalition – attests to the entrenched racialised class inequalities that were demonstrated acutely by the tragedy of Grenfell Tower in 2017. The Midlands also remain fertile ground for exploration, particularly how the polarising logic of the North–South divide erases the vastly differentiated areas of the region. In his examination of postcolonial writing from Nottingham, Leicester, and Birmingham, Thomas Kew notes that '[w]ithin the conceptual framework of the North–South divide, the Midlands are conspicuous only through their absence', becoming 'caught in the middle of a critical landscape that tends to reify, and thereby reinforce, the reductive notion of a North–South divide' (Kew, 2017, p. 2). Kew's call for regional specificity in the Midlands and the aim of *Rewriting the North* are not mutually exclusive. Chapter 3 identified a literary and political tendency in which the North has functioned as a geographically vague shorthand for deindustrialisation and working-class identity, eliding various other marginalised English regions. In this respect, deconstructing the literary North–South divide may simultaneously allow the Midlands to emerge as an equally differentiated literary geography.

Questions regarding Britain's political organisation were given new impetus by the death of Queen Elizabeth II in the autumn of 2022. Britain's longest reigning monarch had for the past seven decades served as the unelected head of a multi-national state form which exists without a written constitution. The BBC's rolling coverage of the proceedings and the designation of an official national mourning period captured the timelessness and ineffability of what Nairn saw as Britain's 'enchanted glass' (Nairn, 2011).[2] Shortly after the activation of Operation London Bridge – triggering several carefully choreographed funeral arrangements – images of Queen Elizabeth and the Union Jack dominated public spaces, television broadcasts, and social media across the country in a recital of national stability through collective commemoration. At the same time, however, the death of Queen Elizabeth as Sovereign revealed the cracks in Britain's constitutional veneer. In parallel to these tributes to the Crown, protests in Scotland and England served as a reminder of the inherently undemocratic character of the monarchy, with a protester in Scotland arrested and charged with 'breaching the peace' for holding a placard which read 'Fuck imperialism, abolish monarchy' (see Quinn, 2022). Regardless of public allegiance to Queen Elizabeth as an emblem of British stability from imperial to post-imperial nation, King Charles III takes the throne when the space separating the Crown from politics is visibly contracting (Schothorne, 2022). The loss of national stability and continuity bound up in Queen Elizabeth represents an interruption in the naturalisation of Britishness, and it is from this faltering that new forms of social and political organisation will appear.

Conclusively, then, the weaving together of culture and politics in Britain has relied upon the codification of 'Northern' regional otherness, and this interdependence must be contended with in future critical examinations of creative work emanating from Northern English regions. If demythologising the North is to help a placed literature of England to emerge, then future critical analyses also need to address the ideological conditions of literary production emanating from governmental cultural policy, alongside form and representation. For contemporary literary studies, the consequences go beyond rewriting the North towards a wider disciplinary 'break up'. A crucial task will be a decentralised critical practice that denaturalises Britishness as a precursor to the complete abandonment of the 'British literature' paradigm. This break between discipline and state would render visible the unitary state logic of the North–South divide and provide the conditions for a post-British, civic English nationalism. As Britain looks outwards to assert itself as a global power, literary production across Northern England is increasingly introspective as writers interrogate the region's political footing. England's 'growing abyss' might, therefore, be less one of cardinal direction, between North and South, than one of optics, between looking out and looking in. The inward look need not be conceived as inherently reactionary; it is also a commitment to the kind of self-reflection that recognises evolution, variance, and change. This heterogeneous, placed literary North is never static, and it is where a post-British literature of England can be activated.

Notes

1 A further limitation is that many of the arts organisations involved in cultural regeneration initiatives temporarily relocate to the city to access funding. For a perceptive critique of this tendency, see Gerry Mooney (2004) 'Cultural Policy as Urban Transformation? Critical Reflections on Glasgow, European City of Culture 1990', *Local Economy*, 19 (4), pp. 327–340.
2 The government sanctioned September 18 as a day of national reflection followed by a bank holiday for the Queen's funeral. See 'The Demise of Her Majesty Queen Elizabeth II: National Mourning Guidance' (DCMS, 2022).

Works Cited

Alexander, C. (2004) 'Imagining the Asian Gang: Ethnicity, Masculinity and Youth after "the Riots"', *Critical Social Policy*, 24 (4), pp. 526–549.

Anderson, B. (1983) *Imagined Communities: Reflections on the Origin and Spread of Nationalism*. London: Verso.

Anderson, P. (1964) 'Origins of the Present Crisis', *New Left Review*, 1 (23), pp. 26–53.

Anderson, P. (1992) *English Questions*. London: Verso.

Arts Council England (2021) 'Strengthening Our Place-Based Approach and Supporting Levelling Up'. Available at: https://www.artscouncil.org.uk/lets-create/deli very-plan-2021-2024/strengthening-our-place-based-approach-and-supporting-level ling (Accessed: 7 October 2022).

Ashbridge, C. (2022) '"All I Need Is Myself": Spatializing Neoliberal Class Consciousness in the Northern Millennial Novel', in S. Lee (ed.) *Locating Classed Subjectivities: Intersections of Space and Working-Class Life in Nineteenth-, Twentieth-, and Twenty-First-Century British Writing*. London: Routledge, pp. 206–225.

Ashcroft, Lord (2016) 'How the United Kingdom Voted on Thursday … and Why'. Available at: https://lordashcroftpolls.com/2016/06/how-the-united-kingdom-voted-and-why.

Aslam, N. (2004) *Maps for Lost Lovers*. London: Faber and Faber.

Augé, M. (1995) *Non-Places: Introduction to an Anthropology of Supermodernity*. Translated by J. Howe. London: Verso.

Aughey, A. (2007) *The Politics of Englishness*. Manchester: Manchester University Press.

Aughey, A. (2013) *The British Question*. Manchester: Manchester University Press.

Araujo, F. (2017) 'Hull Revisited: What Happens When a Brexit Stronghold Becomes City of Culture?' *New Statesman*. 16 January. Available from: www.newstatesman. com/politics/uk/2017/01/hull-revisited-what-happens-whenbrexit-stronghold-becomes-city-culture (Accessed: 17 July 2022).

Back, L. and Mills, K. (2021) '"When You Score You're English, When You Miss You're Black": Euro 2020 and the Racial Politics of a Penalty Shoot-Out', *Soundings: A Journal of Politics and Culture*, 1 (79), pp. 110–121.

Bagguley, P. and Hussain, Y. (2004) *Riotous Citizens: Ethnic Conflict in Multicultural Britain*. Abingdon: Routledge.

Bäing, A.S. and Wong, C. (2018) 'The Impact of Brownfield Regeneration on Neighbourhood Dynamics: The Case of Salford Quays in England', *Town Planning Review*, 89 (5), pp. 513–534.

Ball, J.C. (2004) *Imagining London: Postcolonial Fiction and the Transnational Metropolis*. Toronto: University of Toronto Press.

Barnett, A. (2017) *The Lure of Greatness: England's Brexit and America's Trump.: Why 2016 Blew Away the World Order and How We Must Respond*. London: Unbound.

Barnett, D. (2018) 'Folk Realism: The Literature Exploring England's Legends and Landscapes', *The Independent*, 2 March. Available at: https://www.independent. co.uk/news/long_reads/folk-realism-english-literature-countryside-legends-landscape-nature-gothic-writers-fantasy-a8234691.html (Accessed: 11 October 2019).

Baucom, I. (1999) *Out of Place: Englishness, Empire, and the Locations of Identity*. Princeton, NJ: Princeton University Press.

Bauman, Z. (2004) *Wasted Lives: Modernity and Its Outcasts*. Cambridge: Blackwell.

Bauman, Z. (2017) *Retrotopia*. Cambridge: Polity.

BBC Media Centre (2012) 'London 2012 Olympics Deliver Record Viewing Figures for BBC', 13 August. Available from:www.bbc.co.uk/mediacentre/latestnews/2012/olympic-viewing-figs.html (Accessed: 13 May 2020).

BBC News (1997) 'Stanley Baldwin | Formative Years, Into Parliament, Lloyd George', 18 December. Available at:http://news.bbc.co.uk/1/hi/special_report/1997/uk_politics/stanley_baldwin/40375.stm (Accessed: 17 September 2020).

BBC News (2016) 'Lincolnshire Records UK's Highest Brexit Vote', *BBC News*, 24 June. Available at: https://www.bbc.com/news/uk-politics-eu-referendum-36616740 (Accessed: 22 September 2020).

Beaumont, A. (2015) 'Original Modern or a New Kind of Ordinary', *Alluvium*, 4 (3). Available at: https://www.alluvium-journal.org/2015/06/26/original-modern-or-a-new-kind-of-ordinary (Accessed: 30 December 2017).

Bell, M. (1972) *Primitivism*. London: Methuen and Co Ltd.

Bentley, P. (1941) *The English Regional Novel*. Crows Nest, New South Wales: G. Allen & Unwin.

Berberich, C. (2015) 'Bursting the Bubble: Mythical Englishness, Then and Now', *Journal of Postcolonial Writing*, 51 (2), pp. 158–169.

Berlant, L. (1997) *The Queen of America Goes to Washington City: Essays on Sex and Citizenship*. Durham, NC: Duke University Press.

Berlant, L. (2011) *Cruel Optimism*. Durham, NC: Duke University Press.

Bhabha, H.K. (1994) *The Location of Culture*. London: Routledge.

Blair, T. (1995) 'Leader's Speech, Brighton 1995'. Available at: www.britishpolitica lspeech.org/speech-archive.htm?speech=201 (Accessed: 7 September 2020).

Block, E. and Negrine, R. (2017) 'The Populist Communication Style: Toward a Critical Framework', *International Journal of Communication*, 11, pp. 178–197.

Bluemel, K. (2019) 'The Regional and the Rural', in J. Smith (ed.) *The Cambridge Companion to British Literature of the 1930s*. Cambridge: Cambridge University Press, pp. 160–174.

Bogdanor, V. (1999) *Devolution in the United Kingdom*. Oxford: Oxford University Press.

Bonnett, A. (2010) *Left in the Past: Radicalism and the Politics of Nostalgia*. London: Bloomsbury.

Boym, S. (2001) *The Future of Nostalgia*. New York: Basic Books.

Briggs, H. (2018) 'Lost History of Brown Bears in Britain Revealed', *BBC News*, 4 July. Available at: https://www.bbc.co.uk/news/science-environment-44699233 (Accessed: 28 December 2020).

Brooker, J. (2010) *Literature of the 1980s: After the Watershed*. Edinburgh: Edinburgh University Press.

Brouillette, S. (2014) *Literature and the Creative Economy*. Stanford, CA: Stanford University Press.

Burke, A. (2007) 'Concrete Universality: Tower Blocks, Architectural Modernism, and Realism in Contemporary British Cinema', *New Cinemas: Journal of Contemporary Film*, 5 (3), pp. 177–188.

Burnett, J. (2004) 'Community, Cohesion and the State', *Race & Class*, 45 (3), pp. 1–18.

Burnham, A. (2018) 'English Devolution: The Best Answer to Brexit', in *Full Speech Transcript*. Methodist Central Hall, Westminster: Greater Manchester Central Authority. Available at: https://www.greatermanchester-ca.gov.uk/media/1579/devolution___best_answer_to_brexit_speech.pdf (Accessed: 26 July 2022).

Byrne, K. (2014) 'Adapting Heritage: Class and Conservatism in *Downton Abbey*', *Rethinking History*, 18 (3), pp. 311–327.

Cantle, T. (2001) 'Community Cohesion: A Report of the Independent Review Team'. Home Office. Available at: http://tedcantle.co.uk/pdf/communitycohesion%20cantlereport.pdf (Accessed: 5 September 2020).

Carrington, B. (2021) 'Once England had Tebbit's Cricket Test – Now It's the Penalty Kick Test', *The Guardian*, 14 July. Available at: https://www.theguardian.com/commentisfree/2021/jul/14/england-tebbit-cricket-test-penalty-kick-team-racist (Accessed: 12 September 2022).

Cartwright, A. (2017) *The Cut*. London: Peirene Press.

Challakere, P. (2007) 'Aesthetics of Globalization in Contemporary Fiction: The Function of the Fall of the Berlin Wall in Zadie Smith's *White Teeth* (2000), Nicholas Royle's *Counterparts* (1996), and Philip Hensher's *Pleasured* (1998)', *Theory & Event*, 10 (1), n.p.

Christophers, B. (2008) 'The BBC, the Creative Class, and Neoliberal Urbanism in the North of England', *Environment and Planning A: Economy and Space*, 40 (10), pp. 2313–2329.

Clarke, H.D., Whiteley, P. and Goodwin, M. (2017) *Brexit: Why Britain Voted to Leave the European Union*. Cambridge: Cambridge University Press.

Clarke, T. (2013) *The Cambridge Introduction to Literature and the Environment*. Cambridge: Cambridge University Press.

Clewell, T. (2005) *Modernism and Nostalgia: Bodies, Locations, Aesthetics*. Basingstoke: Palgrave Macmillan.

Cockin, K. (2012) *The Literary North*. Basingstoke: Palgrave Macmillan.

Connell, L. and Marsh, N. (2011) *Literature and Globalization: A Reader*. London: Routledge.

Cottrell, A. (2017) 'The Power of Love: From Feminist Utopia to the Politics of Imperceptibility in Sarah Hall's Fiction', *Textual Practice*, 33 (4), pp. 679–693.

Crawford, R. (1992) *Devolving English Literature*. Oxford: Clarendon Press.

Daddow, O. (2019) 'GlobalBritain[TM]: The Discursive Construction of Britain's Post-Brexit World Role', *Global Affairs*, 5 (1), pp. 5–22.

Davidson, P. (2005) *The Idea of the North*. London: Reaktion.

Deleuze, G. and Guattari, F. (1972) *Anti-Oedipus: Capitalism and Schizophrenia*. London: Continuum.

Deleuze, G. and Guattari, F. (1987) *A Thousand Plateaus: Capitalism and Schizophrenia*. Minneapolis: University of Minnesota Press.

Denham, J. (2001) *Building Cohesive Communities: A Report of the Ministerial Group on Public Order and Community Cohesion. Home Office.* Available at: www.tedcantle.co.uk/publications/005%20Building%20Cohesive%20Communities%20%20%28The%20Denham%20Report%29%202001.pdf (Accessed: 5 September 2020).

Department for Culture, Media and Sport (DCMS) (2014) 'UK City of Culture Consultation' *GOV.UK.* 11 December. Available at: https://www.gov.uk/government/consultations/uk-city-of-culture-consultation (Accessed: 1 October 2022).

Derbyshire, J. (2012) 'Stuart Hall: "We Need to Talk about Englishness"', *New Statesman*, 23 August. Available at: https://www.newstatesman.com/politics/uk-politics/2012/08/stuart-hall-we-need-talk-about-englishness (Accessed: 4 September 2020).

Derrida, J. (1994) *Specters of Marx: The State of the Debt, the Work of Mourning and the New International.* London: Routledge.

Docherty, T. (2017) 'Brexit: Thinking and Resistance', in R. Eaglestone (ed.) *Brexit and Literature: Critical and Cultural Responses.* London: Routledge, pp. 181–195.

Dodd, P. (1990) 'Lowryscapes: Recent Writings about "the North"', *Critical Quarterly*, 32 (2), pp. 17–28.

Dorling, D. (2010) 'Persistent North-South Divides', in N.M. Coe and A. Jones (eds) *The Economic Geography of the UK.* London: SAGE, pp. 12–28.

Duff, K. (2014) *Contemporary British Fiction and Urban Space: After Thatcher.* New York: Palgrave Macmillan.

Ehland, C. (2007) 'Introduction: Northern England and the Spaces of Identity', in C. Ehland (ed.) *Thinking Northern: Textures of Identity in the North of England.* Amsterdam: Rodopi, pp. 15–32.

Electoral Commission. (2019) 'Results and Turnout at the EU Referendum', 25 September. Available at: www.electoralcommission.org.uk/who-we-are-and-what-we-do/elections-and-referendums/past-elections-and-referendums/eu-referendum/results-and-turnout-eu-referendum (Accessed: 22 July 2020).

English, J.F. (2005) 'Introduction: British Fiction in a Global Context', in English (ed.) *A Concise Companion to Contemporary British Fiction.* Oxford: Blackwell.

Etherington, B. (2018) *Literary Primitivism.* Stanford, CA: Stanford University Press.

Evans, G. (2017) 'Brexit Britain: Why We Are All Postindustrial Now', *American Ethnologist*, 44 (2), pp. 215–219.

Featherstone, S. (2009) *Englishness: Twentieth-Century Popular Culture and the Forming of English Identity.* Edinburgh: Edinburgh University Press.

Fisher, M. (2014) *Ghosts of My Life: Writings on Depression, Hauntology and Lost Futures.* Winchester: Zero Books.

Florida, R. (2014) *The Rise of the Creative Class.* New York: Basic Books.

Foreign Affairs Committee (2018) 'Global Britain: Sixth Report of Session 2017–2019'. Available at: https://publications.parliament.uk/pa/cm201719/cmselect/cmfaff/780/780.pdf (Accessed: 31 August 2020).

Forrest, D. (2011) 'Our Friends in the North and the Instability of the Historical Drama as Archive'. *The Journal of British Cinema and Television*, 8 (2), pp. 218–233.

Forrest, D. and Vice, S. (2015) 'A Poetics of the North: Visual and Literary Geographies', in I. Franklin, H. Chignell, and K. Skoog (eds) *Regional Aesthetics: Mapping UK Media Cultures.* London: Palgrave Macmillan, pp. 55–69.

Fowler, C. (2008) 'A Tale of Two Novels: Developing a Devolved Approach to Black British Writing', *The Journal of Commonwealth Literature*, 43 (3), pp. 75–94.

Fowler, C. and Pearce, L. (2013) 'Introduction: Manchester and the Devolution of British Literary Culture', in L. Pearce, C. Fowler, and R. Crawshaw (eds)

Postcolonial Manchester: Diaspora Space and the Devolution of Literary Culture.
Manchester: Manchester University Press, pp. 1–19.

Fukuyama, F. (1989) 'The End of History?', *The National Interest*, 16, pp. 1–18.

Gardiner, M. (2004) *The Cultural Roots of British Devolution.* Edinburgh: Edinburgh University Press.

Gardiner, M. (2007) 'Literature, Theory, Politics: Devolution as Iteration', in B. Schoene (ed.) *Edinburgh Companion to Contemporary Scottish Literature.* Edinburgh: Edinburgh University Press, pp. 43–50.

Gardiner, M. (2012) *The Return of England in English Literature.* Basingstoke: Palgrave Macmillan.

Gardiner, M. (2013) *The Constitution of English Literature.* London: Bloomsbury.

Gardiner, M. and Westall, C. (2016) 'The BBC and British Branding', *Open Democracy*, 7 May. Available at: https://www.opendemocracy.net/en/ourbeeb/bbc-and-british-branding (Accessed: 10 October 2022).

Giblett, R. (1996) *Postmodern Wetlands: Culture, History, Ecology.* Edinburgh: Edinburgh University Press.

Giddens, A. (1990) *The Consequences of Modernity.* Cambridge: Polity.

Gifford, T. (1999) *Pastoral.* London: Taylor & Francis.

Gifford, T. (2012) 'Pastoral, Anti-Pastoral and Post-Pastoral as Reading Strategies', in S. Slovic (ed.) *Critical Insights: Nature and Environment.* Ipswich: Salem Press, pp. 42–61.

Gilroy, P. (2005) *Postcolonial Melancholia.* New York: Columbia University Press.

Gilroy, P. (2013) *There Ain't No Black in the Union Jack: The Cultural Politics of Race and Nation.* London: Routledge.

Giovannini, A. (2020) 'Last Word: COVID-19 and English Devolution', *Political Insight*, 11 (3), p. 40.

Glaze, B. and Blanchard, J. (2016) 'Labour Heartlands Give Huge Backing to Brexit as the North Votes to Leave', *The Mirror*, 24 June. Available at: www.mirror.co.uk/news/uk-news/labour-heartlands-give-huge-backing-8271074 (Accessed: 14 July 2020).

Goodhart, D. (2017) *The Road to Somewhere: The Populist Revolt and the Future of Politics.* London: C. Hurst & Co.

GOV.UK (2022) 'The Demise of Her Majesty Queen Elizabeth II: National Mourning Guidance'. Available at: https://www.gov.uk/government/publications/the-demise-of-her-majesty-queen-elizabeth-ii-national-mourning-guidance/the-demise-of-her-majesty-queen-elizabeth-ii-national-mourning-guidance (Accessed: 7 October 2022).

Groom, B. (2022) *Northerners: A History from the Ice Age to the Present Day.* London: HarperCollins.

Hall, S. (1987) 'Minimal Selves', in L. Appignenesi (ed.) *Identity: The Real Me: Postmodernism and the Question of Identity.* London: ICA (ICA Document 6), pp. 43–447.

Hall, S. (1996) 'New Ethnicities' in K. Chen and , D. Morley (eds) *Stuart Hall: Critical Dialogues in Cultural Studies.* London: Taylor & Francis, pp. 442–451.

Hall, S. (2002) *Haweswater.* London: Faber & Faber.

Hall, S. (2007) *The Carhullan Army.* London: Faber & Faber.

Hall, S. (2015) *The Wolf Border.* London: Faber & Faber.

Hames, S. (2020) *The Literary Politics of Scottish Devolution: Voice, Class, Nation.* Edinburgh: Edinburgh University Press.

Hardt, M. and Negri, A. (2000) *Empire*. Cambridge, MA: Harvard University Press.

Harris, J. (2020) 'The Covid-19 Crisis is Accelerating the Breakup of the UK', *The Guardian*, 23 August. Available at: https://www.theguardian.com/commentisfree/2020/aug/23/covid-19-crisis-breakup-uk-brexit-pandemic-scottish-independence (Accessed: 1 October 2022).

Harvey, D. (1988) 'The Geography of Class Power', *Socialist Register*, (34), pp. 49–74.

Harvey, D. (1989) *The Condition of Postmodernity: An Enquiry into the Origins of Historical Change*. Oxford: Blackwell.

Haslam, D. (1999) *Manchester, England: The Story of a Pop Cult City*. London: Fourth Estate.

Hazeldine, T. (2017) 'The Revolt of the Rustbelt', *New Left Review*, 105 (1), pp. 51–79.

Hazeldine, T. (2020) *The Northern Question: A Political History of the North-South Divide*. London: Verso.

Hazell, R. (2000) *The English Question*. Manchester: Manchester University Press.

Head, D. (2002) *An Introduction to Modern British Fiction*. Cambridge: Cambridge University Press.

Head, D. (2008) *The State of the Novel: Britain and Beyond*. Chichester: Blackwell.

Head, D. (2017) *Modernity and the English Rural Novel*. Cambridge: Cambridge University Press.

Head, D. (2020) 'The Farming Community Revisited: Complex Nostalgia in Sarah Hall and Melissa Harrison', *Green Letters*, 24 (4), pp. 354–366.

Heise, U.K. (2011) 'Deterritorialization and Cosmopolitanism', in L. Connell and N. Marsh (eds) *Literature and Globalisation: A Reader*. London: Routledge, pp. 157–170.

Henderson, A. and Jones, R.W. (2021) *Englishness: The Political Force Transforming Britain*. Oxford: Oxford University Press.

Hess, S. (2012) *William Wordsworth and the Ecology of Authorship: The Roots of Environmentalism in Nineteenth-Century Culture*. Charlottesville: University of Virginia Press.

Hill, J. (1999) *British Cinema in the 1980s: Issues and Themes*. Oxford: Clarendon Press.

Howcroft, M. (2021) 'Pride, Shame, and the Civic Imaginary: Hull as UK City of Culture and Brexit'. PhD Thesis. University of Hull.

Hubble, N. and Tew, P. (2016) *London in Contemporary British Fiction: The City Beyond the City*. London: Bloomsbury.

Huggan, G. (2001) *The Postcolonial Exotic: Marketing the Margins*. London: Routledge.

Huggan, G. (2016) 'Back to the Future: The "New Nature Writing", Ecological Boredom, and the Recall of the Wild', *Prose Studies*, 38 (2), pp. 152–171.

Hughes, T. and Goodwin, F. (1979) *Remains of Elmet*. London: Faber and Faber.

Hull2017 (2013) 'Bid Summary'. Hull City Council. Available at: www.hullcc.gov.uk/pls/portal/docs/PAGE/HOME/CLASMAIN/CLAS_CITY%20OF%20CULTURE%202017/HULL%20UK%20CITY%20OF%20CULTURE%202017%20BID%20SUMMARY_W.PDF (Accessed: 7 October 2022).

Hussain, Y. and Bagguley, P. (2005) 'Citizenship, Ethnicity and Identity: British Pakistanis after the 2001 "Riots"', *Sociology*, 39 (3), pp. 407–425.

Ilott, S. (2015) *New Postcolonial British Genres: Shifting the Boundaries*. Basingstoke: Palgrave Macmillan.

Jackson, J. (2020) *Writing Black Scotland*. Edinburgh: Edinburgh University Press.

Jameson, F. (1991) *Postmodernism: Or, the Cultural Logic of Late Capitalism*. New York: Duke University Press.

Jamie, K. (2008) 'A Lone Enraptured Male', *London Review of Books*, 6 March. Available at: https://www.lrb.co.uk/the-paper/v30/n05/kathleen-jamie/a-lone-enrap tured-male (Accessed: 26 May 2020).

Jewell, H.M. (1994) *The North-South Divide: The Origins of Northern Consciousness in England*. Manchester: Manchester University Press.

Jones, K. (2011) 'Writing the Wolf: Canine Tales and North American Environmental-Literary Tradition', *Environment and History*, 17 (2), pp. 201–228.

Jones, O. (2011) *Chavs: The Demonization of the Working Class*. London: Verso.

Kennedy, J. (2013) 'Terror in the Terroir: Resisting the Rebranding of the Countryside', *The Quietus*, 13 December. Available at: https://thequietus.com/articles/14114-country-life-british-politics-uncanny-music-art (Accessed: 20 December 2019).

Kennedy, J. (2017) 'The Brexit Novel?', *The New Socialist*, 29 October. Available at: https://newsocialist.org.uk/the-brexit-novel (Accessed: 10 October 2019).

Kennedy, J. (2018) *Authentocrats: Culture, Politics and the New Seriousness*. London: Repeater Books.

Kennedy, M. (2017) 'How to be Rich, Popular, and Have It All: Conflicted Attitudes to Wealth and Poverty in Postcolonial Fiction', in H. Ramsey-Kurz and M. Kennedy (eds) *Uncommon Wealths in Postcolonial Fiction*. Boston: Brill, pp. 287–304.

Kenny, M. (2014) *The Politics of English Nationhood*. Oxford: Oxford University Press.

Kenny, M. (2021) 'Governance, Politics and Political Economy – England's Questions after Brexit', *Territory, Politics, Governance*, 10 (5), pp. 1–18.

Kenny, M. and Sheldon, J. (2020) 'Unionism, Conservative Thinking and Brexit', *Centre on Constitutional Change*. Available at: https://www.centreonconstitutiona lchange.ac.uk/news-and-opinion/unionism-conservative-thinking-and-brexit (Accessed: 1 October 2022).

Kew, T. (2017) 'Regional Literary Cultures of the Midlands'. PhD Thesis. University of Leicester.

Kumar, K. (2003) *The Making of English National Identity*. Cambridge: Cambridge University Press.

Kumar, K. (2015) *The Idea of Englishness: English Culture, National Identity and Social Thought*. London: Routledge.

Kundnani, A. (2007) 'Integrationism: The Politics of Anti-Muslim Racism', *Race & Class*, 48 (4), pp. 24–44.

Kundnani, A. (2014) *The Muslims are Coming!: Islamophobia, Extremism, and the War on Terror*. London: Verso.

Kuper, A. (2003) 'The Return of the Native', *Current Anthropology*, 44 (3), pp. 389–402.

Law, D. (2003) '"Guddling for Words": Representing the North and Northernness in Post-1950 South Pennine Literature'. PhD Thesis. University of Lancaster.

Lea, D. (2017) *Twenty-First-Century Fiction: Contemporary British Voices*. Manchester: Manchester University Press.

Lee, N. (2017) 'Powerhouse of Cards? Understanding the "Northern Powerhouse"', *Regional Studies*, 51 (3), pp. 478–489.

Li, V. (2006) *The Neo-Primitivist Turn: Critical Reflections on Alterity, Culture, and Modernity*. Toronto: University of Toronto Press.

Lilley, D. (2016) 'Unsettling Environments: New Pastorals in Kazuo Ishiguro's *Never Let Me Go* and Sarah Hall's *The Carhullan Army*', *Green Letters: Studies in Ecocriticism*, 20 (1), pp. 60–71.

Linkon, S.L. (2014) 'Men Without Work: White Working-Class Masculinity in Deindustrialized Fiction', *Contemporary Literature*, 55 (1), pp. 148–167.

Linkon, S.L. (2018) *The Half-Life of Deindustrialization: Working-Class Writing About Economic Restructuring*. Ann Arbor: University of Michigan Press.

Littler, J. (2013) 'Meritocracy as Plutocracy: The Marketising of "Equality" Under Neoliberalism', *New Formations*, 80 (81), pp. 52–72.

London Organising Committee of the Olympic Games and Paralympic Games (LOCOG) (2012) *London 2012 Olympic Games Opening Ceremony Media Guide*. London: LOCOG, p. 19. Available at: www.london2012.com/mm/Document/ Documents/Publications/01/30/43/40/OPENINGCEREMONYGUIDE_English.pdf (Accessed: 13 May 2020).

MacLeod, G. and Jones, M. (2018) 'Explaining "Brexit Capital": Uneven Development and the Austerity State', *Space and Polity*, 22 (2), pp. 111–136.

Major, K. (2016) 'Why the North of England Will Regret Voting for Brexit', *The Independent*. Available at: www.independent.co.uk/voices/why-the-north-of-engla nd-will-regret-voting-for-brexit-a7101321.html (Accessed: 14 July 2020).

Mance, H. (2016) 'Britain Has Had Enough of Experts, Says Gove', *The Financial Times*, 3 June. Available at: https://www.ft.com/content/3be49734-29cb-11e6-83e4-a bc22d5d108c (Accessed: 11 October 2019).

Mandler, P. (1997) 'Against "Englishness": English Culture and the Limits to Rural Nostalgia, 1850–1940', *Transactions of the Royal Historical Society*, 7, pp. 155–175.

Mansfield, J. (2010) 'Fiction and the Meaning of Place: Writing the North of England, 1845–1855 and 1955–1965'. PhD Thesis. Leeds Metropolitan University.

Markwick, M. (2018) '"Gold put to use of paving stones": Internal Colonialism in Wuthering Heights', *Victorians: A Journal of Culture and Literature*, 134 (1), pp. 125–138.

Massey, D. (1984) *Spatial Divisions of Labour: Social Structures and the Geography of Production*. Basingstoke: Palgrave Macmillan.

Massey, D. (1994) *Space, Place and Gender*. Chichester: Polity.

Massey, D. (2007) *World City*. Cambridge: Polity.

May, T. (2016a) 'Theresa May – Her Full Brexit Speech to Conservative Conference', *The Independent*. 2 October. Available at: https://www.independent.co.uk/news/ uk/politics/theresa-may-conference-speech-article-50-brexit-eu-a7341926.html (Accessed: 25 March 2020).

May, T. (2016b) 'Statement from the New Prime Minister Theresa May', *GOV.UK*. 13 July. Available at: https://www.gov.uk/government/speeches/statement-from-the-new-prime-minister-theresa-may (Accessed: 1 April 2020).

May, T. (2017). Theresa May, 'PM Statement: General Election 2017'. 9 June. Available at: www.gov.uk/government/speeches/pm-statement-general-election-2017 (Accessed: 28 July 2020).

McGregor, J.(2017) *Reservoir 13*. London: HarperCollins.

Mckenzie, L. (2017) 'The Class Politics of Prejudice: Brexit and the Land of No-Hope and Glory', *The British Journal of Sociology*, 68 (1), pp. 265–280.

McLeod, J. (2004) *Postcolonial London*. London: Routledge.

McLeod, J. (2011) 'English Somewheres: Caryl Phillips and the English North', in A. Teverson and S. Upstone (eds) *Postcolonial Spaces: The Politics of Place in Contemporary Culture*. Basingstoke: Palgrave Macmillan, pp. 14–27.

McLeod, J. (2020a) 'Warning Signs: Postcolonial Writing and the Apprehension of Brexit', *Journal of Postcolonial Writing*, 56 (5), pp. 607–620.

McLeod, J. (2020b) 'Reinventing the Nation: Black and Asian British Representations', in N. Sushelia and M. Stein, (eds.) *The Cambridge History of Black and Asian British Writing*. Cambridge: Cambridge University Press, pp. 453–467.

Mendes, A.C. (2019) 'Sunjeev Sahota's Fictions of Failed Cosmopolitan Conviviality', in A. Stevic and P. Tsang (eds) *The Limits of Cosmopolitanism: Globalization and Its Discontents in Contemporary Literature*. New York: Routledge, pp. 53–69.

Miah, S., Sanderson, P. and Thomas, P. (2020) *'Race', Space and Multiculturalism in Northern England: The (M62) Corridor of Uncertainy*. London: Springer Nature.

Mooney, G. (2004) 'Cultural Policy as Urban Transformation? Critical Reflections on Glasgow, European City of Culture 1990', *Local Economy*, 19 (4), pp. 327–340.

Morely, P. (2013) *The North: (and Almost Everything in It)*. London: Bloomsbury.

Morphet, J. (2021) *The Impact of COVID-19 on Devolution: Recentralising the British State Beyond Brexit?* Bristol: Bristol University Press.

Morrison, J. (2017) 'Jihadi Fiction: Radicalisation Narratives in the Contemporary Novel', *Textual Practice*, 31 (3), pp. 567–584.

Morton, H.V. (1927) *In Search of England*. Cambridge: Methuen.

Moss, S. (2018) *Ghost Wall*. London: Granta.

Mozley, F. (2017) *Elmet*. London: John Murray.

Myers, B. (2012) *Pig Iron*. Hebden Bridge: Bluemoose Books.

Myers, B. (2017) *The Gallows Pole*. Hebden Bridge: Bluemoose Books.

Nairn, T. (1977) *The Break-Up of Britain: Crisis and Neo-Nationalism*. London: Atlantic Highlands.

Nairn, T. (1998) 'Virtual Liberation or: British Sovereignty Since the Election', *Scottish Affairs*, 25 (2), pp. 13–37.

Nairn, T. (2000) *After Britain: New Labour and the Return of Scotland*. London: Granta.

Nairn, T. (2011) *The Enchanted Glass: Britain and Its Monarchy*. London: Verso.

Niven, A. (2019) *New Model Island: How to Build a Radical Culture Beyond the Idea of England*. London: Zed.

Niven, A. (2020) 'Why It's Time to Stop Talking about English Identity', *The Guardian*, 15 July. Available at: https://www.theguardian.com/commentisfree/2020/jul/15/english-identity-patriotism-england-independent (Accessed: 15 September 2020).

Noble, S. (2019) 'English Indices of Deprivation 2019: Research Report', GOV.UK [Preprint]. Available at: https://assets.publishing.service.gov.uk/government/uploads/system/uploads/attachment_data/file/833947/IoD2019_Research_Report.pdf (Accessed: 7 October 2022).

O'Brien, P. (2018) 'The Deindustrial Novel: Twenty-First-Century British Fiction and the Working Class', in B. Clarke and N. Hubble (eds) *Working-Class Writing: Theory and Practice*. Basingstoke: Palgrave Macmillan, pp. 229–246.

O'Brien, P. (2020) *The Working Class and Twenty-First-Century British Fiction: Deindustrialisation, Demonisation, Resistance*. London: Routledge.

Olusoga, D. (2017) 'Empire 2.0 is Dangerous Nostalgia for Something that Never Existed', *The Guardian*, 19 March. Available at: https://www.theguardian.com/

commentisfree/2017/mar/19/empire-20-is-dangerous-nostalgia-for-something-that-never-existed (Accessed: 31 August 2020).

O'Neill, D. (2017) 'The (Global) Northern Working Class: Engels Revisited', in E. Mazierska (ed.) *Heading North: The North of England in Film and Television.* Switzerland: Palgrave Macmillan, pp. 279–295.

Orwell, G. (2001 [1973]) *The Road to Wigan Pier.* Edited by P. Davison. London: Penguin Classics.

Osborne, G. (2014) 'Chancellor: "'We Need a Northern Powerhouse"'. GOV.UK. Available at: https://www.gov.uk/government/speeches/chancellor-we-need-a-northern-powerhouse (Accessed: 4 March 2020).

Peace, D. (1999) *Nineteen Seventy Four.* London: Serpent's Tail.

Pearce, L., Fowler, C. and Crawshaw, R. (2013) *Postcolonial Manchester: Diaspora Space and the Devolution of Literary Culture.* Manchester: Manchester University Press.

Perfect, M. (2014) *Contemporary Fictions of Multiculturalism: Diversity and the Millennial London Novel.* Basingstoke: Palgrave Macmillan.

Phillips, C. (2003) *A Distant Shore.* London: Random House.

Phillips, H. (2017) 'A Woman Like that Is not a Woman, Quite. I Have Been Her Kind': Maxine Peake and the Gothic Excess of Northern Femininity', in D. Forrest and S. Vice (eds) *Social Class and Television Drama in Contemporary Britain.* Basingstoke: Palgrave Macmillan, pp. 149–164.

Pitcher, B. (2009) *The Politics of Multiculturalism: Race and Racism in Contemporary Britain.* Basingstoke: Palgrave Macmillan.

Pitcher, B. (2019) 'Racism and Brexit: Notes Towards an Antiracist Populism', *Ethnic and Racial Studies*, 42 (14), pp. 2490–2509.

Pitcher, B. (2022) *Back to the Stone Age: Race and Prehistory in Contemporary Culture.* Montreal: McGill Queens University Press.

Pocock, D.C.D. (1979) 'The Novelist's Image of the North', *Transactions of the Institute of British Geographers*, 4 (1), pp. 62–76.

Procter, J. (2003) *Dwelling Places: Postwar Black British Writing.* Manchester: Manchester University Press.

Procter, J. (2011) 'The Return of the Native: Pat Barker, David Peace and the Regional Novel after Empire', in R. Gilmour and B. Schwartz (eds) *End of Empire and the English Novel Since 1945.* Manchester: Manchester University Press, pp. 203–217.

Quinn, B. (2022) 'Civil Liberties Groups Criticise Police over Arrests of Anti-Monarchy Protesters', *The Guardian*, 12 September. Available at: https://www.theguardian.com/uk-news/2022/sep/12/anti-monarchy-protester-charged-with-a-breach-of-the-peace-edinburgh-queen-death-king (Accessed: 28 October 2022).

Rawnsley, S. (2000) 'Constructing "The North": Space and a Sense of Place', in N. Kirk (ed.) *Northern Identities: Historical Interpretations of 'The North' and 'Northernness'.* Aldershot: Ashgate, pp. 3–22.

Robertson, R. (1992) *Globalization: Social Theory and Global Culture.* London: Sage.

Robinson, N. (2015) *Election Notebook: The Inside Story of the Battle over Britain's Future and My Personal Battle to Report It.* London: Transworld Digital.

Rose, N. (1999) *Powers of Freedom: Reframing Political Thought.* Cambridge: Cambridge University Press.

Ruppin, J. (2017) 'Sarah Hall, Foyles'. Available at: https://www.foyles.co.uk/sarah-hall (Accessed: 17 September 2020).

Rushdie, S. (2012) *Imaginary Homelands: Essays and Criticism, 1981–1991*. London: Granta.

Rushton, P. (2017) 'The Myth and Reality of Brexit City: Sunderland and the 2016 Referendum'. Centre for Applied Social Sciences, University of Sunderland. Available at: http://sure.sunderland.ac.uk/id/eprint/7344 (Accessed: 5 August 2020).

Russell, D. (2004) *Looking North: Northern England and the National Imagination*. Manchester: Manchester University Press.

Russell, D. and Wagg, S. (2004) *Sporting Heroes of the North: Sport, Region and Culture*. Newcastle: Northumbria University Press.

Sahota, S. (2011) *Ours are the Streets*. London: Picador.

Sahota, S. (2015) *The Year of the Runaways*. London: Picador.

Salford City Council (2006) 'Outline Planning Application of Peel Media Ltd.'s Land at Quays Point off Broadway Salford Quays Salford'. Salford City Council Planning Committee. Available at: https://studylib.net/doc/16028838/application-no–06-53168-ou t-applicant (Accessed: 22 June 2020).

Sanders, K. (2009) *Bodies in the Bog and the Archaeological Imagination*. Chicago and London: University of Chicago Press.

Savage, M. (2015) *Social Class in the Twenty-First Century*. London: Pelican.

Schothorne, R. (2022) 'Silence Reigns', *New Statesman*, 14 September. Available at: https://www.newstatesman.com/ideas/2022/09/silence-reigns (Accessed: 13 October 2022).

Shaw, F. (2018) *Outwalkers*. Oxford: *David Fickling Books*.

Shaw, Katy (2017) 'Living by the Pen: In Conversation with Sunjeev Sahota', *English: Journal of the English Association*, 66 (254), pp. 263–271.

Shaw, Kristian (2017) *Cosmopolitanism in Twenty-First Century Fiction*. Basingstoke: Palgrave Macmillan.

Shaw, Kristian (2018) 'BrexLit', in R. Eaglestone (ed.) *Brexit and Literature: Critical and Cultural Responses*. London: Routledge, pp. 15–30.

Shaw, Kristian (2021) *Brexlit*. London: Bloomsbury.

Shields, R. (1991) *Places on the Margin: Alternative Geographies of Modernity*. London: Routledge.

Smith, A. (2017) *Autumn*. London: Hamish Hamilton.

Smith, A. (2019) *Spring: A Novel*. London: Hamish Hamilton.

Smith, A. (2020) *Summer: A Novel*. London: Hamish Hamilton.

Smith, Z. (2018) *Feel Free: Essays*. London: Hamish Hamilton.

Spracklen, K., Laurencic, J. and Kenyon, A. (2013) '"Mine's a Pint of Bitter": Performativity, gender, class and representations of authenticity in real-ale tourism', *Tourist Studies* [Preprint]. Available at: https://doi.org/10.1177/1468797613498165 (Accessed: 17 June 2019).

Squires, C. (2007) *Marketing Literature: The Making of Contemporary Writing in Britain*. Basingstoke: Palgrave Macmillan.

Stone, J. (2021) 'Priti Patel Says Fans Have Right to Boo England Team for Taking the Knee', *The Independent*, 14 June. Available at: https://www.independent.co.uk/news/uk/politics/priti-patel-taking-knee-boo-england-b1865409.html (Accessed: 12 September 2022).

Tannock, S. (1995) 'Nostalgia Critique', *Cultural Studies*, 9 (3), pp. 453–466.

Taylor, C. (2017) 'Elmet Leaves the Metallic Taste of Blood in the Mouth', *New Statesman*, 19 August. Available at: https://www.newstatesman.com/culture/books/2017/08/elmet-leaves-metallic-taste-blood-mouth (Accessed: 11 October 2019).

Horton, T., Tew, P. and Wilson, L. (2014) *The 1980s: A Decade of Contemporary British Fiction*. London: Bloomsbury.

The Daily Mail (2016) 'WHO WILL SPEAK FOR ENGLAND?'. 4 February. Available at: https://www.dailymail.co.uk/debate/article-3430870/DAILY-MAIL-COMMENT-speak-England.html (Accessed: 30 March 2020).

The Electoral Commission (2019) 'Results and Turnout at the EU Referendum'. Available at: https://www.electoralcommission.org.uk/who-we-are-and-what-we-do/elections-and-referendums/past-elections-and-referendums/eu-referendum/results-and-turnout-eu-referendum (Accessed: 22 July 2020).

The Telegraph (2016) '"Britain's Worst Tourist Attraction"' Ferris Wheel Gives Panoramic Views ... of Dudley'. 15 March. Available at: https://www.telegraph.co.uk/news/newstopics/howaboutthat/12194700/Britains-worst-tourist-attraction-Dudley-West-Midlands-ferris-wheel.html (Accessed: 20 November 2019).

Thompson, D. (2011) 'To the North' in K. Shaw (ed.) *Analysing David Peace*. Newcastle upon Tyne: Cambridge Scholars Publishing, pp. 107–114.

Thompson, E.P. (1963) *The Making of the English Working Class*. New York: Pantheon.

Thorpe, A. (2017) *Missing Fay*. London: Jonathan Cape.

Tomaney, J. and Pike, A. (2018) 'Brexit, Devolution and Economic Development in "Left Behind" Regions', *Welsh Economic Review*, 26 (29), pp. 29–37.

Tomaney, J. and Pike, A. (2020) 'Levelling Up?', *The Political Quarterly*, 91 (1), pp. 43–48.

Tyler, I. (2013) *Revolting Subjects: Social Abjection and Resistance in Neoliberal Britain*. London: Zed Books.

Umney, C. and Symon, G. (2020) 'Creative Placemaking and the Cultural Projectariat: Artistic Work in the Wake of Hull City of Culture 2017', *Capital & Class*, 44 (4), pp. 595–615.

Underwood, J. (2019) 'Pit Closure as Art', in E. Pollard and B. Schoene (eds) *British Literature in Transition: Accelerated Times, 1980–2000*. Cambridge: Cambridge University Press, pp. 162–177.

Vardy, C. (2013) 'The Allure of the 1980s', *Alluvium*, 2 (4). Available at: https://www.alluvium-journal.org/2013/07/21/the-allure-of-the-1980s (Accessed: 15 July 2020).

Virdee, S. (2014) *Racism, Class and the Racialized Outsider*. Basingstoke: Red Globe Press.

Virdee, S. and McGeever, B. (2018) 'Racism, Crisis, Brexit', *Ethnic and Racial Studies*, 41 (10), pp. 1802–1819.

Wacquant, L. (2008) *Urban Outcasts: A Comparative Sociology of Advanced Marginality*. Cambridge: Polity.

Walezak, E. (2019) 'Landscape and Identity: Utopian/Dystopian Cumbria in Sarah Hall's *The Carhullan Army*', *Critique: Studies in Contemporary Fiction*, 60 (1), pp. 67–74.

Wellings, B. (2019) *English Nationalism, Brexit and the Anglosphere: Wider Still and Wider*. Manchester: Manchester University Press.

Westall, C. and Gardiner, M. (2013) *Literature of an Independent England: Revisions of England, Englishness, and English Literature*. Basingstoke: Palgrave Macmillan.

Wharton, C., Fenwick, J. and Fawcett, H. (2010) 'Public Policy in the Party City: The Spectacle of Culture, Gender, and Locality', *International Journal of Public Administration*, 33 (14), pp. 779–789.

Whyte, C. (1998) 'Masculinities in Contemporary Scottish Fiction', *Modern Forum for Language Studies*, 34 (2), pp. 274–285.

Wilkies, D. (2006) 'Race Riots Blamed on Millions Paid to Migrant Areas', *Daily Mail Online*, 31 May. Available at: https://www.dailymail.co.uk/news/article-388431/Race-riots-blamed-millions-paid-migrant-areas.html (Accessed: 7 September 2020).

Williams, R. (1977) *Marxism and Literature*. Oxford: Oxford University Press.

Williams, R. (2001) *The Long Revolution*. Peterborough: Broadview.

Williams, R. (2005) *Culture and Materialism*. London: Verso.

Williams, R. (2016) *The Country and the City*. London: Vintage.

Wilson, J. (2017) 'Novels of Flight and Arrival: Abu Bakr Khaal, *African Titanics* (2014 [2008]) and Sunjeev Sahota, *The Year of the Runaways* (2014)', *Postcolonial Text*, 12 (3 and 4), n.p.

Woods, M. (2010) *Rural*. London: Routledge.

Index

Taylor & Francis eBooks

www.taylorfrancis.com

A single destination for eBooks from Taylor & Francis
with increased functionality and an improved user
experience to meet the needs of our customers.

90,000+ eBooks of award-winning academic content in
Humanities, Social Science, Science, Technology, Engineering,
and Medical written by a global network of editors and authors.

TAYLOR & FRANCIS EBOOKS OFFERS:

A streamlined
experience for
our library
customers

A single point
of discovery
for all of our
eBook content

Improved
search and
discovery of
content at both
book and
chapter level

REQUEST A FREE TRIAL
support@taylorfrancis.com

 **Routledge**
Taylor & Francis Group

 **CRC Press**
Taylor & Francis Group